ROMNEY MARSH

ROMNEY MARSH

WALTER J. C. MURRAY

THIRD EDITION

ROBERT HALE · LONDON

ISBN O 7090 0653 5

First published in the Regional Series 1953
Second edition 1972
Reprinted 1975
Third edition 1982

Robert Hale Limited
Clerkenwell House
Clerkenwell Green
London, EC1

Printed in Great Britain by
Redwood Burn Limited, Trowbridge,Wiltshire
and Bound by Western Book Company

CONTENTS

ILLUSTRATIONS

ILLUSTRATIONS

CREDITS

Skyfotos: No 1; Aerofilms Ltd; 8, 12, 17, 27; the remainder are from photographs by the author.

The seven drawings of ships are by Lieut.-Commander Ramsay Harrison, R.N.V.R., and the sketch map of the area was drawn by C.G. Bloomfield.

ACKNOWLEDGMENTS

In my adventures and explorations of Romney Marsh, in my search and research for first-hand knowledge and accurate information, I have met, corresponded with, and bedevilled with questions, a great many people. From the old salt on the beach to the historian in his study, one and all have answered me with a willingness and charm, and with such an earnest desire to be of assistance that I find it difficult indeed to express to them my most sincere thanks. To many I cannot do so in person, for I do not even know their names. We just met and talked of birds and ships and knightly deeds and then went on our separate ways, perhaps never to meet again. Maybe one day, in curiosity, they will glance at this page; if so, this is my warmest "Thank you". Without you this book could never have been written. In fact, writing a book of this kind is like making a mosaic, in which many fragments are fitted together to build up an interesting, colourful and complete picture. How poor the picture is I am to blame, but for the very many beautiful pieces yours is the credit. In particular I am grateful to: Miss J. Maulden, Miss P. Neve, Miss G. Renwick, Miss A. R. Roper, K. A. Ashby, M. F. Barton (Skyways International), C. J. Bloomfield, R. D. Burrowes, H. Catt, R. Cooke (Pett), R. Cooke (east Guldeford), Captain T. Dannreuther, C. H. Dobbie, M.I.C.E., Lieut-Commander Ramsay Harrison, R.N.V.R., J. Harrod (Silver City Airways), P. E. N. Hitchins, H. Hickmott, N. H. Joy, F. C. Mctear, A. W. Reynolds, The Royal Society for the Protection of Birds, Major Teichman-Derville, O.B.E., R. E. Scott, A. Thompson, The Town Clerk of Rye, P. F. White, F. Wright, L. A. Vidler, Councillor Mrs J. Kirkham, Mayor of Rye, Mrs B. Burt, Mr E. G. Burt, Mr Christopher M. Fincken (Romneyrail) and Mr M. B. de Woolfson (Silver City Airways).

I should also like to acknowledge my indebtedness to Mrs George Bambridge and Macmillan & Co. for their kind permission to quote from *Puck of Pook's Hill* by Rudyard Kipling, and to many authors for their books and papers dealing with Romney Marsh. A bibliography is appended.

To
MARION CROOK
this book is dedicated

·Chapter I

THE SIXTH CONTINENT

THE Marsh lies a-dreaming under the summer sun. Its broad acres, its green pastures, irregular as a patchwork quilt, feather-stitched with reedy dyke and glinting sewer, reach as far as the eye can see. Fortunately the day is hazy, the heat shimmers and veils the distance, and from the one-time sandy bluff of the Isle of Oxney, which is our vantage point, we cannot see too much. That is a good thing! It is a mistake when exploring a new country to weary our eyes and overtax our minds with novelty.

We can see enough. To the south there is that unmistakable glare in the sky which means that the sea is not far away. For six or seven miles the levels below us spread away in a fading jig-saw pattern till they merge into the haze and their limits are hidden in mystery. Where the Royal Military Canal is not too reed-choked we can see its waters flash in the sunshine, and we can trace its course by the unending line of elm trees which fringe its banks. There are no towns, we can discern no villages. A church stands alone in a twenty-acre field, the inevitable radar masts loom in the distance. Romney Marsh lies a-dreaming, but already it has cast its spell upon us. It has reached out and touched you. Were it not so, you would never be reading this page. Its spell is potent, you cannot escape its magic.

One day you will come back here to the Isle of Oxney, one winter's day, perhaps, when there is that startling clarity of atmosphere for which the Marsh is famous. Then you may see in one *coup d'œil* the whole of Romney Marsh. You may see all the way from Folkestone to Fairlight, from Appledore to Dungeness.

Those limits are the limits of the region into which we are adventuring, because within those four points lie all the levels and marshes collectively known as Romney Marsh. The four points

I

do not enclose a rectangle, nor yet a quadrilateral, but the sector of a circle. Perhaps a geometrical description will not help many to visualise the shape of the region, so picture instead a birthday cake to which you and your friends have done full justice. You know what it looks like the day after, less than half is left, about two or three slices less than half. Well, there you have almost precisely the shape of Romney Marsh. The centre of the cake, which is now the point of the wedge, represents Dungeness Foreland. The cut edges of the cake correspond to the sea shore from Dungeness to Hythe, and Dungeness to Pett, and the un-cut crust of the cake stands for the rim of low hills which almost unbroken sweeps round from Shorncliffe at Folkestone to Hastings and the cliffs of Fairlight.

The radius of this circle, that is the distance from Dungeness to any point on the rim of hills, is roughly nine miles, and thus we can work out that the area of our region is approximately one hundred square miles. What a small area that is! Why, the area of England alone is 50,823 square miles! Many volumes have been written on the history of England, many a good book has been written about a single county, but a doubtful reader might well wonder if there is enough material in so small an area as Romney Marsh to fill even a chapter.

If that doubtful reader were to take a train journey from Ashford in Kent to Hastings in Sussex, passing through the little junction of Appledore, he would find no reason to change his mind. If half-way along the track he could drag his attention from the magazine he was reading to glance out of the carriage window, there would be nothing to hold his roving eyes, only flat fields, clumps and thin lines of trees, ditches, sheep, an occasional cottage, a farmhouse. Why, he would be back in his magazine or asleep before he reached Rye. If upon waking at Hastings half an hour later a friend should ask him, "What did you think of Romney Marsh?" I can see him rubbing his eyes and answering: "Romney Marsh, old chap? I never noticed it."

This small corner of Kent, with its snip of Sussex, which to the casual traveller appears so little different from other flats and levels, has been called by some The Fifth Quarter of the Globe.

A brave description this, something indeed to catch the eye and provoke curiosity. Nor yet is it too extravagant, for when the four corners of the world came in arms against its people, they did not fail to shock them. They shaped the history of England, and that means they changed the story of mankind.

But it is not in history alone that the Marsh holds the attention. It stirs the imagination in so many other ways. It is a place apart. It is neither Sussex nor Kent. It is not merely the fifth quarter of the globe. It is a "won'erful odd-gates place . . . Romney Marsh. . . . I've heard say the world's divided like into Europe, Ashy, Afriky, Ameriky, Australy, an' Romney Marsh." So says old Tom Shoesmith in the story of the Dymchurch Flit, from Kipling's *Puck of Pook's Hill*. And when Dan says he has only been as far as Rye once, Tom goes on:

> "Ah, that's but the edge. Back behind of her there's steeples settin' beside Churches, an' wise women settin' beside their doors, an' the sea settin' above the land, and ducks herdin' in the diks [he meant ditches]. The Marsh is just-about riddled with diks and sluices, an' tide-gates an' water-lets. You can hear 'em bubblin' and grummelin' when the tide works in 'em, an' you can hear the sea ragin' left and right handed all up along the Wall. You've seen how flat she is—The Marsh? You'd think nothin' easier than to walk eend-on acrost her? Ah, but the diks and the water-lets they twists the roads about as ravelly as witch-yarn on the spindles. So ye get all turned round in broad daylight."

This whimsical and altogether delightful description of "her" —the Marsh—is hard to equal anywhere in the extensive literature that touches upon the area. It makes no mention of historic events, of the Cinque Ports, of the Barons, of the king's ships, of victories and defeats, of disaster, fire and bloody murder. And yet, in its fanciful way, it paints the backcloth before which passes the pageant of all its history. The sea is the dominant feature, the sea that rages left- and right-handed all along the Wall. The sea that is sitting above the land. For it is the sea that has created and destroyed. It is from the sea that the Marsh has been won,

it is on the sea that its men have shouted the name of England,
it is by the sea that liberties have been won, it is from the sea that
the Marsh, lying behind its Walls, must be for ever protected.

And the wise women sitting beside their doors, what counsel
did they give their sons that enabled them to befriend kings and
defeat their enemies? And how did those churches rise from salty
mudflats and shifting shingle? And how do the dykes and the
sewers, the tide-gates and the sluices drain a land which lies below
high-water mark? And those ducks "herdin'" in the diks, isn't
that a touch of nature that must capture the imagination of every
bird-watcher?

Old Tom Shoesmith—or was it Puck?—knew a thing or two,
and if I am to try to answer some of these questions, if I am to
try to tell the story of the Marsh, I can only hope Puck will be
looking over my shoulder. For its history is like its roads, "as
ravelly as witch-yarn on the spindles", and if you know what
that's like, you will think my task is hopeless. Very likely I shall
get all turned round in broad daylight; but just because I have
found my way across some of its winding lanes and just because
you have come with me so far and are prepared to wind the ball
as I unravel the yarn, I am going to carry on.

*   *   *   *   *

To bring you under its spell, we had just now a glimpse of Romney Marsh from the top of the Isle of Oxney. But since we have
decided to explore this region properly, it is important to enter
into it for the first time by the best route. There are many ways
into the Marsh, by road, by rail and by sea. During the war
many a R.A.F. type came in by air, to use the four or five strips
which the levels so conveniently provided. At Lympne, on the
high ground to the north-east, there is an important airfield
today. But by air is not the best way in to begin with; leave that
till later, when you will want to see the whole area spread beneath
you as one vast fascinating map of intricate detail and clean-cut
coast. Neither is the ancient way in by sea to be recommended
today. There are no liners, there is no service. You would make
your landing on the wild beaches of Dungeness, or on the
shallow sands of Camber, or against the Wall at Dymchurch, or

4

the new wall at Pett. There is Rye Harbour, but the chances of finding a fishing-boat making for that narrow and awkward mouth of the Rother would be one in ten thousand. Strange that, when seven centuries ago four of the most famous harbours in Britain would have awaited your choice.

Roads in are many. One could come in from the west over the hills from Hastings and so to Winchelsea, or down through Sussex following the course of the Rother, past Bodiam Castle; through Kent by Tenterden or by Ashford; or again one could come in from the east from Dover and Folkestone over the hills and down to Hythe. But roads are not the ideal way in, not for the first visit—the distractions and responsibilities of the highways are too exacting, and if one walks the transition is too slow, and the distances are too great to be accomplished comfortably. No, the ideal way in is by rail, not by the route the doubtful reader took from Ashford, but the exact opposite. Entrain at Hastings, (I took a return to New Romney), forget the daily papers, leave the favourite magazines on the bookstall and settle down to the simple delight of looking out of the compartment window.

After leaving Ore a tunnel takes the line under the hills, which meet the sea in the fine sandstone cliffs at Fairlight. I like a tunnel, not for its smoke and its vile smells, but for the curiosity it provokes in what may await me at the other end. In our childhood there was an awful fascination about the shrill, then muffled, scream of the engine as it plunged into the bowels of the earth, the rush to close the windows and shut out the demons of the underworld, the fearsome and chaotic glitter and clatter as another entombed train fled by. Then the dazzling light as we emerge, and the windows go down and we breathe again, and, gradually, as our eyes become accustomed to the glare, we discover we are in a new world.

The tunnel beyond Ore was no exception, it belched smoke, for the line had not been electrified. But it is unique in the one respect that it emerges upon the confines of the Sixth Continent. At first perhaps there is nothing unusual to detect in the spring countryside through which it passes. There are abundant primroses and wood anemones upon the banks and carpeting the woods that come down to fringe the track. An orchard on the hillside alight with early cherry blossom certainly suggests Kent, although it is still miles to the county boundary. If we can catch a glimpse of the names of the little halts through which the train rattles, there is a quaint ring about them. Three Oaks and Guestling, Doleham, Snailham; but then the whole English countryside is rich in curious place-names. Yet gradually we become aware that there is a change. A small stream runs parallel with the line on the north side; it is the beginnings of the River Brede, and its narrow, flat-bottomed valley widens and widens. It catches the expectant eye, we are within the catchment of the Rother, this is the first water that goes down to the Marsh, and this flat-bottomed valley is the shadow before, the level sward, its long banks and intersecting ditches are the first hint of things to come.

There are willows, not old pollard willows hanging shaggy on the water, but orderly lines of trees, spaced alternately and on long leggy trunks, standing ten foot clean above the pastures. Their leaves gleam silvery as they turn in the fresh breeze. There are heron motionless along the banks or "knee-deep" in the dykes, leaning forward in that intent way that means any moment they will dart for a fish and whip it out vainly flapping in their huge bills. One can see it done from the compartment window, so familiar are the birds with the passing of a train. In fact, the noise or vibration of the locomotive may be what starts the fish in their direction, and a heron never fails to seize the fleeting opportunity. An experienced eye can pick out the peewits, scores and hundreds of them, scattered over the broad and hedgeless fields. But what a sight they make when, rising in their thousands, a great flock is seen above the low horizon flashing white, then dark, against an April sky!

But it is neither birds nor ruffling water that finally grips the attention. It is the wide open spaces—and the sheep. Were it not for the line of undulating hills on the south, and the low, sandy escarpment to the north, this might be a portion of downland, ironed out flat. The Downs, alas, have few flocks nowadays, but here on the Brede Level are the first flocks of the many thousand sheep which the Marsh supports. Romneys: the name echoes round the world from Argentina to Australia, New Zealand to the Falklands. Romneys, these are the sheep which down the centuries have ousted ships, won pastures from harbours, turned mariners to farmers. Look well at them, big, hardy and well-fleeced; why, those very levels which now they crop so close were at one time an arm of the sea, where the jostling ships of the proud Cinque Ports unloaded their spoils of war.

★   ★   ★   ★   ★

The train slows down at a wayside station. It stops at what seems but little bigger than the three halts through which it has passed. Another quaint name, we wonder, craning our necks to read the title on a rusted railway lamp-post. What does it say? W–I–N—WINCHELSEA. Never shall I forget the shock I received when for the first time I read there that honourable, ancient name, in such tarnished and humble setting. I remembered enough of my classroom history to know that Winchelsea and Rye were the two Antient Towns, that they were numbered with the Cinque Ports, that illustrious Winchelsea was coupled with the name of Edward and with admirals and battles. Admitted these facts were hazy, but they had created in a childish mind an aura of greatness about this historic place, and somehow I had been led to expect at least a castle or battlements, or a town with some vestige of dignity. Yet all I saw was a faded name on the blue glass of a railway lamp in a little wayside station.

"Where," I asked a solitary porter who had just put some empty cans in the van, "where is Winchelsea?"

The old man eyed me for a moment, then seeing I was serious he put one hand on the door handle and pointed with the other across the levels. "This be Winchelsea Station," he said. "But the town sits yonder, a good mile walk from here. Winchelsea be on the hill now, sir."

The hill was a low eminence well furnished with trees. I had noticed it before we drew in to the station, but on closer inspection I could just see a roof or two. But what did he mean by the word "now"?

7

"Do you mean Winchelsea isn't where it was?" I asked rather stupidly.

"Oh no, sir," he replied, stepping clear as the train started again with a noisy jerk. "No, sir. Old Winchelsea lay over yonder . . ." The train wrenched us apart and his last words were drowned in noise and steam, but I thought I caught the words "under the sea" before the smoke engulfed him. I sat back and pondered. Surely there had been no recent disaster, and it must just have been the old porter's manner of speech, "Winchelsea be on the hill now, sir", that suggested such a thing. Yet if there had been another site whereon the ancient town had stood, and if indeed the words I thought I heard were true, then why had I never read in history of so calamitous an event? And where was the sea?

These are questions you too may very well ask as you jog along to Rye. They were questions to which, years ago, I had to find the answers. I will give them to you in the pages that follow, but there is no time now, for unless you lean out of the compartment window and look forward along the track you will miss a view I would not have you miss at any cost. Well . . . that is, I do not want it to cost you your head, and I am not going to have the first pages of this book recommending anything so dangerous. *Ne pas se pencher au dehors.* Even so, I would have liked you to have seen the shape of Rye. For Rye stands where it did. This ancient town is not modest and retiring, like Winchelsea among its trees, but piles up upon its rocky bluff in roofy terraces, conspicuous for all to see for miles around. It is a wonderful shape, not dramatic like St Michael's Mount, not even shapely, but most extraordinarily picturesque, no matter whether seen in broad daylight or romantically silhouetted against the evening glow.

There will be plenty of time later properly to appreciate the shape of Rye, but as the town is barely two miles from its old rival and less from Winchelsea Station, we shall only just get a glimpse of the River Tillingham, a mill, a sluice-gate, before we are at the station of Rye itself. A busy little town this, the meeting-place of routes, the confluence and bridging of three rivers, the western key and market of the Marsh, the Mecca of tens of thousands of visitors, the show-place of the past; borough, Cinque Port. Have I left anything out? Yes, the harbour, but that must come last. In spite of all the vicissitudes brought about by man and nature, in spite of the slough of despond, and mud, into which it stumbled, Rye has won through. It's a large little town today, proud of its past, but not living in it.

We cannot see closely anything of the old part of Rye from the railway. It lies in fact outside the site of the city walls. But as we leave the station we can just see the clock and tower of the great church, and if we know where to look we may see what appear to be two small round turrets of an old castle. As the story of the Marsh unfolds we shall come back to Rye again and again, and then we shall discover that these two turrets are the top of a grand old gateway—the Land Gate, which, in its way, epitomises the Antient Town. For Rye is a gateway to the past, Rye has been a gateway of Old England, and Rye is a gateway to the Marsh.

*   *   *   *   *

With a roar the train thunders over the iron bridge that crosses the Rother. This sentence sounds extravagant, but anyone who has been in Rye for the first time and heard this sound when the wind was in the east will agree it is startling. Being acquainted with the sound of V-twos, I must admit that the first time I heard it, taken unawares, I jumped, and was amazed at the sang-froid of the Ryers. How quickly familiarity breeds deafness! I have stayed in Rye a number of times since and have never noticed it.

As the Rother is crossed and if the tide be low, it will be noticed through what a depth of mud—"slub" as it is still some-times called—the river cuts its way. If a full tide is in, then the river looks quite respectable, small sailing yachts may be enjoying themselves, or some thirty fishing boats may be seen riding considerably above the level of the adjoining recreation ground. Back in Sussex (this is the Sixth Continent, don't forget) we pronounce the name of the River Rother to rhyme with bother, but quite a number of knowledgeable folk down Rye way pro-nounce the first syllable to rhyme with both. So long as we know something of the astonishing story of this river, it is hardly worth becoming involved in a controversy. I like the more sonorous pronunciation, yet, being born and bred in Sussex, it still sounds affected in my ears.

Now at last we are on the Marsh, and if the line were to travel straight on in an E.N.E. direction it would go for fifteen miles on the level and pass through neither town, village nor hamlet. Even when at their prime, no railway company could have contemplated so uneconomical a run, so the line skirts along the north-western margins, going nearly dead straight for Appledore Junction and running parallel to the rim of hills that enclose the Marsh. But the line is not too near these one-time sea cliffs, and when quite suddenly the level crossing at East Guldeford is passed, in an instant the broad breezy spaces of Guldeford Marsh are spread far and wide on either hand.

It would be well at this point to make clear two important facts, for without being in possession of them the reader might very easily become confused. I may already be guilty of causing misunderstanding for not having mentioned in the very first sentence that Romney Marsh is no marsh at all. The reader has probably inferred that tens of thousands of sheep require thousands of acres of pasture, but he will still be wondering, as I did when first exploring the region, where in the area and how much of it is the marshland. After all, one does not call a place a marsh without good reason, and one pictures sedgy swamps, waterlogged depressions, dense reed-beds, or muddy flats and undrained bogs. It comes as something of a shock to learn that there is no marsh in Romney Marsh. In all the 50,000 acres of the levels it is safe to say there are not one hundred acres of real swamp, bog or reed-bed apart from the water-lets.

If you are a lover of marshland, as I am, and delight in the lush vegetation, its wild life, its secrecy, let not this discovery disappoint you. Romney Marsh was marsh once—about that we have much to discover—but it is now dry land. Yet it has such innumerable dykes, ditches, cuts, guts, sewers, sluices, streams, canals, channels, pools and pits that it more than makes amends for its misleading name. Besides, it has the sea, nearly twenty miles of coast and thousands of acres of the most remarkable beachlands in the world, Denge Beach, ending in that astonishing and ever-growing headland, Dungeness. No, don't be disappointed if Romney Marsh is not what you had been led to expect.

This brings me to the second fact, and again it is a matter of names. Romney Marsh is the name popularly given to all the levels between the rim of low hills and the sea from Hythe to Rye. This is not strictly accurate, as Romney Marsh proper is that part of our area which lies east of a line from Appledore to the town of New Romney—roughly half of the levels. West of that line the levels are known as Walland Marsh, Denge Marsh, Denge Beach and Guldeford Marsh; and west of the Rother as Nook Beach and Pett Level. In order that there may be no misunderstanding in the following pages it will be best to refer to each part of the levels by its proper name and to speak of the whole region as The Marsh.

While settling these matters the train has carried us beyond Guldeford Marsh, over the Kent Ditch—though there is no more feeling of being in Kent than there was of being in Sussex—and on through the north-western margins of Walland Marsh. There are more trees on the levels here than were on the breezy spaces of East Guldeford, and on the left the high ground of the Isle of Oxney is less than a mile away. The highest poin⁺ at this end of the "island" is Cliff Farm, 182 feet, but it rises so abruptly above the dead level of Walland Marsh that it seems higher. Its face is quite steep towards the south, but there are no exposed sandstone cliffs such as there are at Rye and Playden. It is plain there must have been in the past, even if the old names of Stone Cliff and Cliff Farm no longer lingered on the map, and it reminds us that at no very remote time the sea washed along the foot of these sandstone hills, and creeks extended so much farther inland that tidal waters completely encircled these four miles of high ground. It appears that the River Rother, entering the creeks at their extreme north-western limit, divided its waters, part going down the creek north of the island and part to the south. The high ground would thus be cut off at high or low tide and become a secure retreat. One can understand how it took the name of the Saxon Isle—Saxoney—Oxney. To call it the Isle of Oxney is one of those redundancies common in names around our coasts, and common too whenever the meaning of an old suffix has been forgotten.

Our train draws in to Appledore Junction, and here we must change, for the line to Lydd and New Romney, coming down from Ashford, strikes off at a sharp angle to the south-east. There is usually an hour to wait, so we can either walk the mile to Appledore village and see the church and the Royal Military Canal, or we can look in at the Station Inn, enjoy a leisurely one, and have some chat with the farmers. Although the Royal Military Canal encircles The Marsh completely from Hythe to Rye, and we must cross it whenever we enter or leave the levels, this particular section of it from Appledore to Warehorne is quite lovely and is worth a visit, especially in late spring, when the wych elms that line its banks are just breaking into leaf. Fortunately these three miles are in the safe-keeping of the National Trust.

But the Canal emphasises another aspect of The Marsh which, while taking this preliminary canter across the region, we should add to our stock of information. From "times out of mind", as the old records so frequently and quaintly express custom, The Marsh has been regarded as the "invasion beach" for the conquest of Britain. Roman, Saxon, Dane, Norman, French, Napoleon and Hitler, one and all, when casting their eyes enviously or vindictively across the narrow waters to the white cliffs and the green and pleasant land of Albion, have considered this area the ideal landing ground, a gateway to England. Hence the story of The Marsh is bound up with the history of Britain, and the history of The Marsh is dependent, in a way almost too extraordinary to be true, upon its changing geography. It is sufficient here to note that the Canal was cut to the direction of Mr William Pitt at that alarming time when Boney was planning his fantastic invasion barges, half-castle, half-raft, to be propelled across La Manche by sail and windmills.

While waiting on the platform at Appledore we shall not fail to notice the curious arrangement of the platforms; they are not opposite one another, as is usual, but are staggered, the up-platform beginning where the down-platform ends. It is the same at Rye. Hence passengers cross the line to get from one platform to the other. Whether this arrangement was to save bridge, tunnel or personnel (or the legs of passengers), no one has been able to explain to me. I have been so sternly brought up to obey the injunction that Passengers Must Not Cross the Line that I feel delightfully like a naughty boy at these stations and want to put a penny on the line for the engine to flatten into an oval medal for me.

If we were boarding our train in summer it would be hard to find a seat in its six or eight crowded brakes, so popular is the coast between Dungeness and Dymchurch. But out of season there is more than enough room in a couple of brakes, and we can choose which side we like. It makes no difference, however, for all The Marsh looks the same to one unfamiliar with it. To the right-hand as we make towards Lydd is Walland Marsh, to the left about a mile away is the boundary of Romney Marsh proper. The boundary is the main road from Appledore to New Romney, and this road follows or runs on the top of an old earthwork known as the Rhee Wall. Unless you knew what to look out for, you would never notice it while motoring along the road, but closer attention would reveal that for most of the way the road runs a few feet above the level of the marshes. It would also be observed that, to the north-east, the level of Romney Marsh is a foot or two lower than the level of Walland Marsh to the south-west. Who made the Rhee Wall has been a vexed question, and it is too early to become involved in the argument just now. It is mentioned, as so many things have to be mentioned, in this introductory chapter to make clear its position and to familiarise the reader with the features of The Marsh which play such an important part in its story.

The Rhee Wall cannot be distinguished from the railway carriage and in fact, after running parallel for three or four miles, road and rail diverge, the Wall to New Romney and the rail to Lydd.

The fine tower of Lydd's great church is soon seen to the south; it is 132 feet high, and in a few minutes we are running into the town whose name is probably better known to most people, soldiers at any rate, than any other in all The Marsh. Nearly a hundred and fifty years ago volunteers were trained here to be prepared to meet Napoleon, and for the past sixty years Lydd has been an artillery camp, having been permanently occupied since 1906. Modern guns soon outdistanced the ranges, and more recently the camp has been a training ground for the Royal Tank Corps. Even if the town is not familiar to those who undergo military training, it is at least familiar in name to them as an explosive. But it somehow seems a shame that a place mentioned by name, Hlyda, in a Saxon charter of the eighth century should only be known in the twentieth in connection with lyddite.

The name Hlyda is said to be derived from the Latin *littus*, a shore or strand, in which case the name originated a good two thousand years ago. Furthermore, it gives another clue to the evolution of The Marsh and the formation of Dungeness, for Lydd is now more than two miles from the sea.

From Lydd Town Station our journey continues for a mile or so across Denge Marsh, and then, suddenly, the big surprise. The line is no longer running through the green levels of The Marsh; it is running on shingle, miles and miles of it, to the right-hand and the left, as far as the eye can see from the carriage window. It looks a vast desert, for it has something of the colour of the desert, much of it is destitute of vegetation of any sort or kind, and the shallow undulating ridges of shingle that ripple its entire surface complete the impression. "What an awful place!" many a visitor has ejaculated on seeing the beachlands of Dungeness for the first time. They can be excused, for it looks, nine months out of twelve, utterly desolate; besides, they have at the back of their minds memories of the excruciating torture beach has for tired and tender feet, whether shod or unshod.

But do not judge this barren waste of shingle from the railway carriage window; neither must it be judged in car comfort, nor indeed from anywhere along the road. Have patience and courage, and I will show you not merely how to walk on the beach in comfort, but, if I may, the peculiar magic of this unique place, its strange beauty, its fascinating ecology.

The preliminary journey of ours is nearly ended. The railway line makes a great bend. The lighthouse, which we saw almost directly ahead, swings round in an unexpected way and falls behind us. We travel north parallel with the sea coast for a mile or two—we can see the bungalows lining the shore—and then into New Romney, railway terminus, but for us the beginning of our adventure.

I have described this journey as I first took it some thirty years ago. Today the line from Appledore to New Romney no longer exists, like so many of our branch lines tiny, uneconomical, delightful, it became redundant. Regretfully you must now make this part of your journey by road.

CHAPTER II

EVOLUTION

COMPARED with the age and geological structure of almost the whole of Britain, The Marsh is very young. A geological map of South-Eastern England, one of those most fascinating maps in a variety of colours showing the disposition and composition of the surface rocks and earths in Kent and Sussex, defines The Marsh as Alluvium and describes it in no uncertain terms as "very recent". The story of the rocks is so long and spans such vast periods of time that a few thousand years are no more in a chapter than the turning of a single page. Yet although the deposition of material that is now The Marsh only occurred, geologically speaking, very recently, it is necessary to push time back at least ten.thousand years to arrive at the period when it began.

It may seem unnecessary in this adventure to travel so far back through time. Personally I have a sneaking admiration for Wells's Time Machine, and whether it went forward or backward I should have been deeply interested in what I found there. When I was discussing some points on the evolution of Romney Marsh with one of the best-known personalities living there, he was inclined to laugh at my earnest desire to get the early part of the story straight. "No one," he said merrily, "nobody is going to worry about the ups and downs of Romney Marsh. And if anybody did, they wouldn't agree with you. Have some more sherry." The sherry was very good, and if I had stayed much longer enjoying such hospitality I might have found that night, on cycling back across the lonely levels, that the ups and downs of Romney Marsh would have been far too much for me. On another occasion I was telling a friend something of what I had learned about the makings of The Marsh, and she was deeply

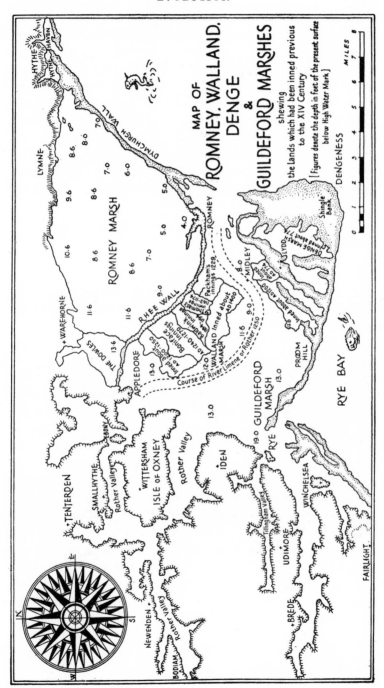

MAP OF
ROMNEY. WALLAND.
DENGE
&
GUILDEFORD MARSHES

shewing
the Lands which had been inned previous
to the XIV Century

[figures denote the depth in feet of the present surface
below High Water Mark]

interested. "But it's the most extraordinary story I've ever heard," she declared. "Let them keep all their old Cinque Ports, you must tell this."

At the George Hotel in Rye I met a young man recently returned from a tour of Australia and New Zealand. It was one of those chance acquaintances which coincidence or good fortune sometimes arranges. He had seen enough sheep recently to have no interest whatever in that side of The Marsh, but he was well versed in maps. "You must show maps," he said enthusiastically. "All this is new to me, as it will be to many others. You must draw maps, consecutive maps, to illustrate these extraordinary changes you describe."

No one can write a book to please everybody. If I were to attempt to do so about The Marsh, I should first put everything in and then, by a process of elimination, in accord with personal dislikes and lack of interest, one by one remove each subject, until the reader was the happy possessor of a pair of good cover boards, the spine of the binding and nothing else. So I shall tell the story in my own way, and although it may start off "Once upon a time" it is no fairy story. It may read like fiction, but it is fact. If then we put our Time Machine into reverse and ride backward ten thousand years, we shall arrive at a period when Palæolithic man was just giving place to his Neolithic counterpart. We shall not disturb either of these primitive men, they did nothing that could alter the course of Nature in the shaping of The Marsh. But they were both in the immediate neighbourhood, and some quite good Neolithic implements have recently been found, several in 1938 and 1940 at Kenardington, about two miles or so north-east of Appledore; and another away south-west, off-shore of Pett Level.

But what those primitive men saw we may see again. There was a broad bay open to the sea. It was twenty miles long and from ten to fifteen miles wide, but its waters were shallow. At low tide probably a great deal of its floor was uncovered and mud-flats and sand-banks were exposed interlaced with watercourses. This great bay was confined by cliffs, which are the self-same semicircle of low hills which rim The Marsh today. Not only were they higher and more rugged, but their extremities reached farther seaward. Fairlight extended one or two miles farther into the Channel. The estimated recession of this headland has been put at one foot per annum. At the other end of the arc was a headland which now no longer exists. It must have jutted well out to sea from where Hythe now stands. Being of Lower Greensand, it was less resistant to all the agents of erosion than the tougher sandstone of Fairlight. At the western end of the bay

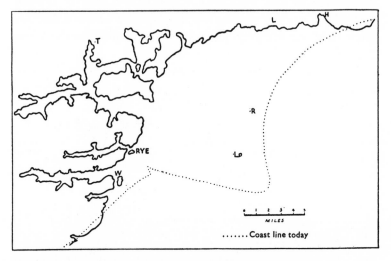

The Great Bay—as it was at the time of the Neolithic Depression. The coastline is approximately that of the 50-ft. contour today.

T=Tenterden	R=New Romney
L=Lymne	Ld=Lydd
H=Hythe	W=Winchelsea

there were six or seven narrow creeks reaching far inland, almost as far as Robertsbridge and Tenterden of today.

Then very gradually a tremendous change took place. The land began to sink. This does not mean only the land of our particular region, but includes half of England and a good deal of north-western France and the Netherlands besides. This was what is known as the Neolithic Depression, and geologists are now pretty well agreed that the fall in the land level was about seventy feet. Or, to put it another way, what had been the seventy-foot contour line was, after the Depression, sea level.

One might well imagine that as a result of this the waters of the bay would have been deepened by that amount and the possibility of new land lost for ever, as indeed so much of Britain was lost at that time. But no; the paradox of The Marsh is that although the land sank deeper and deeper beneath the sea The Marsh gained. How did this happen? For two reasons, first because running into the creeks at the western end of the bay were three or more rivers, draining much of East Sussex and West Kent and bringing down quantities of silt. The Brede, the Tillingham and the Rother are still there now. Sand, mud and other particles are carried in suspension by the impetus of a river.

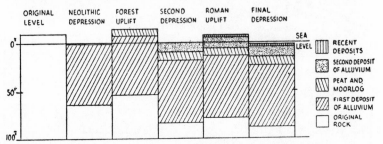

The Paradox: as the land sank below sea level so new land was being created.

When the river is checked on collision with the sea such suspended matter sinks to the bottom and, provided the scour of tides and waves is not too great, remains there. Hence as our bay was already shallow to begin with and free from big wave action, its floor became covered with alluvium. The second reason was that because the sinking of the land was so gradual the deposit could keep pace with it. So although at the climax of the Depression the original sea bed had sunk seventy feet it had been overlaid by river silt, material from the eroded cliffs and marine deposits to almost an equal depth.

Geology has shown again and again that what goes down often comes up again, and our region was no exception. This part of the earth's surface was still far from stable, and a reactionary oscillation occurred. An Uplift commenced. The muddy sands and shallows were gradually raised above the tidal limits. At first no doubt the shallow waters were choked with marine vegetation and plants of the "salts". But as the land rose higher and the water drained off, so its salt-marsh characteristics disappeared and it became firm, dry land. The experts (and I would like here to acknowledge my indebtedness to C. J. Gilbert, F.G.S., for his paper in *Archæologia Cantiana* on "The Evolution of Romney Marsh") say the Uplift was about twenty-five to thirty feet.

This was not Romney Marsh, far from it. This was but the

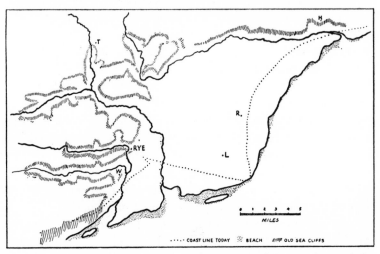

The Forest Uplift—showing the possible position of the coastline and the course of the rivers.

T=Tenterden R=New Romney
H=Hythe   L=Lydd
      W=Winchelsea

foundation. But upon the new land now raised up forests of oaks grew, covering almost the whole area of what is now The Marsh. Farther seaward in fact, for beyond low-tide mark it is still possible to see off Winchelsea Beach and Pett Level ancient tree-trunks, rooted stumps and other debris of that forest exposed. A dark blackish mud is known to lie south of Dungeness beneath the sea, and when one of the first maps of The Marsh was made, by Poker, in 1594, it showed an area in the then wide estuary of the

Rother south-east of Rye called the Black Shore which undoubtedly was another exposure of the same thing.

Along the seaward margins of the Forest Uplift beaches were
thrown up, and one might well have thought conditions were
then stabilised. But it was not so. How long the Uplift lasted
none can say with exactness. But the fact is it did not last in-
definitely. The oscillations of the earth's crust had not yet died
out, and a new depression began. Down, slowly down, went
the land once more. The great forest sank slowly to sea level and
below it. At first it was protected by the beaches which the
waves drove farther and farther inland as the shore deepened. At
length even this protecting rampart failed; it was breached in
places and swept away in others. The sea poured in, and the
whole Forest was submerged.

Once again the rivers did their work, and as the rate of the
depression was slow the deposit of silt kept pace with it. There
were differences, however, this time in the depths of the deposit,
in that the eastern half either did not sink so far as the rest or
because it was still partially protected by beaches; while the
western half was more exposed and scoured more thoroughly
by the waves and tide, which once again beat against the line of
ancient cliffs at Winchelsea and Rye and Oxney.

That was possibly 2000 B.C., when the forest was submerged
and buried; it might have been later. But we have proof positive
that it happened, for almost everywhere on The Marsh where
there have been borings and excavations "moor log" has been
found, sometimes only four or five feet below the surface, sometimes at two or three times that depth. On Pett Marsh it is
twenty-five feet below the surface; at Appledore ten feet. The
thickness of the Submerged Forest layer is some six or seven feet
and includes logs, leaf mould and peat. In some instances the
ancient wood is hard and black as ebony, and in others soft and
rotten, rapidly disintegrating on exposure to the air.

For the last time, so it would appear, there was an upward
movement of this vexed portion of the world's surface, and the
whole area was raised once again a few feet. The muddy shallows
of the eastern end were raised almost to mean sea level, certainly

above low-water mark, while the western half with its varying deposits of mud and sand was still largely well below sea level. As before, the shallowest waters were soon choked with vegetation, which both checked the movement of tidal water and hastened the deposit of yet more alluvium. Considerable parts of the eastern half of this vast marshland, protected as it soon became by new beaches on the shore line, ceased to be regularly submerged at high tide, and portions gradually became firm ground. They were islands in The Marsh—Romney, Midley, Ivey.

Yes, at last we have reached the stage in its evolution where The Marsh is just recognisable; we have passed from geological times and records to historic times; we have entered on the Christian Era. The Romans have arrived.

*   *   *   *   *

This dash across a hundred centuries has been a little breathless. We must pause a moment and collect our thoughts and summarise what has happened. Twice has the land sunk and twice has it been raised again, each oscillation being more feeble than the last. During each depression enormous quantities of alluvium have been deposited, until it has reached depths up to sixty feet. During each uplift vegetation has thrived, and the land has been consolidated, completely during the Forest Uplift, but only partially during the second upheaval. Throughout the centuries the rivers have either poured into the creeks and the bay or have cut their way by devious routes across the new land or across the mud-flats exposed at low tide, The headland at Hythe has disappeared and Fairlight has been cut back more than a mile. During each uplift a new shore line was created, and along it the waves piled new beaches, which during the depressions were either driven inland or broken through, submerged or swept away.

Thus we have arrived at a point in its story no longer remote, barely two thousand years ago, and we should take very careful note of the state of affairs. For now men have come upon the scene, not primitive Stone Age men, but able, purposeful, civilised men. The history of Britain has begun.

How did The Marsh appear at the time of the Roman occupation? This was towards the end of the second period of upheaval, and there is little doubt that the greater part of Romney Marsh proper was at that time consolidated. Roman remains have been found over most of the eastern half. Nevertheless much of it must have been marshland and subject to flooding at exceptional high tides. It should be noted also that such slope as The Marsh has is not towards the sea but inland. That is to say to the south about Lydd, Romney and The Warren, the land was above sea level, whereas towards the north, the backlands, particularly about

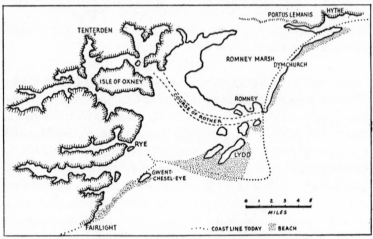

Romney Marsh at the time of the Roman Occupation.

Appledore in an area called The Dowles, the land was below sea level.

The western half of The Marsh was by no means consolidated. Indeed every high tide completely covered it. The sea reached far up into the river creeks and washed against the cliffs of Rye and Playden, Peasmarsh and Oxney. At low tide most of the area was exposed as mud-flats intersected by innumerable channels and watercourses, which carried off the tidal water, and by the meandering beds of the rivers Rother, Tillingham and Brede.

Another noticeable feature of the period which must not and could not be overlooked was the enormous bars and beds of

24

shingle which were accumulating in the shallows across the whole width of the bay from Fairlight to Hythe, but in particular about the islands of Lydd and Romney. The full story of the shingle must be kept for another chapter, but we cannot here pass over its effect upon the evolution of The Marsh. We have already seen that beaches thrown up along the shores during an uplift protected in some measure the land behind during a depression. And not only did these beaches act as a protecting barrier against the waves, but they also helped to hold up the flood waters and tidal waters. This steadying of ebb and flow created quieter conditions in the lagoons behind, which hastened the deposition of silt and hindered its removal by tidal scour. Thus, the more beach the more the build-up of alluvium; and the stronger the shingle bars the greater protection given to the low-lying land behind. As we shall see later, the shingle was continuously on the move, and where in one place it may have been piled up, later that same place would become subject to a scour, become thin, and finally the waves of the Channel would break through. When this happened a complete alteration might occur in the distribution of the silt; the rivers and tidal waters would find a new exit to the sea, and new-claimed land would be flooded. The people who came to live on the newly consolidated marshlands discovered themselves to be always in danger of such disaster, and they began to take it upon themselves to strengthen the defences against the sea. Men began to take a hand in the shaping of The Marsh.

But Nature had one more trick up her dainty sleeve. Feeble as the last uplift had been, the oscillations had not yet quite died away, and there was to be one more depression. Probably this movement had already commenced during the Roman occupation, but its full effect was not felt until the thirteenth century. It is possible we may still be experiencing the last tremor today; and there are several authorities on the subject who are convinced that the whole area is still sinking, very, very gradually, at the rate of some six inches per century.

The oscillations of The Marsh might be illustrated diagrammatically as a highly damped alternating curve.

Such a graphical representation does not pretend to be accurate. It only attempts to make it easier for the reader to grasp what has happened. The dating can be little more than guesswork, as written records can carry us back no further than Julius Cæsar. But a point that the diagram does make clear is the initiation of the movements, for it will be observed that an uplift commences at the very pit of a depression, and a downward movement must perforce begin at the very apex of an uplift. This of course assumes that depression followed uplift and uplift depression in a series of excessively slow but continuous movements. There is practically nothing to show from geological study whether when one movement was completed there was a pause

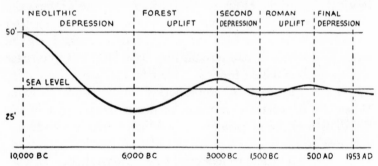

Oscillations of the land during the past 12,000 years.

before the next oscillation. Even if there were pauses it is the fact that a new movement commences at the peak of the previous movement that makes it so difficult to describe clearly.

The ups and downs of The Marsh and the principal events in its evolution might be tabulated as follows:

TABULATION OF EVENTS

Before 12,000 years ago

Earth's crust 70 feet above present level. High bare cliffs surrounding a shallow bay probably exposed at low tide.

Neolithic Depression 10,000–6,000 B.C.

Land sinks 70 feet, but deposits of marine and river silt keep pace. Headlands off Hythe and Fairlight cut back one to two miles. Sandstone cliffs scoured and eroded. Creeks reach far inland.

Forest Uplift 6,000–3,000 B.C.

Land raised from 25 to 30 feet. Covered by oak forests and moorland. The whole leaves a deposit of from 6 to 8 feet of leaf mould, moor log and peat. A shore beach forms at the seaward boundary of the uplifted area.

2nd Depression 3,000–1,500 B.C.

Land sinks again below sea level. At first lagoons form behind the shore line, but beach defences are breached and high tides flood the whole area. Again marine and river silt keeps pace with depression. Now a real marsh choked with marine vegetation.

Roman Uplift 1,500 B.C.–500 A.D.

Land raised 10 to 15 feet above sea level. Water-logged marsh consolidated to the east. Alluvium deepened to the west. Formation of Dungeness initiated. Shore defences strengthened by new beach bars and shingle spits.

Final Depression 500 A.D.–*today*

Land again sinks below sea level. Innings commenced. Period of great storms. Romney Haven blocked and course of Rother changed. Winchelsea lost, Promehill lost, Cinque Ports left high and dry. Artificial sea walls constructed, as the whole of The Marsh below high-water mark. Accumulation of shingle at Dungeness grows steadily greater. Sand dunes forming at Camber and Greatstone.

However inaccurate the above may be in detail, it does at least give an outline of the extraordinary sequence of events which brought about The Marsh. All that happened we can never know until that Time Machine is invented; we shall never know all the scenes in the drama. But we do know the five Acts, for we have complete proof of the story in the tremendous depth of alluvium which would only have been deposited as marine and river silt in a comparatively sheltered and shallow bay. We have proof of the Forest Uplift in moor log and peaty strata which lie above the first great bed of silt. We know that this sank again, for the moor log is deeply buried by another layer of alluvium. We have the vast shingle beds of Dungeness still corrugated by the storm beaches cast up century after century. And finally we have two thousand years of history, written records of the last amazing Act upon which the curtain has not yet fallen.

*   *   *   *   *

Before we leave the story of the evolution of The Marsh and before the stirring pageant of history passes on its stage before us, it is necessary to know a little bit more about the behaviour of the rivers, particularly the Rother. These rivers drained the Weald of East Sussex and West Kent and until comparatively recent times all that area was heavily forested. G. W. Lamplugh, F.R.S., has described the valleys as being continually choked by fallen timber and the like until, as may be seen in Canada and parts of Scandinavia at the present day, the whole bottom of a valley is a wet swamp. It is probable too that the rainfall was very much heavier than it is now, for as A. D. Hall and E. J. Russell have pointed out "the present rivers seem to overflow too rarely and to leave too little deposit behind to account for the considerable depth and extent of alluvial soil that has accumulated."

The Rother, the Brede and the Tillingham, and possibly others, found their way into the bay by narrow V-shaped estuaries, and, as we have seen, unloaded their burden of silt there. Except during the uplifts the floor of this bay was commonly exposed at low tide, hence the rivers had to find their way through and among the mud-flats and sand-banks and out through the beaches and shingle spits to reach the open Channel. This meant that their courses to the sea were constantly subject to variation. Winds and tides, currents and eddies would cause continuous changes in the deposition of silt and the shape and extent of the shingle bars. Thus at high tide the whole or part of the bay was open water, deep enough for the first boats to navigate easily, while at low tide the area was a series of shallows, lagoons, marshes, islands and salts, intersected by the beds of the rivers, often cutting deeply through the silt, as indeed the Brede and the Rother can be seen to do round about Rye to this very day.

28

When the beach bars and beds of shingle were very extensive and, except for breaches here and there, almost shut in the bay from the open sea, then the outlets for the escape of tidal and flood and river water were very much restricted, and the shallows would barely have time to empty before the next high tide came surging in. When such conditions prevailed, and they did over nearly the whole of the western half during the first twelve centuries of the Christian Era, then The Marsh was in very truth a marsh and the beach-locked bays and flooded creeks were the ideal harbourages and the Cinque Ports were at their prime.

But to get back to the Rother—the river which created The Marsh, which was responsible for the power and importance of at least three Cinque Ports and which finally brought them to utter impotence. The Rother it would appear has had no less than seven courses across The Marsh. I am very much indebted to Mr C. G. Bloomfield, of the Kent Rivers Board and Rye, for information on this difficult subject. If anyone knows his maps, ancient and modern, from A to Z, Mr Bloomfield does; furthermore he has given enthusiastic and original study and research to the evolution of The Marsh and the formation of Dungeness. In his opinion the earliest course of the Rother was north of the Isle of Oxney, along the line of the cliffs eastward, to reach the sea near Hythe.

When this course was last in use is a very vexed question, and about it high argument and long has raged for years. Julius Cæsar wrote a good deal about his invasion of Britain but was extremely vague on geography. Furthermore Roman map makers left much to be desired and their coastal outlines were hopeless in matters of detail. T. Lewin, in his book *Cæsar's Invasion of Britain*, presumes that when the Romans first arrived in 55 B.C. they found the whole of The Marsh under water, certainly at high tide, except for the island or islands round about New Romney and the beds and bars of shingle which were piled up against them and spread out across the bay. They called this sheltered water the Limene. At low tide, as we have seen, the rivers made their way across the exposed mud-flats and cut deep channels which made good harbours. The Rother had

certainly cut such a channel to sea at Hythe, for it was commanding this deep inlet that the Romans built a castra, the ruins of
which can still be seen, but which are now known as Stutfall
Castle. The harbour was the Portus Lemanis.

While the Hythe inlet was certainly there, and indeed it per-
sisted for many centuries after the Romans had left, it is now
considered extremely doubtful that the Rother was running in
that course during their occupation. In fact Dr Gordon Ward,
who has given a great deal of study to the Roman and Saxon
occupation of The Marsh, is convinced, and geologists on both
sides of the Channel support him, that the Roman occupation
coincided with the end of the last uplift and that the level of the
eastern half of The Marsh, Romney Marsh proper, was probably
ten feet higher than it is today. The Rother no doubt was then
running in its second bed, which took it from Appledore in a
south-easterly direction to New Romney, where it reached the
sea in a widish estuary between the islands and Lydd.

Its channel, together with the banks which began to be constructed along it and which were the beginnings of the Rhee Wall,
assisted very greatly in protecting the low-lying levels of Romney
Marsh when the final depression began to be felt. In fact as the
sea began to flood more and more ominously into the as-yet-
unreclaimed western half of The Marsh, the Teutonic settlers
who followed the Romans became increasingly aware of the
dangers which threatened them. Gradually a most complex
organisation was built up whereby vigilance, money and labour
were marshalled so that drainage, sea defence and repair might
always be effected at a moment's notice. As we shall see later,
the famous "Laws and Constitutions of Romney Marsh" were
thus formulated and became, as Lambarde wrote in 1576, "a
patterne and exemplar to all the like places of the whole realme
whereby to be governed".

Whether the Romans did anything to further the reclamation
of marshland is a moot point, though it is generally conceded
that they were the first to strengthen the sea defences of Romney
Marsh eastwards, where the Dymchurch Wall runs today. It
appears that the Romans were forced to do something here,

because Roman remains, in particular pottery, have been found seaward of the wall. The tidal currents had in fact already begun to scour away the beach defences, built up there in earlier times, which protected the east shore of The Marsh. The wear and tear has been going on ever since, and for fifteen centuries it has been the unceasing task of the "Lords of Romney Marsh" to repair, rebuild, strengthen, lengthen and heighten the Dymchurch Wall. It is today a tremendous affair more than three miles long, reaching as far as Littlestone, faced with massive concrete and in places incorporating some of the latest ideas on sea defence.

It seems probable that the Romans did little else in the defence or reclamation of the marshland. No doubt it was not necessary in their time. But in the three or four centuries that immediately followed their departure changes occurred. First there was the continued fall in the level of The Marsh and the ever-increasing threat of the sea to burst in and flood it, but at the same time we see the ever-growing efforts of men not only to defend such consolidated land as they already possessed but to reclaim new land.

All the time that any part of The Marsh was subject to regular tidal flooding, marine and river silt was continuously being deposited there. As the land sank, the deeper became the alluvium. This, as we have seen, is the paradox of The Marsh, but it is a fact that must always be borne in mind, as otherwise the reclaiming of new land, or "innings", as they were called, is quite inexplicable. Where the sea piled up shingle barriers the innings of The Marsh thus sheltered was automatic, it was natural. In the quiet shallow water vegetation grew apace, mud and sand settled down among it and by degrees it was consolidated. We can see something of the same sort happening in any disused mill-pond. The stream flowing into it drops its silt when checked by the body of water of the pond, and the pond shallows. Reeds and other water plants thrive in it and slowly choke it, their roots mass and with more silt gradually consolidate until the whole mill-pond is filled, leaving no more than a narrow channel for the stream to find its way through.

Thus about the islands and especially about Lydd natural reclamation had taken place. We have actual written record of this in Saxon charters of the eighth century, in one of which the king grants to the Church of Christ in Canterbury "the pasture for 150 beasts near the marsh which is called Bisceopeswic (in Lydd) as far as Rhip Wood and the borders of South Saxony".

It seems likely that the monks, or their superiors, perceiving the way in which new land was being created by natural agents, caught the idea of hastening nature by their own labours. They could see that by shutting out the tidal movements of the water by means of shingle banks or earth walls or dykes the inned marsh or mud-flats could be consolidated, and with proper drainage become firm and profitable land. The monks were set to work, and they in their turn recruited labour from among the fisherfolk and herdsmen who already occupied the higher land and the islands.

The traditional method of reclaiming land, and it is the method which is still employed in areas around The Wash, is by means of walls of clay dug from the landward side, so that an area of marshland is enclosed and protected from the sea and tidal movements. The ditches which were excavated as the result of the wall building proved useful for drainage purposes, and everywhere on The Marsh the walls are clearly visible and it is possible to trace out the progress of nearly every innings.

Small innings continued to be made during the next two hundred years, but by the eleventh and twelfth centuries the idea had caught on, so to speak, like wild fire. Practice and experience developed skill, and successive Archbishops of Canterbury undertook really big works.

Beckett, who is only known to many people as the archbishop murdered in the cathedral, "the turbulent priest", scarcely strikes us as a man who would stoop to such mundane work as reclaiming marshland. The fact is, however, that Canterbury was not only the centre of Christianity in Kent, but the centre of civilisation and of learning, and owned vast estates over which it wielded both temporal and spiritual power. The Church commanded a pool of labour among its own personnel, the monks, of whom manual labour was expected, nay demanded, just as much as spiritual exercises and pastoral care. Thomas Beckett, always full of zeal for the Church, observing the success of minor innings when on visits to the estates of Lyminge, those about Romney and about Lydd, conceived the idea of winning for the Church new territories. Round about 1162 he was responsible for the first really big innings west of the Rhee Wall, a work which proved to be the first step in the reclamation of Walland Marsh and ultimately of the whole of The Marsh.

It will be remembered that the second course of the Rother was along the line of the Rhee Wall, and that its bed, and the banks which came to be built along it as rough sea defences, protected the low-lying Romney Marsh behind. As St Thomas's innings adjoin almost directly on, it seems likely that the work could only have been undertaken if there had been a change in the Rother's course. At any rate we know from records that by the middle of the thirteenth century the course which the Rother was then cutting through mud-flats and marshland of Walland Marsh was a great curve, due south from Appledore, sweeping round north-east at Midley and reaching the sea in a lagoon-like harbour at Romney.

Whether this change was as a result of the innings or whether the innings were made possible as a result of the change it will never be possible to determine. For not only did Archbishop Beckett reclaim at least a square mile, but his successors, Baldwin, Boniface and Peckham, all completed major works. Boniface's innings alone cover more than a thousand acres. It appears the two things went together, and there is no doubt at all that once these innings became firmly established, well drained and protected by banks against tidal flooding, the influence upon the course of the Rother and indeed upon the whole movement of tidal water over the remaining area of The Marsh was profound.

It will be seen that as dry land replaced tidal levels so the volume of water that moved in and out of the river mouths and gaps in the shingle bars was reduced. This meant that tidal scour was slowly but steadily lessening, with the results that the river courses tended to silt up and the shingle which was for ever being drifted along the coast in unbelievable quantities, steadily, and on occasion with startling rapidity, was closing the gaps.

The more The Marsh was inned so much the more did the task of making every new innings become easier. But little could those fervent archbishops, those hard-working monks, those busy Marshmen, their "Lords, bailiffs and jurats" have known that what they were doing which seemed so good, praiseworthy and profitable, and which indeed led to the reclamation of the entire Marsh, was at the same time to bring utter stagnation and ruin to the proud Cinque Ports, New Romney, Winchelsea and Rye, to their Limbs and Members and to all the seafaring folk who lived beside those tidal waters. Slowly and surely new land took the place of those historic waters, and only when it was much too late did the seafarers realise that their brothers the Marshmen had robbed them of their birthright.

★   ★   ★   ★   ★

Nature had another trump to play, however. During the eleventh and twelfth and thirteenth centuries a series of great storms raged along the coasts of Britain and Northern Europe. It is not possible to say if they were in any way the result of or connected with the sinking of the land. Their occurrence, however, did coincide with the crucial period of the last depression, and it may well be that the causes of the ups and downs, in the tidal movements, as it were, of the earth's crust in this part of Europe, were also the causes of the terrific storms.

All the old writers record these fearful tempests. We know that in 1097 an island off the coast of Kent was completely overwhelmed; the position is marked by the Goodwin Sands. In the twelfth century heavy storms and high seas were frequently recorded along the coasts of France and the British Isles, but it was in the thirteenth century that they reached a climax.

Holinshed writes:

"On the first day of October, 1250, the moon, upon her change appearing red and swelled, began to show tokens of the great tempest of wind that followed, which was so huge and mightie, both by land and sea, that the like had not been lightlie knowne, and seldome, or rather never, heard of by men then alive. The sea, forced contrarie to his natural course, flowed twice without ebbing, yielding such a rooring that the same was heard (not without great wonder) a far distance from the shore. Moreover the same sea appeared in the dark of the night to burne as it had been on fire, and the waves to strive and fight together after a marvellous sort, so that the mariners could not devise how to save their ships where they laie at anchor by no cunning or shift which they could devise. At Hert-burne three tall ships perished without recoverie, besides other smaller vessels. At Winchelsey, besides other hurte that was doone, in bridges, milles, breakes and banks, there were three hundred houses and some churches drowned with the high rising of the water course."

Winchelsea had grown up upon a very low island somewhere south-east of its present position on the hill. Its old name, Gwent-chesel-ey, means the shingle isle on the level. It may perhaps have been another of the islands which remained just above high-water mark, as did Lydd and Romney, at the time of the Roman occupation. It may have been on a shingle spit or bed. It would almost certainly have been banked and beached with shingle. Before the era of the great storms we know that it was linked to the new land and beach about Lydd. It had a remarkable, if precarious, situation and, as we shall see later, this accounted for its greatness and high rank among the Cinque Ports.

Early storms did considerable damage and broke the link with the land to the east. The tempest of 1250 half ruined the town, which before this had comprised some "700 houses and 50 inns". And then in 1287 came the final disaster, for yet another storm, and fortunately the last in the series, roared up the Channel, and what remained of Old Winchelsea was utterly destroyed. In fact the island and its beaches were swept away leaving no trace, and no one to this day can point with any exactness to a site and say with confidence, "There stood Winchelsea". Curiously enough what was swept away and submerged by the sea less than seven centuries ago is now dry land.

It was not only Winchelsea that suffered. As we have seen,

for nearly a thousand years preceding this disaster the land had been sinking, and while the deposition of silt had kept pace with it, there is little doubt that the coastal defences, i.e. the beaches and shingle bars, were weakened. Great changes had been taking place in the eastward movement of the shingle. The formation of Dungeness, initiated during the former uplift, had accelerated, and the enormous agglomeration of shingle around and south of Lydd was affecting waves, currents and tides. Where previously shingle had accumulated along the seaward shallows of the bay it was now scoured and removed, and at other points it began to accumulate where formerly it was scanty. Thus the shingle banks, bars and beaches between Pett and Bromhill (just east of Old Winchelsea) were thinning and building up at Dungeness, while from New Romney to Dymchurch the scour was increasing and the shingle was being carried along to mass at Hythe and to smother the entrance to Hythe Haven.

Hence the defences of The Marsh were weakened both to the west and the east, and it was something of a miracle that the whole area was not inundated and the reclaimed land, so recently inned, completely ruined. Indeed, had Romney been but a few feet lower it is hard to see how it could have escaped the terrible fate of Winchelsea. As it was the great storm of 1287 gave the people of New Romney a terrifying time. Monstrous waves breaking in to the lagoon-like harbour flung masses of mud, sand and shingle through the town, burying the houses, inns and churches in many feet of storm debris. Loss of life, of ships, property and livestock was severe, and after the "hideous storm" abated the townsmen were faced with the stupendous task of clearing away the mess. It proved indeed beyond their powers. Water must have stood in the church for weeks, for the mark of it upon the pillars is still visible. And the accumulation of debris about the building was so great that to this day one has to descend five steps from street level to the floor of the nave.

Terrible as this ordeal was, the storm had been responsible for something even more momentous. As the people of New Romney dragged themselves from their drowned and buried houses and took stock of the appalling havoc wrought by the storm they must have stood stunned by what was the "most unkindest cut of all". The Rother had changed its course. Their river, the river which was their waterway, the river which flowed into the Great Bay of Romney and kept it open, had left them. Its mouth had been choked with shingle, sand and the debris of the tempest. As Camden records:

> "The sea ... made pitiful waste of people, of cattle and houses in every place, as having quite drowned Bromhill, a pretty town well frequented, and made the Rother forsake his own channel and stopped his mouth to pass into the sea by Rhie."

★   ★   ★   ★   ★

The new course of the Rother, its fourth, is difficult to determine, for when a river breaks away from an old bed, especially in such tempestuous circumstances as this, it often takes some time to settle down in a permanent bed. As in any case its course was across mud-flats uncovered at low tide, it must have been subject to several variations. Bloomfield is of the opinion that it doubled back, about two miles east of Midley, and reached the sea south-east of Rye by the Wenenay Creek—what is now the Wainway Sewer.

There is a good deal to support this theory, for it appears a natural result after the blockage at Romney and the destruction of the shingle bars at Bromehill. Furthermore the Wenenay Creek must have been a pronounced feature of the new landscape, for even on the maps of Symonson, 1594, and Poker, 1617, it is strongly marked, that is three centuries later.

Yet we know it did not remain for long in this bed, and fourteenth-century records show that it had straightened its course and flowed then almost direct from Appledore to Rye. Thus the Rother, the Tillingham and the Brede all reached the sea round and about and under the cliffs of Rye; and the haven and bay which New Romney had had now Rye had in triple measure, and benefited enormously thereby.

With the outlet to the sea at Romney blocked the river and tidal waters had now only the one outlet to the open Channel south and south-east of Rye. Shingle very soon began to pile up

37

against this (how this happens and the full story of the shingle will be told in the chapter on Dungeness), and gradually even this outlet was narrowed. Thus with the Rother gone from Walland Marsh and the volume of the tidal waters which flooded it for ever decreasing, this marshland was ripe for reclamation. The Church no longer had the monopoly of labour and money, and new lords and landowners seeing the possibility of creating and acquiring fresh lands for grazing their sheep seized the opportunity, and vast new innings were undertaken.

The whole of Walland Marsh was reclaimed. At the beginning of the seventeenth century a new cut was made through the Wittersham Level, and the Rother was turned permanently into its course south of the Isle of Oxney. About the same time, Sir Robert Guldeford had taken in hand the innings of the marsh, which has taken his name, between Rye and Lydd, and by 1661 the whole of the bay, except for the estuary south of Rye, had become dry land.

Without the Rother the Great Bay of Romney rapidly silted up. In a despairing effort to restore their fortunes the people of Romney tried to bring the river back by digging out the old course of the Rother along the Rhee Wall from Appledore. It was a tremendous task for the manual tools and limited labour of those days. Even today such a cut eight miles long would be an awkward and tiresome task for modern excavators, for as everybody knows who attempts an artificial dyke or a deep excavation these days on The Marsh, the work becomes tricky and aggravating in the extreme, for there is little or no cohesion in the alluvium and the sides and banks of a digging are for ever falling and caving in. It has been said that only on a natural waterway will the banks hold without piles and continuous dredging. Be that as it may, the people of Romney failed to coax the Rother back along the old course. The new-old cut rapidly silted up, and the Great Bay of Romney, without the scour of the river to keep it clear and with the onward march of the shingle shutting out the tides, silted up also. Ships which had tied up to the walls of the church could no longer approach; the great Cinque Port of New Romney became a little inland town.

Romney Marsh and Dungeness

Gateway to the Marsh - the Land Gate, Rye

The South or Strand Gate, Rye. From an old print by G.H. Grimm, dated 1784

Mermaid Street, Rye

The restored Ypres Tower, now an award-winning museum, Rye

St Mary's, Rye, dominates the ancient town

The Shape of Rye, low tide on the Rother

The Old Hospital, Rye

Sheep on the famous
pastures

St Nicholas, New Romney. Ships once tied up to the wall of this church

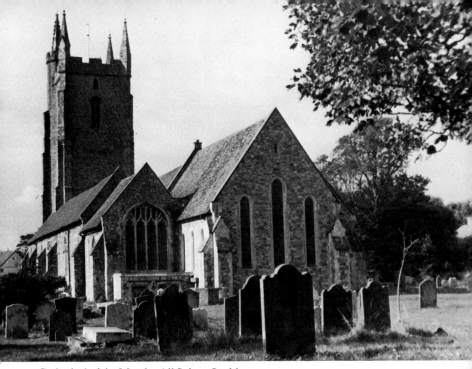

Cathedral of the Marsh - All Saints, Lydd

The Norman doorway of St Nicholas Church, New Romney

The Cinque Port of New Romney – sheep have replaced ships

Today the noble church of St Nicholas is a mile and a half from the sea; where in days of yore the great stone and the little stone marked the entrance to the haven, the modern craze for seaside holidays, seaside hotels, houses, bungalows, beach huts, hostels, caravan sites, holiday camps and golf has brought into being Greatstone and Littlestone, seaside resorts of ever-growing popularity.

The Cinque Port of Hythe suffered a similar fate, and only the two Antient Towns maintained their seafaring estate. But the writing was on the wall—one might be excused for saying on the Wall's End (Walland Marsh). New Winchelsea had been built on a hill over against Rye, and when Edward I planned it, it bordered the new Rother estuary with the long tidal creek of the Brede running several miles inland behind it. It shared with Rye, in fact, a most excellent and sheltered harbour which was known as the Camber, a word derived from Camera or La Chambre. As we shall see later, it became the port for the assembly of the royal forces and produced in Gervase Alard the first Admiral of an English Fleet.

For two centuries Winchelsea on the hill prospered greatly, but the unseen struggle between ships and sheep—we should call it a cold war nowadays—was still raging, and the sheep were winning. Walland Marsh was inned. Guldeford Marsh was inned. The creek of the Brede was silted up and inned. Masses of shingle flung across the Camber reduced tidal scour and created mud-flats and shallows, and the salts before Winchelsea became the levels of Pett. When there was a royal inquiry into the state of things at this Antient Town and Cinque Port in 1587, it was reported that there were "no ships, captains or mariners belonging to the town, but only one sailor named William Bucston".

Thus only Rye remained. Of all the bay, the openings, creeks, harbours, havens and ports there were none, save only the combined estuaries of the Brede, the Tillingham and the Rother, which reached the sea just south of Rye. But towards the end of the sixteenth century even this harbour was in a sorry plight. There was a storm in 1572 which drove so violently inland that the sea broke into the low-lying land behind the town on the north-west. At first the people of Rye thought it a God-send, for it seemed as though their harbour was enlarged and the sea had returned to their assistance. Nothing came of it, and matters worsened. Experts were called in, and vast sums of money spent by the harbour commissioners on a New Harbour, the idea of John Smeaton.

Smeaton's plan was to give the Rother a new outlet to the sea. This was done first by making a cut from the river Brede, at a point known as Reed's Battery, to the sea across the neck of Pett Level. The distance was about 1600 yards. Secondly another cut was made from the original course of the Rother, just east of Rye, to the Gun Garden Rocks; it was known as the Rock Channel. This channel turned the waters of the Rother into the Brede, so together with the Tillingham all three discharged their waters by the new channel out to sea by a new estuary about two miles west of the old one. In theory at least the scour of the combined rivers should have kept this new and narrow harbour channel clear of silt. But Smeaton had reckoned without the shingle. An enormous bar developed across the mouth of the new harbour; it grew at an incredible rate, 160 feet in one year. It was impossible to check. In fifteen years the New Harbour was hopeless and abandoned. It had cost some £60,000.

The Rother returned to his old course, now narrow and silted up. The Camber was no more than salts and shingle and sand. The salts were inned in the nineteenth century, and with the shingle piling up against it the mouth of the Rother continued to advance seaward. It still is advancing. Rye is left high and dry, its cliffs rise queerly above dry land, its harbour, such as it is, is a mile down stream, and the shingle-threatened harbour-mouth itself half a mile even beyond that.

Although but the half of it is told, what a story! The map of England has been enlarged. Some hundred square miles of the richest agricultural land in Britain have been added to her territory. How great was the cost, how much was lost and won remain to be assessed. So much then for the ups and downs of Romney Marsh. Let us turn to the glittering pageant of history, for which the arena is now prepared.

CHAPTER III

THE PAGEANT OF HISTORY I

PREPARATION

THE people who came to live on The Marsh and to adventure upon the sea from the shelter of its creeks and bays were destined to play a decisive part in the fortunes and affairs of England.

But who were they? Where did they come from? Were they in any way different from the other people of southern England? What were their opportunities? What put power into their hands? Who were the "Barons"? What were the Cinque Ports? How was it, in the words of Montagu Burrows, that these people "enjoyed the singular felicity of having taken on the one hand a leading part in establishing the constitutional liberties of England, and on the other of having supplied the chief weapon used by its kings in the consolidation of its territory and the restoration of its sovereignty in the Narrow Seas"?

These and innumerable other questions will come tumbling over one another as we glance at the programme of the pageant to be enacted before us. If it were possible to answer them all simultaneously the art of the Pageant Master would fall into desuetude and the comprehension of history be simplified. But it is no more possible than taking the whole of our banquet in one vast mouthful. Episode must follow episode, scene react on scene, personalities tower and wane, and all the time the tramp–tramp–tramp of the masses, of the people, the real actors, must beat out the march of history till they accomplish their destiny.

The trouble with most of us and with the history books which we last saw in the classroom was that we were either all too anxious to close those books at the sound of the bell or the books were so unenlightening that they asked to be closed anyway. Facts and events make a dull catalogue and children live only for the present. We can be excused. But as we grow older we realise it is the people that interest us; the events and the dates are no more than finger-posts and milestones along the route of their march. It is the lives of the people that grip our attention, their thoughts, what impels their choice at the cross-roads, their training, their blind search for the four freedoms, their failures and their successes.

The people who came to live about The Marsh, on its islands and along its forest-fringed creeks, after the Roman occupation had ended, came with no other idea than that of most settlers to live and make a living there. They may have had to fight, but the Britons and such remnants of the Belgic tribes as had engaged Cæsar so gallantly offered little serious resistance to the Teutonic invaders. The English conquest of South Britain began with the landing of Hengist and Horsa in Kent, and it would not have been long before their ships feeling their way southwards through the Straits would discover the sheltered tidal waters of the bay—as we saw it towards the end of the Roman uplift.

Here they found conditions with which they were not only familiar, but which perfectly suited their way of life. The marshes and sunken land were like the zees and lagoons of the Netherlands, and the islands and river creeks like the Frisians and estuaries of Germany. Furthermore the long narrow estuaries running deep inland were ideal harbours and hide-outs for their ships, for it must be remembered they had become an adventuresome sea-going people; and the low-lying pastures on the east side of the bay, Romney Marsh, provided them with good lands for their animals.

From the very first these settlers seemed to divide their interests between life on the land and life on the water. No doubt the herdsman was on many occasions pirate and fisherman, and the seafarer was equally handy with the animals and rough tillage. But as the centuries slid by, the distinctions, the standing, the liberties, the divergent interests of each became ever more marked.

During the sixth and seventh centuries the Marshmen accepted conditions as they found them and did nothing towards improving or enlarging their pastures. All the emphasis was upon sea-going, shipbuilding, upon adventure, plunder and pillage, upon fishing; and, as intercourse and conflict with friends and foes across the Narrow Seas increased, their skill and seamanship was in ever greater demand, not always so much in their own interests, though these were ever present in their minds, as in service to others.

It is difficult to gather together all the threads which went to make the strength of the Marshmen and the Portsmen, it is still more difficult to assess the particular importance of any one cause which accounted for the power they came to wield. By and large, however, it was their boat-building skill coupled with their seamanship that enabled them to grasp opportunities and shape events. This "land" of their choice had peculiar advantages, for as we may see in many other parts of the world, sheltered waters, long estuaries, fiords, tidal creeks and good beaches often develop a maritime breed. There was also the forest behind, the Andred Weald, which provided them with timber and to spare. The forest had another influence in so far as it tended very much to isolate the area around the bay. Both Marshmen and Portsmen developed a marked independence.

The Portsmen, however, were no quicker to improve their ships than the Marshmen their pastures, and it was only under the spur of first raids and then invasion that attempts were made to build better ships. The double-ended ships of the Vikings were copied by Alfred the Great; furthermore he employed his new ships as a fighting force, as a navy, to go forth on the high seas and attack the invaders before they landed. Under Edgar, his successor, this navy had grown during the tenth century to several hundred ships, and a real organisation had begun for the building of ships, for their manning, and for their terms of service.

An immense amount of research has been done in the effort to discover who was responsible for such an organisation, how and when it affected the south-east coast of England, and what brought about a confederation of the ports. For by the end of the tenth century it is clear that there were indeed ports. Small towns had grown up on suitable sites wherever ships could be built, launched and harboured. They were on islands, estuaries, creeks or

sheltered bays, and in our area alone there were Winchelsea on
the low shingle-covered island, Rye on cliff-girt hill, Lydd on
the shingle, New Romney on the estuary of the Rother, Hythe
on the old haven of the Limene. Nearabouts were Hastings to
the west and Dover and Sandwich to the east, together with a
number of other smaller places.

In her book, *The Constitutional History of the Cinque Ports*,
Miss K. M. E. Murray, who probably has done more thorough
research work of this kind than anyone else, comes to the conclusion that

"the five Head Ports were selected by the king (Edward the
Confessor) as the most important harbours situated at fairly
regular intervals on the south-east coast. Each was made
responsible for the provision of a definite quota of ships, and
was given a suitable reward for the trouble, but it was tacitly
understood that these ships might be partly drawn from the
lesser creeks in the area of each Head Port. It was a method of
concentrating the naval resources at five points, thereby
facilitating the summons of the fleet and increasing its
efficiency."

The king, however, did not group these ports and these seamen
together for convenience and without regard to a fellowship and
a common interest which already existed among them. There
was, as Miss K. M. E. Murray says, "the economic motive which
seems to lie at the root of all mediæval confederations of towns".
In the case of the Portsmen this interest was in fishing and in the
yearly fair held at Yarmouth.

It may sound an extravagance to assign to the herring an
important place in the history of England. But we must do so;
in fact, we must rank the fish higher than the sheep. For, in
mediæval times at any rate, herrings formed a most important
part of the nation's food supply; and, as we are beginning to see,
it was the fisheries which attracted the Portsmen, provided them
with a livelihood and evoked in them qualities and a skill in
seamanship which stood the country in good stead in times of
dire need.

Thus it came about that the Portsmen, having a common interest and a corporate desire to share and protect that interest, having the ships and the seamanship to pursue it, and enjoying at the same time a unique geographical position with regard to the control of the Narrow Seas, the defence of the coasts, and for trade and transport, came to be regarded as one body, an association, independent yet prepared to perform a common duty or task, at command and at a price.

★   ★   ★   ★   ★

The second episode might properly commence with a flourish of trumpets and enter the Portsmen proudly wearing the arms of the Cinque Ports upon their "cotes of white coton". For now indeed they have come into their own. The eleventh, twelfth and thirteenth centuries see them at their prime.

It would be well at this point to make quite clear which were the Cinque Ports, for it has been my experience that nine persons out of every ten are very hazy on the matter. Believing cinque to mean five, it becomes all the more confusing to discover that it might mean twenty-five or even more. However, it did mean five originally, and the five were Hastings, Romney, Hythe, Dover and Sandwich. We still very properly call them the Head Ports, not merely to avoid confusion, but because this in actual fact is what they became and how indeed they were addressed by the others.

It will be seen that in the area of The Marsh two only of the original five were situated, Romney and Hythe. But it must be remembered that in the beginning not the most far-sighted being could ever have imagined the growth and spread of the confederacy that did occur. The five Head Ports were selected as being conveniently spaced along the most critical section of the south-east coast. They were equals, though it must be admitted that a good deal has been said and written to prove or disprove the superiority of one port over another. The fact that Hastings is or was always named first in the list probably means no more than reading from west to east, a geographical order. Dover is sometimes regarded as the superior on account of the fact that the Lord Warden of the Cinque Ports had his residence in Dover

45

Castle. The truth is that the fortunes of the individual ports waxed and waned for a variety of reasons, not the least being the fickle behaviour of the sea. Any special importance that a port assumed would be on account of the size and weight of its ship service.

This ship service was of course the *raison d'être* of the Cinque Ports. The king needed the ships and the men to man them, for the defence of the realm, for expeditions against his enemies, for safe transport. In all, the Ports were to provide annually fifty-seven ships, with a period of fifteen days' service for each. This was a very considerable task to perform and a serious duty to discharge, and naturally it was not done for nothing. The whole history of the Cinque Ports is loaded with the charters, privileges, liberties, rights, honours, titles and ancient customs that became theirs and which they jealously guarded.

During the twelfth century, possibly earlier, Rye and Winchelsea were fully included in this service. They were superbly situated, Rye in a strong position above its cliffs and commanding the bay and the long creeks running deep inland, Winchelsea, the old Gwent-chesel-ey, at sea level controlling the western entrance to the bay. They were even then, in 1190, referred to as the Ancient Towns, and although they were strictly speaking "Members" of Hastings they did nevertheless enjoy all the rights and privileges of the Head Ports and were regarded as their equals. Thus the Cinque Ports numbered seven, and it is worthy of note that our area, The Marsh, claims four of the seven.

It would perhaps be tedious to give a complete list of all the privileges and rights that were conferred upon the Ports or which they claimed. Being the rewards for ship service, however, they were of great importance, both in the realm of civil liberties and in the enjoyment of economic advantages. Besides, they were honourable, colourful and not without a dash of bravado. In the first place they were immune from national jurisdiction and exempt from taxation as normally assessed. They did not pay scutage or tallage. They had the right to "den and strand" at Yarmouth, which meant that during the fishing season they could land and repair their nets on the shore there. Furthermore at the Yarmouth annual herring fair the Portsmen were in control and responsible for law and order. Their freemen took the title of "Barones", which was a word as Edmund Vale points out "handed down from times prior to its association with a title conferring social rank". It was of course a title of distinction, the Barons of the Cinque Ports, and the Portsmen were proud of it; and while perhaps it would be a little unkind to say they became a bit swollen-headed about it, especially after their heroic deeds in the thirteenth century, they did nevertheless get confused over title and rank. As Miss K. M. E. Murray says:

> "The Portsmen themselves, however, like the Aldermen of London, interpreted the title of 'Barones' as carrying with it some of the privileges of the Bishops, Abbots and temporal Barons of the realm. In 1299 they claimed to receive justice in the king's court 'at the hands of their peers, earls and barons', and in the custumal of Sandwich it is stated that 'they ought not to be judged except by their peers and combarons who are the Archbishops, Bishops, Earls and Barons of England', and that they should enjoy all liberties 'sicut et alii Barones Anglie'."

The highest dignity of all that fell to the Barons of the Cinque Ports was the granting of "honours at court". This was the privilege of holding a canopy above the king as he walked from St Stephen's Palace to Westminster Abbey for his coronation and of attending the banquet which followed. For many centuries they performed these honours, and although they declined in rank and in the order of their seating, it was not until the days when the sovereign rode in a carriage to the Abbey that the service became unnecessary. Fairly recently something of the old honour and tradition has been revived in that an invitation to attend the sovereign in the Abbey has been extended to eighteen Barons of the Cinque Ports.

A story is told, on the first occasion of its revival, of a famous Earl Marshal who was superintending the rehearsal of coronation pageantry in the Abbey. One of his greatest problems was to find space and place for all those with the right to attend. We can imagine the noble lord's vexation and amazement upon suddenly being confronted by eighteen unexpected figures in mediæval costume.

"Who the devil are you?"

"We, my lord," was the urbane reply, "we are the Barons of the Cinque Ports."

★　　★　　★　　★　　★

It was to be expected that other towns and villages suitably situated on the creeks, about the bay or along the shores would want to give ship service, so that they too might enjoy the privileges and share the spoils of the Head Ports. While the Head Ports were jealous of their rights, it certainly was convenient for them to have assistance in the arduous task of shipbuilding. They needed large supplies of timber, the demand for equipment was heavy and continuous, and as the ships increased in size the problem of fully manning them grew steadily more difficult.

Hence it was not long before such an extension of the organisation took place. We have seen how Rye and Winchelsea were originally Members of Hastings, although very early in the history of the Ports they took equal standing with the five original Head Ports. The system of members was thus extended, and such towns were known as "Corporate Members" when the arrangement had received confirmation by royal charter. In our area we find Tenterden as a Member of Rye and Lydd as a Member of Romney. While just beyond the confines of The Marsh, Hastings secured Pevensey and Seaford, and Dover secured Folkestone and Faversham. Even this did not complete the confederacy, for many smaller places joined in as "Limbs", or Non-corporate Members, until there were at one time or another more than thirty places joined to the Head Ports. Some of these were quite a distance inland and some had comparatively small burdens to bear in the discharge of ship service, but they all pulled together, and they provided a force which friend or foe could only disregard at his peril.

Traffic between England and the Continent was not inconsiderable before the Norman conquest, and in the hundred and fifty years following that event it greatly increased. The new king of England was king both sides of the Channel. England and France had already been linked by the advent of Christianity and the conversion of Kent at the end of the sixth century. We have already seen the important part the Church played in the early reclamation of The Marsh and how kings gave grants of land to the Church "for the salvation of their souls". Thus Rye and Winchelsea came to be held by the Abbey of Fécamp. Hence there was for several hundred years, in spite of growing national boundaries, the over-all estate of Christendom, and this undoubtedly encouraged traffic, and then trade, to and fro across the Narrow Seas.

Furthermore there was the challenge of the Crusades. We witness the amazing spectacle of kings and emperors, knights and men making their proud, fantastic but arduous journey by land and sea to the Holy Land. Now was adventure afoot, and the Portsmen were not only in great demand for ships and the men to man them, but they were ready themselves to take part.

Of those noble failures, of many of those cruel, jealous and stupid acts we need take no special notice here. The things that concern us are what the Portsmen learnt and the experience they gained, especially when some of them made the remarkable journey in their little ships to the Mediterranean Sea, to join the expedition which in 1190 Richard, the Lion-hearted, organised to join the Third Crusade.

★ ★ ★ ★ ★

Ships—a whole book could be written about them. No other invention of man has had such a profound effect upon his history —at any rate until the twentieth century—and they figure so largely in the story of The Marsh that it is impossible to overlook them here. Ships were the be-all and the end-all of the Portsmen. How they began, how they were made, how they improved, how they triumphed and how they failed, that is also the history of the Portsmen.

It comes as something of a surprise to most people to learn that the ships of the Portsmen in mediæval times were so primitive. We have got so used to the appearance of the full-rigged sailing ships of the sixteenth and seventeenth centuries, thanks to the artists of the Elizabethan era, that it is fixed in the minds of many people that this was the kind of "old-fashioned" ship employed in mediæval times. Compare Drake's *Golden Hind* to the *Queen*

Elizabeth of today, and the progress made during the last four hundred years needs no underlining. There is perhaps no comparison between sail and steam; but even if we compare the *Pelican* with the tea-clippers of a century ago we cannot fail to observe the tremendous improvements in every line and detail of build, rig and control.

Put back the story of ships four hundred years *before* the *Golden Hind* and it calls for some imagination to picture the size, shape and rig of ships of the eleventh and twelth centuries. Imagination

Fifteenth-century Cog—probably the largest type of vessel that was built at, or could use, Rye Harbour before it silted up.

is not far from being the right word, for it is a curious fact that illustrations and descriptions of those ships are very, very rare. Only on the Bayeux Tapestry and on the seals of the Cinque Ports, and a few other ports of the Continent, have we any sort of picture or guide as to their shape and appearance.

The Bayeux Tapestry was made at least fifty years after the Norman invasion, and it was the work, or so it is believed, of Matilda, consort of the Conqueror, assisted by other ladies or sewing women. While it is possible they had never seen a ship, experts are generally agreed that someone with a knowledge both of ships and their handling must have given the tapestry workers guidance and information. Both profile and detail are satisfying and convincing, particularly when allowance is made for the medium in which the work is carried out.

The seals of the Cinque Ports dating back to the fourteenth century show ships of a slightly later period and in a very different medium. Instead of the comparative spaciousness and freedom of the tapestry, they are presented within the formal and restricted central area of a circular seal. They are, however, the work of

Probable appearance of Saxon ship of tenth to eleventh centuries. The stages of development from Longship, mainly propelled by oars, to thirteenth century "Round" ship, propelled by sail, are clear.

men on the spot who knew their ships, and though the craftsmen may have been very vague about the rules of perspective, at least the detail was finely cut. Documents bearing the seals of Romney, Winchelsea, Folkestone, Sandwich and Pevensey still exist and all show a ship as their chief feature.

From these two sources we are able to gather a very fair idea of the ships of the Portsmen. To begin with, their craft could have been no other than the longships of the Norsemen, built of oak with high stem and stern posts, probably about 80 feet long, breadth 16 feet and a depth of 6–7 feet. They were propelled by oars, usually sixteen a side, but a mast was stepped and carried a large square sail. In the first place these Viking ships were essentially warships and carried the shields of the warriors hung in a row along the sides of the vessel. They were double-ended, meaning bow and stern were the same shape, and thus could be propelled backward as easily as forward by oars. Their rudder an oar-shaped board, secured to the starboard quarter by ropes and manipulated by a tiller which passed at right angles to the

Eighth- to tenth-century Norse Longship, as used in the Norse and Anglo-Saxon invasions of England.

blade through the head of it. The sail was used only when there was a following wind, and it took a long time before these early seafarers learnt the art of setting their sails and staying their masts to make use of a beam wind, or to sail close-hauled.

No doubt these longships were modified considerably for trade, passengers and fishing. Such modifications, however, were only in length and beam and no doubt in less careful building. The warships demanded speed with long lines, bows finely sheered and the whole streamlined; but for cargoes and fishing, capacity was all that mattered.

We have no drawings or descriptions of these early craft, as used by the Portsmen before the Norman Conquest. Nevertheless we have for reference those wonderfully preserved ships of Scandinavia. As has been the custom of men in many parts of the world, their great chiefs have been buried beneath huge mounds. Among the Vikings it was the custom to bury the chief within his own ship and above it to raise a great mound of earth and stones. Within the last eighty years several of these Norwegian and Danish burial-mounds have been discovered and uncovered. In one or two instances where the soil was clay the preservation of the woodwork has been almost perfect. The ship found at Gokstad, near Oslo, in 1880 is the finest example known and dates from the tenth century. It was possible to remove it from the mound, and it can now be seen in the Oslo museum. A replica model, complete in every detail, can be seen in the Science Museum at South Kensington. It is an absorbing study, for it was by means of such a ship that Leif Ericsson crossed the North Atlantic in A.D. 1000, reaching Labrador—and he succeeded in returning. By such ships the Vikings explored and raided all the countries of Northern Europe and even reached the Mediterranean Sea. Such ships must have been the type of ship to have been seen moored at Rye, drawn upon the beach at Winchelsea, in Romney Bay, being built in Hythe Haven.

The Bayeux Tapestry, which shows both Norman and Saxon ships, illustrates for the first time ships of the Narrow Seas. Superficially there are no very marked changes from the Viking double-ended ships, but they appear to have been broader and reduced in length. They are of course not decked, and as the heads of horses can be seen above the gunwale it would seem that the depth amidships could not be much more than four feet. Although most of the ships illustrated in the Tapestry show a line of oar-ports in the top plank, it is interesting to note that no oars are shown in use. This cannot be taken to mean that oars as a means of propulsion had fallen out of use; indeed we know that great ships employing banks of oars were in service till at least the end of the sixteenth century. But it does give some indication that sail was being used to greater purpose, that in the Narrow

Seas at any rate seamanship and skill were developing in the handling and management of sailing ships.

With increasing experience and a clearer understanding of the requirements of sail more attention was given to the shape of ships. The longship, which admirably suited propulsion by oars, began to change to the "round" ship, which had a fuller-bodied hull, and which gave better sailing qualities. During the two cen-

Twelfth- to thirteenth-century Cinque Ports "Round" ship.

turies following the Norman invasion such boats increased in size, and everyone will remember the sad story in their history books of the king, Henry I, who never smiled again after his son William had been drowned off the coast of Normandy. The White Ship, the *Blanche Nef*, which went on the rocks in a storm in A.D. 1120, was said to have had aboard three hundred persons.

54

That must have been quite a good-sized vessel, though even then it was not much more than a big open boat.

But two most important changes were at hand; one was an English conception, the forecastles and the aftercastles, and the other was a Mediterranean idea, the rudder on the sternpost. The seals of the Cinque Ports are almost the only authority that we have illustrating these revolutionary changes. The thirteenth-century seal of Winchelsea, one of the earliest English ports' seals in existence, shows the familiar double-ended ship, with mast amidships, and still shows in clear detail the whole of the side rudder, but the innovation of "castles" fore and aft is also clearly depicted. These wooden structures were not a part of the hull, that is to say they were not built in, but they were erected upon bow and stern when the exigencies of battle demanded. In the first place they were no more than raised and protected platforms upon which the archers could take their stand and thus be enabled to direct their arrow-fire at their enemies sheltering behind the sides of their ship.

The enormous advantage such castles gave in battle, particularly to English archers, who were famous for their marksmanship, led not only to general use but to very large and imposing structures. All the time that ships were two-purpose vessels such castles were only temporary platforms. A craft might be a fishing vessel or a wine-ship one day and the next a man-of-war, for she would carry all the timbers aboard ready for erection at a moment's notice. No doubt the protection such platforms afforded to the ship against weather and sea partly suggested the idea of decking the boat, and from the thirteenth century onwards we see this improvement slowly spreading.

The other revolutionary change was the rudder on the centre line. It seems rather extraordinary to us that this idea should not have occurred to the clever and ingenious boat-builders of the preceding thousand years—three thousand if we take Egypt into account. Yet it is a fact that there is no record of a stern rudder in use on any ship before the twelfth century. No one knows for certain whose the idea was and what nation's ships were the first to use it. It is known, however, that when English sailors joined

Richard's great expedition to support the Third Crusade they met and engaged in the Mediterranean near Beirut a huge three-masted ship of the Saracens. She had such high-built sides that the English were unable to board her and had to resort to their favourite tactics of ramming her. While she displayed a number of other novelties to English eyes, her most important features were the rudder on the centre line and her fighting tops.

It may have been the importance attached to propelling a boat forward or backward by oars that delayed the adoption of the idea in the North, and while it was not impossible to affix a rudder at one end of a double-ended ship, i.e. to a curved sternpost, it was certainly difficult, and would ultimately mean reshaping the stern. After a thousand years of longship building it was not easy to break from tradition; nevertheless we have seen that the ships of the Cinque Ports were changing, round ships were replacing longships, sail was replacing oars, and a decked ship replacing the open boat. The time was ripe for a change. Finally they were almost forced to make the change, for as they learnt to sail, more and more making use of a wind on the beam, so did they find when the wind was on the starboard beam that the ship, heeling to the wind, would lift her steering blade right out of the water and the vessel would be out of control. This could be countered, and was in some instances, by using two steering boards, one on each quarter. Not only was this clumsy, but awkward when bringing the vessel ashore or to port.

It is interesting to note in passing that the steering board was always affixed to the right-hand side of the vessel and gave that side its name—starboard; and to avoid damage to the steering board a vessel was laid with its left side against the quay when in port—hence the port side.

None of the seals of the Cinque Ports in Kent and Sussex shows a stern rudder, but the thirteenth-century seals of Poole and Ipswich show such a rudder and also modifications in the line of the ship and build of the stern. The English gold noble, a coin issued by Edward III in 1344 to commemorate the battle of Sluys, clearly shows a stern rudder. We shall hear more of this famous naval engagement later, it is sufficient here to note that the ships of the Cinque Ports took an important part in it; and thus the new rudder must have been common to all English ships of the period.

The difficulty with seals, and similarly with coins, is that such things were struck or made after the event, and because such details as are illustrated must have had considerable common usage before they came to be recognised as an essential part of the picture, it is clear the date of such a seal does not necessarily date the introduction of any innovation. Furthermore the seals of

Three-masted Lugger—circa 1820–45, as built at Rye.

those mediæval towns are only known to us as the imprints on the documents to which they are affixed, and the date of the document is the only guide to the date of the seal. Hence there might well be a lapse of fifty or a hundred years between the actual fact and its first recording.

There was one other innovation which makes its appearance on all the later seals of the Ports, and that is the top castle. This idea appears also to have come from the Mediterranean. These small wooden platforms or turrets were hoisted on the mast to a position above the mainsail. As with the forecastles and after-castles they were originally only put in position for battle, and very effective use could be made of them. Later, as ships came to be used for different purposes, the "top" came to be a permanent feature, and while the word aftercastle has disappeared, fo'c'sle is in common use throughout the seven seas.

By the beginning of the thirteenth century all that had gone to the preparation and training of the men of The Marsh had reached completion. It was as though the Supreme Pageant Master had planned all, for the curtain rises on the next scene, a scene of battle, with everyone in his place, trained, experienced, with all his props in readiness.

The closer we study all the circumstances of the period the

Rye River Barge as used on the Rivers Rother, Brede and Tillingham. The general design remained substantially unchanged from about 1500 to the present day.

more remarkable does the coincidence of events appear. For while half The Marsh itself was already dry land, and the archbishops and others had inned at least a third of what was left of the tidal bay, yet there was still sufficient water in the bay and in the creeks and in the harbours to sail a great fleet. There was sufficient depth of water in and about the ports of Winchelsea, Rye, Romney, Hythe and Lydd both to launch and float boats of the deepest draught then made and sailed. The one-masted sailing ship of the Portsmen, while to our eyes far from perfection, was a thoroughly serviceable boat; they built them, they manned them, over the long centuries they had gained experience in them, and built up such a tradition in seamanship as made England the maritime power she has ever been.

There was one other thing of the greatest importance which had grown alongside, within and around the rest; that was organisation. Without organisation this powerful weapon, this instrument of defence, this fishing and trading fleet would have been ineffective and unreliable. As it was, through remarkable opportunities, unique geographical position and the sturdy independence of its people a Confederation had been established which

Modern Hastings Lugger *Industry*. It is actually over fifty years old, but still in service.

linked and most effectively controlled all the activities of the Portsmen, and at the same time protected their rights and privileges. Curiously enough this Confederation was based on no more than customs and usages which had been the practice "from times out of mind", yet those rights were confirmed again and again by royal charter. It made its own laws, held its own courts, appointed its own judges. It pretty well decided what taxes it should pay to the king. It bargained with kings. It was so loosely knit that as we have seen it was the economic motive that really held it together, yet it was so strong that none could break it—only The Marsh and the sea could do that.

The Marsh was behind all, beneath all, the cause of all. Slowly and surely it had perfected everything that had brought the Barons their power and pride of place. Slowly and surely with an inevitability that is hypnotising to watch, it was removing all.

CHAPTER IV

THE PAGEANT OF HISTORY II

BATTLE

IMAGINE the scene, as we might have beheld it in A.D. 1213, from the cliff-top at Rye. It is during the uneasy and tempestuous reign of King John. Astounding news has set all the Cinque Ports aflame, for Lewis of France, at the behest of Pope Innocent III, is preparing to sail against England. John has done dastardly, terrible things, but invasion by Frenchmen would be ten times worse. To arms!

The bay is alive with ships. Rye's squadron, some eight or more strong, is already drawing slowly away to the shouts and cries of the excited crowds that throng the cliffs overlooking the bay southwards. The castles are in place, pennants fly, yards are hoisted, and the big square sails flap and billow in the breeze. The flag of the Cinque Ports, the three lions of England, dimidiated with the sterns of ships, swells out. A mile or so across the bay south-eastwards the ships of Winchelsea are on the move. Their squadron numbers nearly twice that of Rye. It is a sight indeed, this forest of masts and spars and sails and bloody pennons, as the vessels jockey for position to make the open sea. To the east the smaller contingents of Lydd with Romney can just be descried preparing sail.

Two of the king's longships, propelled by sixteen pairs of oars, make out from the creek behind Rye and organise the mustering of the squadrons. These galleys are strictly speaking the naval core of the fleet, a scheme dating from times more ancient. They had now themselves become the auxiliaries, for the ships of the Portsmen far outnumbered them and considerably outweighed them. But they are still in service, for they are still faster than sail, with a greater manœuvrability, and independent of wind.

The church bells clang noisily. The Barons are ready for battle. Hubert de Burgh is in command of the Ports, he is the Lord Warden of the Cinque Ports. Long has there been friction between the Portsmen and their rivals across the Channel, in trade and commerce and on the fishing grounds. There have been many private battles, feuds, raids and piracy. Now there is a chance to settle these differences, to fly at the throats of their rivals. The long-bowmen are aboard, the quarrels for the cross-bowmen are stacked, hooks are affixed to the yards for slashing the enemies' rigging, the top castles are secured. The Portsmen are ready for battle.

Yet before ever the whole fleet is mustered and under way comes messenger on bloody spur from Dover. Too late! Lewis has slipped out of Boulogne. The invasion of England is off. John has capitulated to the Pope. On bended knee he gave his crown to the legate, Cardinal Pandulf, who handed it back as a gift from the Pope—oh, degradation!—at a fee of one thousand marks per annum! Philip of France has turned his attention to Flanders and has directed his son Lewis to sail with all his forces to Gravelines and Damme.

Turn back? That would not have been in the nature of the Portsmen. But for the details of our little scene I cannot vouch, I can only vouch for the historic facts. The Cinque Ports fleet certainly did follow close upon the French fleet, and while the forces of Philip were concentrating upon Bruges there was a furious engagement at Damme. Half the French fleet was taken or destroyed and the remainder was blockaded in the port. In vain did Philip hasten to their assistance; he could do nothing but burn and destroy the ships left to him and only so save them from the hands of the Portsmen.

The fleet returned in triumph and the Portsmen with some spoils. They had had a crack at the Frenchman who, although he had been taken at some disadvantage, suffered a good hiding. But while this success did not count for much in the opening phase of the struggle between England and France—indeed, it was only in the following year that Philip won a resounding victory at Bouvines against the allies of John—the important thing about the scrap at Damme was that it gave enormous confidence to the Portsmen and gave them their first experience of concerted naval action under one leader.

More was soon to follow. As we all know, the ink was scarcely dry on the Great Charter than John was breaking his solemn oath. The lords in their despair called upon Lewis the French Prince to help them rid England of their false and treacherous sovereign, and indeed offered Lewis the crown of England in return. In haste came Lewis across the Narrow Seas and landed at Sandwich —one of the Cinque Ports, of all places. Now was the fat in the fire, for while the French Prince was welcomed by the lords of the land and the city of London, it was more than the Portsmen could stomach. They refused to support Lewis. As Montagu Burrows says: "With sailorlike straightforwardness they determined to stand by their own Sovereign, and leave the question of his conduct to the future. It was the first and only time that London and the Cinque Ports took opposite sides."

Well, indeed it was. Within five months John was dead. William the Marshal, with astonishing sagacity and speed, had young Prince Henry crowned at Gloucester. So what further need was there now for Lewis of France when the king of England was only an innocent boy of ten? Lewis must go; the "French vermin" must be got rid of.

Lewis had other ideas and was already besieging Dover, where Hubert de Burgh, the Warden, was gallantly holding out. The Barons of the Cinque Ports, heartened by the news, stepped up their harassing attacks upon the French ships. Lewis had to raise the siege and prepare to meet the Marshal, who was gathering a strong force against him. Those who had supported the Prince were now deserting him, and at the affray in Lincoln streets the Prince suffered a severe set-back.

Events had reached a critical stage. Heavy reinforcements were mustered in France by Blanche of Castile to send in support of her husband Lewis. About fifty ships were assembled in France's northern ports and a great number of knights and soldiers embarked, with London as their destination.

The Barons of the Cinque Ports, for ever on the alert, saw

their opportunity. Hubert de Burgh, who had now complete control of the fleets—and their full confidence—set sail with all speed and made to join battle. According to all accounts this was a feint, and instead of rushing directly into the attack with the usual ram-and-board-'em tactics the Cinque Ports ships passed astern of the enemy and appeared to be avoiding conflict. Not for long, however, for getting well to windward they then turned abruptly up Channel and bore down upon the Frenchmen from a most advantageous position. Furthermore every ship from the Ports had been provided with a quantity of quicklime, which, at the critical moment just before each vessel grappled with her chosen opponent, was flung into the air and blown into the eyes of the enemy.

The manoeuvre and the surprise tactics were too much for the Frenchmen; they were soon in confusion. Many of the ships were rammed and sunk, others were boarded, and desperate fights ensued. It seemed safer for some to leap into the sea rather than fall into the hands of the infuriated Portsmen. Robert de Courtenay was captured, Eustace the traitor was executed, many knights were taken prisoner, eventually to be held to ransom, and, according to accounts, barely fifteen of the French ships escaped.

Burrows says: "The result was not inferior to the success of Trafalgar." That is true enough, for only remoteness in time makes the Battle of Dover appear insignificant. We have but to imagine how accounts and results of the Battle of Trafalgar will read in A.D. 2553. For today, with the Nelson relics still with us, that battle stands head and shoulders above all others. In another six hundred years' time, when the Federation of the World is grappling with the problems of interplanetary invasion, the affair in Cadiz Bay will then seem just as small beer as that battle of the Straits seems to us today.

To the people of Kent who on St Bartholomew's Day watched the fight from the cliffs and the walls of Dover Castle in 1217, it was a glorious victory. To them it meant not only defeat of the hated Frenchmen, but freedom. England's ghastly error in seeking foreign succour was righted. With all speed Lewis made his peace and returned home. And the young king, Henry III, joyfully acclaimed throughout the land, made haste, too, to acknowledge his debt of gratitude to the Barons of the Cinque Ports, the "Guardians of the Sea".

It was plain enough now that who held the Cinque Ports held the gateway to England. The Barons themselves became more aware of their opportunities, of their bargaining powers. They were continually being called together to discuss their allegiance during the civil wars which followed between Henry and the Barons, and as Miss Murray writes:

"These assemblies trained the Portsmen in the use of machinery for association, and accustomed them to plan their actions to a certain extent by discussion together. . . . It developed the self-consciousness and prestige of the Ports, it accustomed them to treatment as a unit both politically and administratively."

*　　*　　*　　*　　*

It is neither the purpose nor the intention of this book to write a history of the Cinque Ports. The authors already quoted, and a number of others, have done this with distinction and with thoroughness, and to them the reader may turn, if so inclined, for the intricate and complex details. But many readers will not have the time, nor even the opportunity, for close study, and the purpose of this book is an attempt to present The Marsh and its people from different angles, in different lights, so that like a jewel it may live today aglow with the lights and fires of yesteryear.

A ruin, a breezy level, a village street, apart from their intrinsic charm, may not mean much. A mere catalogue of events associated with each would surely be tedious. Instead such scenes should conjure in the mind's eye a vista down time, of battles which changed the course of history, of mighty conflicting forces through which The Marsh evolved, of sturdy, rugged, independent men who in the struggle for freedom learnt to govern themselves.

How quiet a scene does Winchelsea present today! Winchelsea on the hill, with the fragment of its great church, the chancel still standing in its wide green tranquil yard and with the canopied tomb of the Alards within. Winchelsea with its planned streets, its gates, its cellars, its ruins. . . . How can this exquisite fragment of mediæval England evoke the fiery Gwent-chesel-ey of seven centuries agone?

No, we must plunge once more into the bloody battles and murderous piracy of the Portsmen. We must set sail on those stormy seas; we must ride out such a hurricane as never before and never since has been recorded. Only so can we know and feel the full force of the stirring events which shaped, destroyed and cast up on the shores of time this delicate shell which is Winchelsea.

By the time that Henry was engaged in the bitter struggle with Simon de Montfort, Winchelsea, on the shingle spit at the western entrance to the bay, was a place of considerable size as towns went those days. Matthew Paris writes: "Winchelsea, a place extremely important to the English, and especially to the Londoners." It had grown rapidly, probably on account of its excellent position and harbour and the importance of its wine trade. It must have had a population of four or five thousand, for there were more than 700 houses, grouped in "quarters", besides inns, mills, warehouses and churches.

Its ship service was especially noteworthy, for when Rye was supplying 9 ships and 156 men, when Romney was providing 4 ships and 65 men, Hythe 6 ships and 122 men, Hastings only 5 ships and 96 men, Winchelsea was sending the astonishing number of 21 ships and 596 men. This eclipsed even Dover, whose ships numbered 16 and men 336. As Burrows, whose figures these are, says, there was "more individuality about this port and its leading families than about any of its six fellows".

These qualities must have been brought out by the calamitous events its people survived, for surely no town experienced such an amazing fifty years as Gwent-chesel-ey did for the last half of the thirteenth century. Not merely did it engage in wars and feuds with the French, not only did it take a lead in the tussle with Yarmouth, not only did it suffer onslaught and severe punishment for supporting the lost cause of the de Montforts, but it was engaged in a terrific and, as it proved, a hopeless struggle with the sea.

Slowly and surely the land was sinking; it had been for hundreds of years. From times out of mind the Portsmen of Winchelsea had expended money and labour upon their sea defences, upon the sea-walls and their dykes. There had already been minor disasters. But the great storms for which the century was remarkable were now reaching their climax, and in 1250, 1252 and again two years later furious tempests drove across the British Isles. Huge seas prevailed in the Channel, the sea-walls were breached and partly carried away, and nearly half Winchelsea smashed and drowned.

In 1264 the Battle of Lewes seemed to decide for good that Winchelsea had indeed backed the winner. The young Prince Edward was a prisoner in Dover Castle, and de Montfort won himself a niche in the hall of fame by summoning in the king's name, on 20th January 1265, the first representative Parliament to meet at Westminster.

Yet with what finesse the Fates play! In less than twelve months Earl Simon lay dead on the field of Evesham and Prince Edward stood victor and well-nigh king. The baronial party melted away and only the staunchest of the de Montfort supporters took refuge in Winchelsea to make their last stand. In spite of the capitulation of the other Cinque Ports Winchelsea resisted until Edward himself came with powers against it, stormed the walls and taught the Barons such a lesson as might well have cowed them for ever.

Yet his visit was a blessing in disguise, for Edward, in spite of the stubborn yet courageous resistance he had met, in spite of his many other preoccupations, including a crusade to the Holy Land, saw two things clearly. The importance of the Cinque Ports to England was paramount—he himself became the Lord Warden. The importance of Winchelsea to the Cinque Ports was no less important in its own sphere, but the king had seen for himself that the port was in dire distress. Something must be done and quickly if Winchelsea were to be saved from utter ruin by the sea. It must have been obvious to the king that any repetition of the gales that had already done so much damage would bring disaster. The sea-walls were so badly breached and eroded, and tide water stood so high, that their effective repair could not be contemplated.

The king acted, and not only with statesmanship but with generosity. He decided that Winchelsea must be evacuated and re-established. He gave the land from his own manor and sited the new town on the hill at the eastern end of the Brede creek, about a mile and a half south-west of Rye. It was a wonderful position, quite the equal of Rye, girt by low cliffs on three sides, with a good harbour on the east side and the sheltered creek behind to the north, with the western outlet of the bay before it towards the open sea.

Edward concerned himself personally with the planning of the new town, and it was laid out in what we should call these days the modern style. There were rectangular blocks of houses intersected by streets at right angles, and while this was after the manner of Edward's new towns in Wales, it was no doubt a "tidy" arrangement of the "quarters" which had existed in the old town. It was certainly planned on a grand scale. It comes as a big surprise today, after leaving the houses round the church-yard to travel nearly three-quarters of a mile along country lanes, when suddenly on turning a steep corner there is New Gate majestically striding the road, completely alone—no walls, no houses anywhere in sight, just this great stone arch among the fields and trees. I shall never forget the first time I stumbled across it. I was cycling quietly along from Winchelsea to Pett enjoying a glorious spring day. The laughing cry of the green woodpecker followed me merrily along the lovely lanes. Suddenly there was the Great Gate, and I passed beneath too astonished to brake and I heard the echo of my passing from its ancient walls. I stopped and turned, mumbling aloud in my astonishment. It was beautiful in the sunshine, and to my inexperienced eyes it looked like an Arc de Triomphe dropped from the heavens.

This was New Gate. What an enormous area the New Winchelsea must have covered! Yet there are no traces of any buildings near here, and there are no walls left anywhere.

Edward certainly planned, and indeed carried out his plan, on the grand scale. He may indeed have regarded Winchelsea as the

premier port and taken a soldier's fancy for its bold and courageous inhabitants. And the people themselves, with "their public
spirit and dashing enterprise", spared nothing in money, labour
and goods to co-operate with the king in making their new town
a success.

How timely was the plan to move the port. The arrangements
for the removal of the inhabitants had scarcely been put into
effect, the distribution of the new property hardly completed, in
fact the ink was barely dry on Charter and Conveyance, when
befell the hideous tempest of 1287 which changed the whole
history of The Marsh. Old Winchelsea was destroyed. It was not
merely inundation and further damage of the already half-ruined
town, it was utter destruction. No West Indian hurricane more
completely wiped out a town than did this storm. The size and
weight of the waves smashed the badly damaged sea-walls, swept
away the wooden buildings like so much matchwood and indeed
scoured away the very foundations of sand and shingle upon
which the town was built. There was nothing left. Had the place
been occupied it would have been a disaster of the first magnitude.
It might have looked like the judgment of heaven. It certainly
was an illustration for those who build their house upon sand.
In actual fact it was a great mercy, and to the king, whose fame
as a warrior often blinds us to his other qualities, an added lustre
is given.

One wonders how the Barons and "the multitude" of Winchelsea felt during those terrible hours as the gigantic waves
stormed across the bay and thundered against the cliffs of their
new stronghold. One pictures them crouched against the brow
of the hill peering through the blinding spray and under the lash
of a hurricane. It must have seemed like the end of the world, the
sea gone mad, and in that fury of the waters was their old home.
In their hearts they must have known it was the end, and to them
it must have seemed the end of the Ports and the end of The
Marsh. How could anything survive? Lydd out there on the
shingle? Romney on the mouth of the Rother? The lowlands of
Romney Marsh crouching behind Dymchurch Wall? Hythe on
the old haven?

When the blown spume withered and the cold light of a terri-
fied calm silhouetted the horizon, Gwent-chesel-ey was no more.
The Rother had changed its course. Romney, half buried in
sand and shingle, had lost its river and its port. Hythe Haven
was nearly closed. Romney Marsh, badly flooded, with breaches
in its walls, was still there. Lydd stood where it did, with its
buttresses of shingle grown vaster than ever, but Bromehill, the
little town to the west between Lydd and Old Winchelsea, had
disappeared for ever. The wreckage of ships and houses, of
churches and inns, the bodies of animals and men strewed the
shores for many a ghastly mile.

★   ★   ★   ★   ★

This was the last in the series of great storms of the thirteenth
century. The battle with the elements was over. So speedily
did the Cinque Ports recover that a contemporary observer
might well have said that they had won the victory. As we know,
it was not so, it was the beginning of the end, for like the ups
and downs of The Marsh, a depression begins even at the moment
when the uplift is at its height. Thus the Cinque Ports during the
reign of Edward I reached the very summit of their power. The
valiant deeds of their fleet amazed Europe. Their Great Charter,
granted by the king, confirmed all the rights and privileges
which they had ever claimed. It is still preserved at Hythe. They
were a law unto themselves it is true, but the king, by generous,
judicious and firm handling, not only disciplined them but
further improved their organisation and made them the first
power in the land.

The conflict with England's enemies was far from over. After
the battle off Sandwich in the Straits of Dover the Portsmen were
continually embroiled in dog-fights with the French. This grew
to such a pitch that although open war had not been declared
between the two countries the seamen on both sides of the Channel were so infuriated by the dastardly conduct of their opposite
numbers that they arranged a "private" battle.

In its way this was one of the most remarkable naval engagements ever fought. The Portsmen, goaded in particular by the
French parading up and down the Channel with their prisoners

hanging dead at the yard-arms, sent a challenge to the Frenchmen to fight it out if they dared. The meeting-place was off St Mahé on the coast of Brittany. The challenge was accepted, and both sides mustered all the help their friends and allies could give them. On April 14th, 1293, this naval duel, for that is a proper description of it, took place in a howling gale. It was a bloody affair: no quarter was asked or given. The Portsmen had a habit of throwing into the sea anyone not worth a ransom. The French were ready to do anything the English could do, though it transpired they were not the equals of the Portsmen in seamanship or at any rate in conducting a naval engagement in a full gale. They were swept off the face of the sea. It was a resounding victory for the Portsmen.

But this was a serious matter for Edward. The enraged Philip of France summoned him as his vassal—because of Edward's possessions in Guienne and Gascony—to appear before him to answer for the slaughter. The king of England refused, so Philip took possession of his French dominions. This was open war.

The conquest of Wales and the invasion of Scotland, in both of which the Cinque Ports fleet assisted, did not deter Edward from marshalling his powers. He sailed for Swyn with a considerable force, transported and escorted by the ships of Yarmouth and the Cinque Ports. Here befell another astonishing affair, less creditable to the Portsmen, but typical of one side of their fiery character, their revengeful nature.

For many years, it would not be wrong to say for several centuries, there had been friction between the men of Yarmouth and the Barons. At first the Barons had had all their own way, with every right and royal sanction to land there. The town was small, though the harbourage was good and the situation with regard to the North Sea herring fishery ideal. As the years passed, the annual Herring Fair assumed great importance, and the Barons were responsible for its conduct. They took the matter really seriously, went to immense trouble to select the bailiffs, and in fact the famous Court of Brodhull was developed as a result.

Naturally the herring trade attracted and employed many other seafarers besides the Portsmen. Yarmouth steadily grew and by the thirteenth century was a serious rival of the fishermen from the Channel: bickerings and jealousies, slights and insults, law making and breaking, grew into a regular feud. Furthermore Yarmouth itself was performing ship service; and when the sum total of ships from Winchelsea, Rye, Romney and Hythe was forty vessels, Yarmouth was sending forty-three, and over a thousand men.

But to return to the affair at Swyn. According to the account of Walter de Hemingburgh, the king had scarcely gone ashore, and the troops were in the act of being landed, when the Barons and the men of Yarmouth flew at one another's throats. "Enflamed by their inveterate hatred" the Portsmen "rushed to arms, and in the fury of the attack burnt more than 20 of their ships, putting to the sword as many of their crews as they could lay their hands on; nor, though the king commanded them to desist, was he able to restrain their insane violence."

They were violent times and bred violent men. As Miss K. M. E. Murray says:

"They were men of the fiercest character, thinking nothing of killing merchants, throwing their bodies into the sea, and robbing them of their goods, ships and letters of safe conduct. When the Jews were expelled in 1290, many were attacked in mid-ocean by men of the Ports, robbed of their money, and inhumanly slain and thrown into the sea; others were left on a sandbank which was afterwards submerged by the tide. In 1293 the Cistercian Abbots dared not leave England for fear of the Portsmen."

    ★   ★   ★   ★   ★

Two other great naval battles must be mentioned before we leave these stirring scenes. For not only are they of historic importance, but they are finger-posts of destiny. Each in its way exhibits a symptom which, while unrecognised at the time, was a sure sign of things to come.

Both engagements occurred in the reign of Edward III. The Hundred Years War had begun. The king's first expedition to Flanders to attack France from the north had been a costly failure, and after two years he was forced to return to England to procure more money. This was hard to come by, the Commons were in no mood. They even declared that since the Barons of the Ports were "reaping profits beyond number both on shore and at sea . . . they were bound to guard the sea, as the Commons did the land, without asking or taking wages."

But suddenly came the news that Philip VI of France was gathering a great flotilla, first to attack Edward's allies in Flanders and then to invade England. Edward's appeal to the merchants of London and the Cinque Ports was not in vain, and very soon, himself aboard the Cog *Thomas*, he was leading a very considerable fleet to attack the enemy as they lay in the Flemish harbour of Sluys. This fleet comprised some two hundred vessels, and while the Cinque Ports ships provided the experienced core, there were ships from many other English ports: London, Portsmouth, Dartmouth, Fowey, Yarmouth. Furthermore, several of the ships were cogs, vessels of considerable size in those days, with a displacement of three or four times that which had normally been in use by the Portsmen.

The battle has sometimes been called a land-battle on sea, because Edward employed his forces very much after the manner of a general deploying his forces in the field. He made full use of the "matchless English bowmen" in quickly moving smaller craft to "sweep the decks of the French ships" enabling the bigger vessels carrying the knights and men-at-arms to grapple and board. It was a terrific twelve-hour fight, more than four hundred ships being engaged and tens of thousands of men. (What a chance for a modern film company! But the Cinque Ports seem to have been neglected on the screen.) In the end the victory was Edward's. Nearly the entire French fleet was captured, and trustworthy records go to show that they lost some 30,000 men. Hundreds leapt into the sea to avoid death or capture. "What cowards these English are!" said the royal jester, the only man brave enough to acquaint his sovereign of the disaster. "Because they did not dare to leap into the sea as our brave Frenchmen did."

The last battle of which we are going to take special note was

fought ten years later in 1350, and so close home that all Winchelsea could actually watch it from the vantage point of their sea-
cliffs. This, curiously enough, was not against any particular
enemy of England, but against a horde of Spanish pirates who
had been playing havoc with merchant shipping from Finisterre
to Gris Nez.

For some years English over-sea trade had been steadily
increasing. The wine trade with Bordeaux and Northern Spain
had grown enormously, and, as we have seen, Rye and particularly Winchelsea specialised in the trade. The great Alard family
were vintners. Besides this, Winchelsea, a favourite of both
Edward I and Edward III, had become one of the ports on the
South Coast to receive the royal mandate for the regulation of
the trade in wool which was now England's chief export. Add to
this, traffic in timber and charcoal, cloth and corn, salt and iron,
wax and dairy produce, to say nothing of the herring industry,
and it will be seen that seamanship was already laying the foundations of England's great merchant navy and her supreme position
in world trade.

Pirates were the curse of those times, however, and when they
banded together as this gang of Spaniards had done, even armed
merchant ships stood no chance. Edward was determined to rid
English traders of this curse, and he made Winchelsea his headquarters in preparation for the attack. It was indeed a royal occasion, for the queen attended the king, the Prince of Wales was
there spoiling for the fray, Sir John Chandos, the boy John of
Gaunt, the great nobles, earls and barons, knight and squire.
The Cinque Ports fleets, ships from other ports, and several of the
king's ships were gathered in the bay and crowded the harbour.

The Spaniards had already passed up the Channel and were
doing some trade with Flanders. They were informed that the
English fleet would waylay them, so they were fully prepared
and indeed anxious to engage on the return journey. Froissart
writes:

"When they weighed anchor the wind was favourable to
them; there were forty large vessels of such a size, and so

beautiful, it was a fine sight to see them under sail. Near the top of their masts were small castles, full of flints and stones, with a soldier to guard them. . . . The Spaniards were full ten thousand men . . . and this made them feel sufficient courage not to fear the combat with the king of England."

Edward was now at sea awaiting the return of the pirates. Froissart continues:

"The king posted himself in the fore part of his own ship: he was dressed in a black velvet jacket, and wore on his head a small hat of beaver, which became him much. He was that day, as I was told by those who were present, as joyous as he ever was in his life, and ordered his minstrels to play before him a German dance which Sir John Chandos had lately introduced. For his amusement he made the same knight sing with his minstrels which delighted him greatly. From time to time he looked up to the castle on his mast, where he had placed a watch to inform him when the Spaniards were in sight.

"While the king was amusing himself thus with his knights, who were happy in seeing him so gay, the watch who had observed a fleet cried out: 'Ho, I spy a ship, and it appears to me to be a Spaniard.'

"The minstrels were silenced; and he asked if there were more than one: soon after he replied: 'Yes, I see two, three, four, and so many that, God help me, I cannot count them.'"

The Spaniards being under full sail might very easily have passed Edward's fleet; instead they chose to do battle and bore down upon the English fleet.

"When the king of England saw from his ship their order of battle, he ordered the person who managed his vessel, saying 'Lay me along the Spaniard who is bearing down on us, for I will have a tilt with him.' The master dared not disobey the king's order, but laid his ship ready for the Spaniard who was coming full sail. The king's ship was large and stiff; otherwise she would have been sunk, for that of the enemy was a great one, and the shock of their meeting was more like the crash of a torrent or tempest; the rebound caused the castle in the king's ship to encounter that of the Spaniard: so that the mast of the latter was broken, and all in the castle fell with it into the sea, when they were drowned."

The king's ship suffered damage and began to leak. Shortly afterwards another Spanish ship grappled with him and the fight began in earnest.

"The English had not any advantage, and the Spanish ships were much larger and higher than their opponents, which gave them a great superiority in shooting and casting stones and iron bars on board their enemy, which annoyed them exceedingly. The knights on board the king's ship were in danger of sinking for the leak still admitted water: this made them more eager to conquer the vessel they were grappled to: many gallant deeds were done; and at last they gained the ship, and flung all they found in it overboard. . . . They continued the combat against the Spaniards, who fought valiantly, and whose cross-bowmen shot such bolts of iron as greatly distressed the English."

The young Prince of Wales found himself in an even worse plight than the king—proof of the size and weight of the pirates' ships. Had it not been for the Duke of Lancaster perceiving his plight and promptly coming to his aid shouting "Derby to the rescue", he might well have been drowned. But the ship was taken in the nick of time. "The Prince and his men instantly embarked on board the Spaniard; and scarcely had they done so when his own vessel sank."

One English ship, the *Salle du Roi*, was grappled by a great Spaniard, who taking "advantage of the wind set all their sails the more effectually to succeed in carrying her off. . . . As they were thus towed they (the English) passed near the king's ship to whom they cried out 'Rescue the *Salle du Roi*', but were not heard. . . . The Spaniards would have carried away with ease this prize, if it had not been for a gallant act of one Hanequin . . . who with his drawn sword on his wrist leaped on board the enemy, ran to the mast, and cut the large cable which held the main sail, by which it became unmanageable; and with great agility he cut four other principal ropes, so that the sails fell on the deck, and the course of the ship was stopped. Lord Robert seeing this, advanced with his men, and, boarding the Spaniard sword in hand, attacked the crew so vigorously that all were slain or thrown overboard, and the vessel won.

"However, at last, victory declared for the English: the Spaniards lost fourteen ships: the others saved themselves by flight. When it was completely over, and the king saw that he had none to fight with, he ordered his trumpets to sound the retreat and made for England. They anchored at Rye and Winchelsea, a little after nightfall, when the king, and the Prince of Wales . . . took horses in the town, and rode to the mansion where the queen was, scarcely two English leagues distant." The queen's attendants "had seen from the hills of the coast the whole of the battle, as the weather was clear and fine" and "had told her that the Spaniards had forty ships: she was therefore much comforted by their safe return. The king with those knights who had attended him, passed the night in revelry with the ladies, conversing of arms and amours."

Such, in part, is Froissart's delightful description of this gallant affair. It rings so true, it has such a savour of chivalrous deeds, its human touch, the emphasis it lays on what was best in those violent times, make these passages a fitting climax to the greatness of the Portsmen.

CHAPTER V

THE PAGEANT OF HISTORY III

DESUETUDE

THE Battle of Sluys and the Battle of Lespagnols-sur-mer force upon our attention two things which were the shadows of coming events, portents of fate. At Sluys we have seen how much bigger ships, cogs, were being favoured. The size of ships was already measured in "tunnes", but these tunnes were large barrels of wine and certainly not tons. Nevertheless for comparison purposes a tunne is as good as a ton, and when we read that the cogs had a carrying capacity of 300 tunnes then we are able to compare them with earlier vessels of 60 to 100 tunnes. It is thus clear ships were larger, broader in the beam and with greater draught. Such ships needed deeper water, they found that the harbours, bays and creeks were poor accommodation for them. They sought ports elsewhere. Add to this the steady silting up of the bay, which had been going on for hundreds of years, but which was accelerating due to the speed at which The Marsh was being inned, and the writing on the wall is plain to read.

The battle of Lespagnols-sur-mer underlines this point about the increasing size of ships, for the pirates' vessels were considerably larger than those in the Cinque Ports fleet. But it stresses an altogether different matter which in its way was just as fateful. The Spanish pirates preyed on merchant shipping. This was not only the shipping of the Cinque Ports, nor was it only the shipping of England, but included the merchantmen of the Netherlands, Germany and the Hanseatic ports, of France, Portugal and Spain. Seaborne trade of many nations was growing apace; the old overland routes along which merchandise was sent slowly, with difficulty and in small quantity, were going out of fashion. Merchants and traders both in northern and southern Europe were finding the seaways enormously profitable.

Pirates were a menace, but so were the brigands and robbers of the highways. Already there was keen competition for carrying the trade.

The Portsmen, while jealous of the trade which in particular interested them, such as the herring fishery and the wine business, were to their misfortune turning their attention more and more to fighting, raiding and, let it be said, piracy. As guardians of the Narrow Seas, fighting had been forced upon them, and their ship service constrained them to fight the king's battles. They had carried Crusaders, fought the French on many occasions, been sea support for the conquest of Wales and Anglesey, assisted in the invasion of Scotland. The very fact that Edward III had his headquarters at Winchelsea when preparing to attack the Spanish pirates underlines the point that the Cinque Ports fleet was regarded first and foremost as a fighting force. It is interesting to dwell on the results of the battle of Lespagnols-sur-mer. The gold coin struck by Edward described him as "The Avenger of Merchants"; he was known far and wide as "Le Roi de la Mier", The King of the Sea. The men of Winchelsea and Rye, Romney and Hythe had won a glorious victory in that they made the sea safe for merchants and traders. But in very truth the Portsmen were only a very small part of those merchants and traders; the greater part were their rivals.

★   ★   ★   ★   ★

In our history books Edward's grand victories on French soil are writ large: Crécy, Calais and Poictiers. But in how few do we read about the furious and disastrous attacks upon the Ports which the French made in retaliation. Just when it seemed the enemy had been brought to a standstill, and Edward, while preparing a vast new army for invasion, had given orders that all English craft be drawn ashore out of harm's way, the French fleet made its attack. The full force of this fell upon Winchelsea. What those Barons could have been doing, or whether it was over-confidence that bred contempt and carelessness, no one can say. But they were taken completely by surprise. The fact that it was a Sunday can hardly excuse them for lack of vigilance. The "multitude" were undoubtedly in church, yet the French ships sailed un-molested into the bay, made their landing and fell upon the town with fire and sword.

Yet more extraordinary is the fact that exactly one year later to the very day another and yet more ferocious attack was made upon Winchelsea. Its great church was largely destroyed, out-rages and atrocities committed, buildings burned, goods and treasures carried off.

If such things could happen to the Portsmen and to that Ancient Town which was the pride and favourite of the king, then England was in a bad way. That indeed was the truth. For nearly forty out of the hundred years of war the English lost command of the sea. The French played havoc along the South Coast. It rather shocks us to learn that, becoming bolder and bolder, they sacked and burnt such towns as Portsmouth and Dartmouth, Hastings and Folkestone. They attacked Yarmouth, they pene-trated the estuary of the Thames as far as Gravesend, and Lon-doners saw the red light of its burning.

In 1377 the French once again began an attack upon Winchel-sea and swept into the bay almost unchallenged. But finding Winchelsea better prepared to meet them—it was under the com-mand of the Abbot of Battle—they made a diversion and fell first upon Rye. This port, although in a commanding position, was not yet a walled town as Winchelsea was, and the attackers had an easy task. The place was sacked, its beautiful church damaged and its bells stolen, houses burned, and among other things forty-two casks of wine were among the spoils.

Next turning their attention to Winchelsea, the raiders found the place too strongly held and were forced to call off their attack until the following year. But besides being a priest the Abbot of Battle was a clever and courageous soldier, and yet again he contemptuously rejected their demands for the surrender of the town and compelled them to break off their attack and retreat. But the third time, in 1380, the French came with an overwhelming force, and the Abbot was obliged to evacuate the port. Poor Winchelsea, left to its fate, suffered such terrible destruction that it never fully recovered.

Had the Fates been kind and left it with a harbour and deep water, there is little doubt the town would have regained its pre-eminent position among the Cinque Ports. But it was not to be, for while for two centuries it carried on and took an important part in the control of the fishing industry, the creeks on either side of it were already silted up, the harbour followed, and by the end of the seventeenth century sheep grazed where ships had anchored.

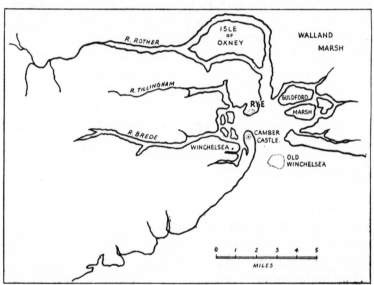

Rye Harbour, early seventeenth century (from an old map), showing the position of Old Winchelsea drowned, and Camber Castle before being land-locked by shingle.

Rye, though badly hit, did not suffer so grievously as Winchelsea. The port pulled itself together, executed as traitors some of its inhabitants who were held responsible for their failure to protect the town, petitioned Parliament for assistance to build itself walls and manned an expedition to revenge themselves upon the French and to recover their church bells. All of which they successfully achieved.

Rye was fortunate: the Rother did not desert her, she clung to her port and her egress to the sea. As Winchelsea waned, Rye's fortunes waxed. Romney was finished as a port; Lydd was almost land-locked—beach-locked might be a better description; Hythe was silted up. Hythe had in fact suffered treble disaster, for apart from damage by the enemy the town had experienced plague, fire and storm. The fire destroyed, so records say, some two hundred houses, and the people were in such extremity that they determined the curse upon their town was more than they could bear and prepared to leave it. This the king prevented and excused them ship service for a period so that they might recover. But like Winchelsea, Hythe had suffered too much.

Of all the busy ports around the bay none was left but Rye. During the sixteenth century Rye was the most frequently used port for passage to France and still supplied ships for war purposes. Queen Elizabeth honoured the town with a visit in 1573, and when the urgent demand for ships to meet the Armada came post-haste to the Cinque Ports Rye provided ships, whereas poor Romney with Lydd had to find £300 to hire a ship to perform their ship service. And, let it be told, the owner of the ship was never paid in full even then.

But all was not well with Rye. All Walland Marsh had long since been inned, and now the Guldeford family were busy reclaiming all the marshland to the east and north-east of Rye. The volume of tidal water moving in and out of Rye Bay—for it was no more than *Rye* Bay now—had been enormously reduced. The Barons of the town were fully aware that in spite of the Rother continuing its course beneath the very cliffs of the port this did not mean that their port and harbour were safe. At last they were beginning to understand that what had been stealthily going on for centuries—the deposition of silt and the reclamation of the marsh land—was robbing them of their birthright.

A survey had been made in 1562 of the Rother's course from Newenden to Rye. This was the long creek that almost encircled the Isle of Oxney on the north and then led westwards towards Bodiam. It showed that what had been a channel varying between 200 and 300 feet wide had in places narrowed to between 16 and 25 feet across. One has only to study Philip Symonson's map of 1594 or Poker's map of 1617 and the one prepared for Sir Robert Guldeford by Samuel Newman and Fran. Hill in 1700, to realise the speed at which the land was gaining upon the sea.

It was not only the silting up of the creeks above Rye that caused concern, but also the rapid reduction in the width and depth of the bay itself. About a mile from Rye to the south stands Camber Castle. This was built by Henry VIII about 1539 and was one of his many coast defence forts, which were built from Scilly to Tilbury. It was something new in the way of castles, having been designed to stand up to bombardment by cannon. It comprised a central citadel, looped for cannon, a ring of semicircular casements and a broad, deep moat. It is low—it seems to squat; and although a great deal of Camber Castle still stands, many visitors miss seeing it while motoring along the road from Winchelsea to Rye.

This fort was built on the fringe of a great shingle spit that was piling up along the edge of the bay which had now silted up south of Winchelsea. Its cannon commanded Rye Bay, in fact the fort itself was probably not much more than a hundred yards from the shore. Its whole purpose was to defend the harbour and port. But the shingle (of which more in the next chapter) was sweeping along from Fairlight Head and heaping up in enormous quantities against the outflow of the Rother and the tidal waters of the estuary.

Quite soon, due to scour in one place and deposition in another, a second huge shingle spit, now called Nook Beach, "grew" from a point south of Winchelsea in a north-easterly direction towards the outlet of the bay. The marshy salts between the spits then filled, and Camber Castle found itself half a mile from the sea. Since then a third spit has been piling up, once again leaving a low, marshy hollow which still contains several pools or "pits" of water.

The result of all this has been that Henry's fort is a mile and a half from the sea at its nearest approach, whereas from the mouth of the Rother, which it was intended to defend, it is two and a half miles. Sheep graze on the pastures around it, and those people who see the most of it are the golfers on the links beside it.

But Camber Castle was out of date almost before the building was completed. It fired no cannon at any enemy ship, it bears no honourable scars. It may perhaps be regarded as yet another monument to an invasion scare, or as a mark of Bluff Hal's determination to be prepared and to go his own way. It might be more rightly regarded, however, as the seal of fate. For what was happening there that so soon and so completely caused it to fall into innocuous desuetude was the last event in the closing of the great bay and the consolidation of the whole Marsh.

Only the waters of the Rother prevented the huge shingle spits of the west joining with the vast accumulations of Dungeness to the east. But nothing could now stop the silting up of the whole of Rye Haven. The salt pans, which had provided such a valuable article of trade ever since the fourteenth century, had gradually been lost; reclamation both natural and artificial went on apace, and the last "salts" before Rye were inned during the nineteenth century.

Today the Rother, joined by the Brede and the Tillingham just below Rye, takes a long, curving, narrow course to the south-east and reaches the open sea nearly three miles away. Up this long, sinuous course small vessels have to make their way at high tide to reach The Strand at Rye. A small place known as Rye Harbour has grown up a mile and a half from the old town, but the mouth of the river is so difficult that no vessels of any size can reach it. One side of the river mouth, the west side, is a huge shingle bed for ever encroaching and only held back by massive groyning, which must continually grow out to sea if the river estuary is not to be turned; and on the other side, to the east, are the vast sands of Camber, also increasing and at the same time blowing and creating a line of dunes just above high-water mark.

*　　*　　*　　*　　*

Every ancient port lies stranded high and dry. How aptly have they been called the "ports of stranded pride"! It is not that the sea has deserted them, but that The Marsh has won this extraordinary round in the struggle between land and sea.

Every inch of the ancient bay has been reclaimed. Some hundred square miles of dry land takes its place. The Marshman has replaced the Portsman, sheep have replaced ships. The pageant of mediæval history, with its kings and princes, its longships and galleys, its archers and crossbowmen, its barons and bailiffs, its heroic battles and burnings, its storms and disasters, has crossed the arena of time. Today replaces yesterday.

CHAPTER VI

DUNGENESS

FORMATION OF THE FORELAND

THOSE who have never seen Dungeness have a surprise awaiting them. For those who love wild, open, desolate spaces the wide beachlands hold a rare pleasure in store. And for those who love a problem the formation of the Ness is as intricate and puzzling a development as one could wish to find anywhere around our coasts. It is, as C. J. Gilbert says, the most remarkable shingle promontory in the world. "It is of such a distinctive character that British sailors have attached its name to similar formations in such distant localities as Paget Sound and the southern shore of Patagonia."

Before we can begin to grapple with its problems, and before we can delight our souls with its flowers and birds, we should have a clear idea of its size and shape as presented to us today. A glance at the map will show that Dungeness is a triangular, or more accurately a cuspate, headland, with its apex pointing almost directly towards the French shore twenty-seven miles away. Its southern edge runs very nearly due east and west and its eastern shore approximately north and south. If along these shores four miles be marked off north and west from the tip of the foreland, and the two points joined, then the whole of the apex enclosed is unbroken beachland, known as Denge Beach.

But this is by no means all the shingle, for there is another vast triangular-shaped area, with Lydd as its apex and its base on the southern shore of the Ness and contiguous with Denge Beach. It is difficult to describe this without reference to the map, but roughly what it amounts to is that for six miles west of the point and for four miles north the whole of the backlands as far as Lydd are shingle, except for the small circular patch of reclaimed marshland south-east of Lydd known as Denge Marsh.

86

Winchelsea still shows the town planning of Edward I

In the churchyard of St Thomas, Winchelsea

The Col. Body Memorial on the Pett Wall

Sheld-drake

The sea-wall protecting Pett Level

Coastal defence - wartime scene

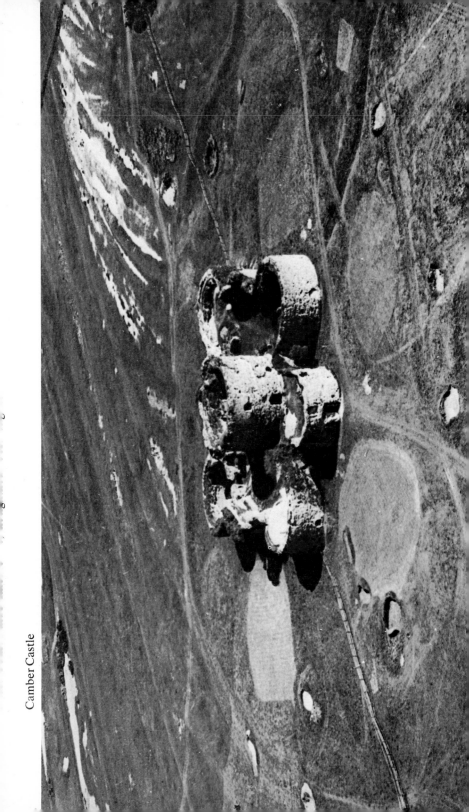

Camber Castle

New Gate, Winchelsea

Seen from a distance or from above, Dungeness looks as flat as a pancake. But at close quarters or from an aeroplane when the level light of the rising sun strikes across it, it is discovered to be undulating. From the air it looks to be furrowed like a ploughed field, but when walking over it the shingle is found to be heaped up in long rounded ridges alternating with shallow hollows. It is a gentle sea of shingle.

These ridges, or fulls as they should be called, if not the key are at least the data of the problem to be solved, for their direction, position and height give the first clues to the formation of the promontory. Each full was at one time a sea beach.

The reader must many a time have spent lazy happy hours "sitting on the beach" doing perhaps no more than sunbathing or casting an idle pebble at the wavelets. But he will have noticed that the slope of the beach is broken up by a series of small banks or ridges parallel to the line of the incoming waves. If today's high tide is higher than yesterday's the last ridge will be farther up the beach than it was the day before. But if today's tide is lower or the waves smaller, then the last ridge will also be smaller, besides being lower down the slope of the beach than it was yesterday. On a spring tide the bank of shingle left will be well up the beach and all previous ridges will have been removed.

If the holiday-maker visited that beach in winter when a full gale was blowing, he would see the great waves pounding on the beach and violently casting up the shingle in a huge bank close under the promenade—perhaps right over the promenade! This would leave behind a full which, if no greater storm occurred, would remain as the highest and at the same time the most inland ridge on the beach. Imagine now that more shingle is being continually brought and piled up along this shore and then in a year, or two or three years' time, another big storm occurs. Once again a storm ridge is flung up, but on account of the increase in the quantity of shingle accumulated, this ridge, though as high, will not be heaped up so far inland. Thus we should have two fulls, parallel to the line of the waves and separated by a hollow. In such a way as this the fulls of Dungeness were formed.

Of the many questions that one wants answered the first naturally are: Where does all the shingle come from and why does it accumulate here? How long has it been piling up and is it still doing so? In which direction do the fulls run? Is Dungeness more recent than The Marsh? And how—but there is no end to the questions we can ask, and the more we think we know the more puzzling do certain features become.

In the first place the shingle is mostly derived from the flints that were formed and embedded in the chalk hills of Sussex. During the centuries these hills have been continuously cut back by all the agents of erosion, exposing the familiar white cliffs we all know so well. After a fall of cliff the sea soon dissolves away the chalk, but the flints remain and are ground and pounded and trundled about by every wave that breaks among the rocks. As the prevailing wind in the Channel is south-west the wave action is such that it sweeps the shingle along the beaches from west to east. Visit any Sussex seaside resort and it will be noticed at once that groynes have had to be built to check this movement of the shingle; and it will also be observed that the shingle is always banked up against these groynes on their west sides, and scoured away from the other side to such an extent that there is often a difference in level of as much as ten feet. The piling up of the shingle is never reversed.

This is proof positive of what is known as the Eastward Drift. In some places where the shore line is such that the scour of the waves is increased, such as at Seaford, even groyning is insufficient to prevent the shingle from being swept away, and that unfortunate but charming seaside town is now faced with the prospect of losing all its beach. In other places, particularly in the lee of a headland, shingle accumulates. This can be seen on a small scale in the lee of Seaford Head at Cuckmere Haven; on a much larger scale at the Crumbles, east of Eastbourne in the lee of Beachy Head; and on a vast scale in the lee of Fairlight in the Camber Castle beaches and at Dungeness in its own lee.

Wave action sweeps shingle along any south- or south-west-fronting shore. If that shore, as at a headland, bends suddenly north-eastwards, then the movement is checked or halted because wave direction is both altered and weakened. Shingle accumulates. If the water is deep to the east of the headland, the shingle will not be moved across it, or only very slowly, because shingle is moved by wave action and scarcely at all by currents and eddies. In such a case the accumulating shingle will gradually be drifted along the north-east side of the headland until such time as it reaches a point where the full force of the waves once again hurries its eastward movement.

If, however, the water is shallow to the east of the promontory, that is, not deeper than about ten feet at high water, then the shingle which is accumulating in the lee of the headland will be carried across the shallows by wave action, and a bar or spit may develop. This spit would tend to take a direction that was a continuation of the coastline where it commenced. The beaches which developed before Camber Castle are an excellent example of this phenomenon.

There is another aspect of the behaviour of shingle which must not be overlooked. This is when rivers or tidal inlets discharge their waters across its path. This volume of water rushing out to sea for some twelve or fourteen hours out of every twenty-four acts as a wave break and at the same time as a barrier to the drifting shingle. The result is that the pebbles begin to pile up on the west side of the river estuary and may be in such quantity that by degrees the accumulation will turn the river mouth more and more eastwards. This is exactly what has been happening to the Rother during the last four centuries and is still going on today. Were it not for the massive groyning of the west pier the mouth of the Rother would be facing east with a long shingle spit running parallel to it and between it and the open sea.

This, as has already been recounted, actually happened, when John Smeaton attempted to give Rye a new harbour. The discharge of water from the new outlet was so feeble that it was unable to hold back the drifting shingle for any length of time, with the result that an enormous spit developed, turning its mouth due east. This shingle spit grew at the astonishing rate of one hundred and sixty feet per year. Again at Shoreham-by-Sea the River Adur has had its mouth turned and runs parallel to the sea coast for more than a mile, while a massive shingle bar several hundred yards wide separates it from the sea. Bungalow Town is built on the bar, as no doubt Old Winchelsea was built on a similar spit a thousand years ago. But let us see how the shingle first began to accumulate on the seaward edge of The Marsh.

* * * * *

If we go back to the time of the Forest Uplift, there must have been then a shore which ran in a fairly straight line from Fairlight Head to the Hythe Headland. W. V. Lewis, in his admirable paper on "The Formation of Dungeness Foreland" which appeared in *The Geographical Journal*, is of the opinion that the Eastward Drift of shingle along the Channel was operating much the same as it is today. This would mean that a fairly even beach would have fringed this shore, though allowance would have to be made for the outlet of the three rivers, the Brede, the Tillingham and the Rother. As the land sank, the shingle beaches would not disappear under the waves, but would be driven back by them upon the land. When the land finally sank below high-water mark it did so so gradually that, as we have seen, the deposition of river and marine silt was able to keep pace with it. Similarly the accumulation of shingle was able to keep pace both with the fall of the land and the deposit of silt.

But by then an important new factor was taking effect: this was the immense volume of tidal water which, after flooding the bay for six hours, ebbed and had to find its way back through the bars and spits, and coupled with it was of course the water of the three rivers. This would mean large breaks were made in the old beach line, and furthermore heavy accumulations of shingle would occur to the west of each outlet. These outlets were probably where Hythe, Romney and Rye or Winchelsea are today.

An uplift followed, the pre-Roman uplift, and nearly half the bay, most of Romney Marsh proper, became dry land. There was no longer an outlet at Hythe; the Rother went out at Romney and the Brede and Tillingham south of Rye. Lydd and Midley and Romney were islands.

The shingle now began to shape up rather differently, though

90

obeying of course the same laws. There was a beach along the south-eastern edge of Romney Marsh, probably just a little seaward of the present site of the Dymchurch Wall; shingle was building up around Lydd west of the Rother estuary; and shingle bars were formed from Fairlight across the bay towards Midley and Lydd, but broken by the egress of the Brede and Tillingham and some of the tidal water. The ends of two of these shingle beds can still be seen six miles west of the Ness at what is known as The Midrips and The Wicks. These two beaches are a few feet lower than the beaches farther east, and their fulls run in a north-easterly direction. It was upon one of these spits towards its western end that Gwent-chesel-ey was built.

The last depression, which began in Roman times, then began to take effect. Before we can fully appreciate what happened during the last 1,500 years there are two or three points about the behaviour of shingle bars which should be understood. As we already know, fulls build up parallel to the line of the breaking waves; if, however, a shingle bar first accumulates and then lengthens in a north-easterly direction as it is swept round a headland, two things may happen. Either a new spit will form, branching out from the previous one and taking a more easterly direction, or the bar itself will tend to swing round—by the waves scouring more shingle from its western end and drifting it along towards its eastern end. Thus it will face more directly the oncoming waves driven by the prevailing south-west winds. The shingle spits which developed before Camber Castle from the sixteenth century onwards are an excellent and recent example of this and give a clear indication as to the formation of Dungeness.

When The Marsh began to sink for the last time the eastern half, Romney Marsh, was in grave danger of inundation. As we know, it sank below high-water mark, and at the Appledore end, which is considerably lower than the seaward edge, there was serious flooding and the Marshmen were hard put to it to build walls to hold out the tidal waters. The "Great Wall" and the "Little Wall" of Apuldre are continually referred to in ancient documents. The Walls, together with the silting up and inning of Walland Marsh, held off the danger in this quarter, and a much more serious threat developed along the seaward edge. If it had not been for the shingle which had been piled along it during the previous uplift Romney Marsh would have again become a tidal bay. But this beach was driven in as the land sank and formed a temporary barrier from the mouth of the Rother, about the position of Littlestone, through Dymchurch towards Hythe.

But the outlet of the Rother checked the supply of shingle to this beach, and, obeying the law described above, the bar began to wear thin at its south-western end while shingle accumulated towards its eastern end. Break-throughs occurred, and it became plain to the Marshmen that this was where the greatest danger threatened. Almost all their attention and energies were then directed to this margin and the strengthening of this old beach or the embankment which replaced it. Such was the beginning of the Dymchurch Wall.

In the meantime immense shingle spits had developed across the mouth of the western bay from Fairlight toward Lydd. Once again the tendency was to wear away south of Rye and accumulate towards the east. As Lydd was above high-water mark these masses of accumulated shingle found a lodgement against it. This tended to increase the deposition of silt, and, as we have seen, land reclamation took place around Lydd as early as the eighth century. The new land in its turn encouraged the piling up of more shingle. The two things took place together, and wherever an exposure is made today in the marginal lands between shingle and reclaimed marshland it can be seen how pebbles, sand and river silt are superimposed in layers and in various mixtures.

The last and final factor in the shaping of Dungeness now comes into play. All this time we have only considered the wave action as a result of the prevailing south-west winds coming up Channel. We have taken no account of wave action driven by winds coming through the Straits of Dover. It has not been necessary to take any account of these before because as the beaches and shingle spits ran roughly south-west to north-east a change from the prevailing wind to an easterly wind would do little more than commence a brief drift of shingle in the opposite direction.

This would soon be returned when the south-westerlies began to blow again. But the great accumulation of shingle at Lydd was in a different case: it was in a much more exposed position and began to experience the full force of waves from the east. These created fulls facing east, that is the shingle was driven up in long ridges running roughly north and south. The waves from the south-west, however, were piling up fulls running east and west. The tendency was therefore for a point to develop.

If the lines of the fulls be inspected in the great beachlands south of Lydd, in particular from the air, or upon an air mosaic photograph, the gradual development of the promontory is quite easily discernible. In the Holmstone and the West Ripe beaches the "bend" was in the neighbourhood of ninety degrees, a little less and a little more. Farther east, south of Brickwall Farm, the point rapidly becomes acute, the fulls almost bending back upon themselves, pointing towards Lydd. Farther east still the point becomes flatter again, and at Dungeness today the angle between the two sides of the promontory, that is to say the amount of bend, is slightly more than a right angle.

The critical moment in the final formation and shaping of the headland came in the thirteenth century when the great storms occurred. The shingle spit upon which Old Winchelsea was built was first broken and then scoured clean away and the Rother's mouth at Romney was blocked, and the river had to find a new outlet by Rye. The forces controlling the shingle drift were thus considerably altered. Shingle was checked to the west of the new estuary, but to the east of it wave-action coupled with the shortage of new material began to scour away the shingle, sweeping it along, as we have just seen, to build up the point. The effect of this over the past six centuries has been to remove completely the western half of the massive shingle beds which end in the Holmstone and West Ripe beaches of today.

This severe scour is still going on, and just east of the little new seaside resort of Camber the visitor will be astonished at the slightness of the embankment which protects the low-lying Marsh on the one hand from the open sea on the other. When the tide is high at this place one can appreciate the words of old Tom

Shoesmith about the " sea settin' above the land". It most certainly does, some twelve feet, and it has been necessary to construct costly coastal defences in the form of concrete ramps to prevent a break-through.

It will be noticed that along this shore of Dungeness—the West Beach—scour is going on at one end near Camber while build-up and accumulation is going on at the Ness end. This means that there is a nodal point, popularly called "the noodle" by those whose business it is to study the coastal defences. This point, where the shingle scoured away is equalled by fresh material drifted along from the west, does not remain constant. Accurate observations and carefully kept records show that "the noodle" is itself gradually moving east, roughly at the same rate that the Ness itself is growing east. Hence the range of scour is being steadily extended eastwards and the defences of The Marsh from Camber to the Midrips being continuously attacked; if it had not been for man's intervention here the present century would have seen The Marsh flooded.

In fact it might not be out of place at this point to mention that during the Second World War when danger of invasion was imminent it was planned to flood The Marsh in an emergency. The scheme was to breach the sea-wall here and at Dymchurch, and engineers anticipated that three high tides would be sufficient to inundate the whole of the levels. As the entire marshland lies between high- and low-water mark, this was a practical proposition and would have meant the evacuation of the whole population and the livestock and would have done incalculable damage to property. Thank God it was never necessary.

It is also of peculiar interest to read the *Kentish Gazette* of Sept. 11, 1804.

"On Thursday last, Mr Pitt accompanied by Generals Twiss and Moore, met the Lords and Bailiff of the Level of Romney Marsh at New Hall, near Dymchurch, to consider of the best mode of inundating The Marsh in case of invasion, when it was determined that, on the appearance of the enemy on the coast, the sluices should be opened to admit the sea so as to fill the dykes, which should be accomplished in one tide, and in the case of actual invasion remain open another tide, which would be sufficient to inundate the whole Level."

That was to complicate matters for Napoleon.

Nearly one hundred and fifty years later, on Pett Level, in 1940, when Hitler's invasion scare reached its peak, a smaller flooding scheme was actually carried out, and the extraordinary effect this had upon the bird life of the area is·described in another chapter.

On the east shore of the Ness, the East Beach, much the same thing is happening as along the West Beach. Immediately in the lee of the promontory, shingle, drifted round the point, steadily accumulates and, as we have seen, is slowly straightening the East Beach to form a right angle with the West Beach. But farther north from Littlestone onwards past Dymchurch the scour which began seven centuries ago is just as persistent as ever. During all these years generation after generation of Marshmen have worked upon the famous Wall. But in spite of all their efforts it was hard to keep pace with the erosion.

As M. Teichman-Derville writes in his book *The Level and the Liberty of Romney Marsh*, no

"grant of land was made in the Marsh without some provision for the upkeep of the Walls . . . and where lands lying in the heart of the Marsh might yet suffer by the neglect of a Wall or waterway several miles off, a more elaborate system of mutual obligation and co-operation between the owners and tenants of the various manors became essential. As early as the twelfth century there had thus come into existence a recognised body of custom referred to as the Lex Marisci ('secundum legem marisci') which by the thirteenth century is found in force with special officials to administer it. These officials consisted, by 1250, of XXIV sworn men or Jurats, elected by the commonalty, to enforce the contributions of land-holders within the Marsh towards the maintenance of sea walls and water courses for the common benefit and safety."

We have seen that the Great and the Small Walls of Apuldre were the important defences up to the thirteenth century. But the progressive inning of Walland Marsh and then the change in the Rother's course, gradually made these defences no longer necessary. In the meantime the vast build-up of shingle about Lydd was steadily increasing the scour effect along the East Beach, and by the fifteenth century the Dymchurch Wall was the critical defence, and has been ever since. Tremendous effort has been expended to reinforce it against both continuous erosion and shock storms, but even so, serious breaches have now and again occurred. M. Teichman-Derville quotes: "On the 19th December, 1705 (the like unknown in this levell since the memory of man), the sea broke through at Eastfleet and High Knock, and so shattered the Wall elsewhere that the level is in great danger of total inundation."

One hundred years later the danger was as serious as ever. In fact, the more the Ness grows eastwards the greater becomes the scour, for the shingle is built up and held at and in the lee of the point and little or none is drifted up the East Beach. It became essential that a really efficient sea-wall should be constructed. Groynes and embankments, brushwood and piles can only be temporary measures against relentless erosion. So at last in 1803–4 what was then a first-rate modern sea-wall was constructed by Rennie, and in the main is the Dymchurch Wall of the present time. It is some three miles long and reaches as far south as Littlestone. Even this substantial defence has needed continuous repair and some twentieth-century modernising. There is very little shingle along the Wall, and at high tides the sea is right up to it, but at low tides there is a wonderful expanse of sand.

At the very tip of Dungeness the continuing accumulation of shingle is simply astonishing. Over a number of years during which records have been kept the estimated yearly advance of the Ness towards the east is from eight to twelve feet per annum. Temporary annual advances are frequently much more. W. V. Lewis describes how in 1931 "the Ness extended eastwards by a further 20 yards". These rapid advances occur after continuous south-westerly winds, when a spit is built up. A big easterly storm will remove and redistribute most of the shingle of such a spit; only for yet more to be piled up under the wave-action of the prevailing wind to replace it and ultimately to become permanent beachland.

The lighthouses which have been built at various times at the tip of the promontory are conclusive proof of the growth of Dungeness. There have been four. In the third which still stands, but now 600 yards from the sea, there is a plaque which reads:

"This lighthouse was erected by Thomas William Coke Efq of Holkam Houfe in the County of Norfolk instead of the old lighthouse which originally ftood 540 yards to the northward and which by means of the land increafing from the Violence of the Sea became ufelefs to Navigation. A.D. 1792 Diftant from the Sea 100 yds at low water."

The present lighthouse, the fourth, ultra modern, semi-automatic, superbly equipped, was opened on June 29, 1960, by the Duke of Gloucester, then Master of Trinity House. It is within both sight and sound of the sea.

Another most interesting fact about the Ness is the great depth of water immediately offshore. A glance at the ordnance maps will show that the 5-fathom and the 10-fathom submarine contour lines almost touch one another at the extremity of the Ness. The 5-fathom line, that is 30 feet of water, skirts the beach for half a mile, and the 10-fathom line, which indicates a depth of 60 feet of water, is barely a hundred yards south-east of it. If this proximity to deep water be compared with the distance of Rye Harbour from the same contour lines, it is all the more striking, for off the mouth of the Rother the 5-fathom line is three and a half miles offshore, and the 10-fathom line over five miles.

This great depth of water immediately off Dungeness allows shipping to approach amazingly close, literally within a stone's throw. It is commonly reported that small packages have actually been flung from shore to ship and ship to shore. I have not seen it done, but can well picture it happening. While distances across water are most deceptive, it is nevertheless an incredible and a

97

most fascinating sight to see these great vessels cruising along the beach, which at high tide and from a little distance they seem to be doing.

For those interested in shipping on the high seas there is no place like Dungeness. Being in the direct line of all that shipping passing through the Straits of Dover and making its way south-west to pass down Channel, the Ness is the perfect grandstand, and the procession of vessels never fails. Like boys on the railway platform, one can sit on the beach and take the names of ships without need of either field-glass or telescope.

Obviously Dungeness is no place for children to go paddling or swimming; let them enjoy all the delights of hundreds of acres of sand at Camber or Greatstone. But the fishermen can have great sport here, for from the beach he can cast his sinker into thirty feet of water, which is probably impossible from any other beach around our shores.

I witnessed an amusing incident just near the place on the East Beach where the deep water gives place to the shallows of the East Road. A fellow and his girl had slithered down the steep beach to enter the water for a bathe. He was first and waded bravely in. She was not far behind, and when he turned round to call her to follow she was already waist-deep. But at the moment the man's back was turned to the open sea what should the young woman to her horror observe but a triangular black fin break the surface, barely three yards away from her sweet-heart.

With a shriek of horror she flung up her arms, stared for one agonised moment, and then turned and fled. There can be no more nightmare task than getting out of deepish water and up a steeply shelving bank of shingle, but she accomplished the feat in seconds.

He, dismayed, turned to see what the horror was, and at the critical moment a second porpoise in the school making its way round the Ness saw fit, in a moment of frolic, to show another fin. He saw it, and then he too was floundering for the shore. It was a neck-and-neck race for their clothes, where she sank down on the beach a nervous wreck. He tried to console her, like a big wet dog trying to lick a half-drowned kitten. I was about to go over and assure them there was no call for alarm, but was forestalled by an old salt who, leaving the winch that had been supporting him, sauntered down to them. He knocked his pipe out on his heel and, gesticulating with it in a manner worthy of a Millais canvas, told them no doubt a real shark story.

But the girl, I am sure, will to her dying day declare that the Dungeness monster had all but swallowed up her romance. To my thinking it clinched the engagement.

What the future of Dungeness may be we may well wonder. Its tip has reached such a depth of water that it seems reasonable to suppose that the growth eastwards must now be slowed up on account of the vast quantities of shingle which must be deposited in the depths before new spits can appear above the surface. On the other hand the deposit of sand in its lee, between the point and Littlestone, has been enormous, and again at Camber and Broomhill Sands the area is very great. The shallowing of both the East Road and the West Road will have a marked effect both on tidal currents, which carry sand, and on the force of the waves which drift shingle. Coupled with this it must not be overlooked that man has taken a hand in causing changes. The great new sea-wall at Pett will prevent any more erosion and drift from the old shingle beds of Camber Castle, and the continuous extension of the piers at the mouth of the Rother will still further check the drift of shingle, besides creating a greater eddy to the east where sand is being deposited.

From this it would appear that "the monster" can only increase by its own erosion, that any growth farther east can only be at the expense of wastage from its West Beach, in which case the Ness will become more and more acute as "the Noodle" moves east. There is, however, the possibility that the two shoals, Stevenson's Shoal two and a half miles to the south-west and the Newcombe Sand-bank three miles to the north-east, may continue to develop and cause shallower water. This will not only cause a change in tidal currents and wave force, but may give the opportunity for the Ness to throw out spits north-east, eventually to part enclose the East Road.

This may sound extravagant, but when one surveys the whole history of the shingle and the extraordinary way in which the great spits grew out from the lee of Fairlight towards Lydd, and did eventually enclose the whole western half of The Marsh, nothing seems impossible to Dungeness.

CHAPTER VIII

DUNGENESS

FLOWERS OF THE FORELAND

HOWEVER it may have been formed, whatever may be its future, Dungeness is unique. On that account alone, as one of the Seven Wonders of Britain, it is worthy of a visit. But there is so much more to it than geography; it has such charm, such spaciousness, such wildness; it is a desert island between the sounding sea and the dreamy levels of The Marsh; it has its own exquisite flora, its rare birds, its insects; it is a place where few come or go.

Many come and go along the principal roads from Lydd and Greatstone, and still more come in the holiday months by way of the Miniature Railway from Hythe and New Romney. A few come to fish, some to watch the passing ships, but most just to see the lighthouse—there is nothing much else for the tripper to see—and the lighthouse is certainly a bit unusual, in so much as you can walk right up to it, round it, up it, and lean your back against it and eat an orange, if you want to, in its shade.

But more than that the average visitor to Dungeness does not do—more's the pity. There are reasons though: lack of time; the miniature trains return in an hour; or it's a long journey home by car; there doesn't seem anything much to see now we've got here; the month is August and the sun too grilling to make one want to do anything more than find a spot of shade or a "stop-me-and-buy-one"; or there is a general disinclination to walk any distance at all on loose shingle.

All good reasons for not staying long. I remember the first time I ever went there, many years ago, in a friend's car. We parked of course near the lighthouse, which was temporarily closed to visitors, so the first and only thing we could do was to walk to the seashore. This, under a roasting sun across two or three hundred yards of loose shingle, was torture to our thinly shod feet and bare heads. We found the sea and found also that the beach was no more comfortable and no less oily than any other beach. There was nothing to see but one small tramp steamer passing close inshore. In an hour we were done; in fact, if it had not been for the thought of that journey back across the shingle we should have gone before. We trudged to the car, which was hot enough to bake bread in, and made all speed for the green and shady lanes of Sussex. My wife vowed she would never go to Dungeness again—it was "too awful".

That is indeed a dreary picture, but as far as it goes it is nevertheless a true one. The Ness can be the dreariest, weariest sunscorched desolation that ever one set tired eyes upon; and, in winter, the bleakest desert, with its skimpy vegetation dark and stark, and its pits full of cold grey water swept by harsh winds. Few places in Britain can equal it for exposure. To walk three miles across its yielding, stodgy shingle in the teeth of a streaming south-westerly gale is one of those dreadful numbing experiences that makes you think the whole world is relentlessly against you. Or when a north-easter, unhampered since it left the Arctic, is screaming in the few remaining wires that bulge between the telegraph poles, you might well think Dungeness was the last place God made, when there was nothing left but sticks and stones to make it with.

In one sense it is. But as the prophet says, "The desert shall rejoice and blossom as the rose". And that is the magical thing about Dungeness; it blossoms. Once seen its flowers can never be forgotten, and their delicious fragrance haunts the memory. For if by chance in some far-off spot one sniffs unawares a faint copy of that perfume, instantly it evokes in the mind, in that mysterious smell memory of ours, the sweetness of the original, and we see again the beachlands decked with gay flowers, the shingly hollows pink-carpeted with thrift, the foxgloves, the broom, the narrow blue riband of the encircling sea and the vast sky.

Everything depends upon when and where you go and how. May and June are the right months, and the centre to make for is Lydd. Avoid the lighthouse and the East Beach—these are trippery and inclined to be somewhat ramshackle; they can be visited later. Stay at Lydd for a day or two; there are the Dolphin Hotel and the George Hotel, where you can be comfortable and well looked after. Forget about the car, buy or borrow a map, and early one fine morning—do try to make it early—set off for a walk towards the shore.

There are four roads to the sea from Lydd. The one to the south-east goes to the lighthouse, that to the south-west goes to Camber, only use the car on these. Two go to the south—choose either of these; one goes past the Camp to the British Sailor, the other bears to the left and eventually reaches the sea at the Hope and Anchor. Do not be deceived into thinking that refreshment can be obtained at either of these jolly-sounding inns. You cannot get even a drink of water—they are derelict ruins. But don't let that put you off; we are in search of flowers, not fluids.

There is no charm about the Military Camp, with its huts and wire, though to be quite fair it is nothing like as bad as it might have been. In any case the glory of the June morning puts everything in its place. The quality of the light is something I find quite impossible to describe. I do not know whether the cause is the sun rising out of the sea, or the almost insular character of the promontory, or the reflections of the beachlands, or the strange effect of horizontal beams of light as the sun's rays stream across the levels unimpeded. It is altogether unearthly, ethereal. Small things cast long shadows, slight unevennesses create pools of rich deep tones, yet every full and tussock flushes and gilds, and the flowers glow and the gorse burns.

There are wisps of bird song, lark in the zenith and linnet in the furze, but their slender music only accentuates the profound stillness. If you are sensitive to such moments, you will find yourself walking a-tiptoe or stealing along the verges so that no footfall prevents your hearing the breathless breathing of the awakening day. You'll stop; many times you'll stop, to see, to breathe, to hear. You'll stop to watch a hare loping along the shingle, and there is his mate. They have a merry frolic in and out among clumps of blue and purple bugloss, quite oblivious of your presence, as most animals always seem to be early in the morning.

They twist and leap, jumping clean over each other, and then speed away along the top of a ridge, their black-tipped ears clearly seen above the wispy fescue grass.

You'll stop to hear the sea long before you reach it. On a full tide and a windless day the gentle swell lifts into little crystal-clear waves which plash in unceasing rhythm all along those long, long miles of beach. This is not Tennyson's long ripple washing mournfully in the reeds. It is a fairy music, of cymbals and glass bells. Just to hear it from far off on a fine morning is to put one in tune with all the fairy lore that was ever written or imagined. The Pharisees have from time immemorial been much in the minds of The Marsh folk. According to old Tom Shoe-smith all the fairies had quitted the shores of one-time Merrie England, so miserable had become their lot. An old wise woman, in response to their wailings and their grief, had permitted her deaf-and-dumb son to ferry them over the sea, and one and all departed in the Dymchurch Flit. He, poor fellow, had been un-able to hear or to tell anything that he had seen.

But to quote Tom Shoesmith's own words, I think "'Twas a passel o' no-sense talk about the Pharisees". Or if the little folk did indeed leave our shores centuries ago, they have certainly returned. If you don't see them yourself you'll believe it once you have been down to the beachlands in June.

You'll stop longest of all for the flowers. Whilst vast stretches of the beach are still as bare and destitute of vegetation as the foreshore, it is nevertheless dotted with innumerable green oases. Colonies of plants, some small, some extensive, have everywhere succeeded in establishing themselves. Where such communities have been in existence a long time the mat of roots and decayed vegetation, together with such wind-blown debris as has accumu-lated, produces a "soil" which holds a certain amount of moisture and in which many species of plants can thrive. Such colonies may cover an area as large as a tennis court or as small as a pocket handkerchief.

Quite a number of plants succeed without any such mat of soil. One of the most delightful surprises for me was the common broom, which on account of the force of the wind crouches low to the shingle, like a porcupine. In spite of the exposure and barrenness of the situation, maybe because of it, these close-set, shrubby brooms burst into a profusion of blossom. Normally brooms grow ragged and leggy, their beauty spoilt by a lot of deadwood. The brooms of Dungeness are prostrate, dwarfs, sweeps' brooms; but what they lose in stature they more than make up in blossom. The sight of dozens, no, scores of these knee-high shrubs smothered in lemon-gold butterfly flowers set in the naked shingle is something one can never forget.

Thrift, the sea pink, is a plant which one more normally associates with the seaside. I have seen it in places as far apart as the Coolins of Skye and the chalk cliffs of Sussex; it is a common plant from Cornwall to Kent. But never have I seen it anywhere as it grows on the beachlands of Dungeness. It is not a large-flowered variety and it is short in the stem, but in those places where it has colonised acres of shingle the effect is indescribably lovely. Thrift is naturally a very compact, close-growing, "mossy" type of plant. Exposure accentuates this characteristic, and this together with the gentle undulations of the fulls creates much more than a carpet effect—a rosy mist seems to cling to the shingle, and one feels that at any moment a breath of sea breeze may blow it away.

How it is that foxgloves have come to succeed here is hard to say. I have always associated them with woodland clearings where two years before the woodman's axe had been busy; half-shade and leaf mould seems their natural habitat. Yet on the naked shingle and exposed to the intense light of these shadowless beachlands foxgloves are in places abundant. True, they are barely half the height of their stately sisters, but they are sturdy and richly coloured, and they succeed by sending long roots deep down in the shingle, where moisture is present.

There is water under all the beachlands. On an average the depth of the shingle is twelve feet. As we have seen, it lies piled up upon the old peaty clay of the Forest Uplift; and above this old bed, water gathers in the shingle. Wherever shingle has been or is being removed and pits of sufficient depth are left, water fills them. This is fresh water, it is neither salt nor brackish. In fact, this natural reservoir is of the greatest importance to the rapidly increasing population, which has come to stay, along the East Beach. Without this supply it is doubtful if Greatstone could ever have grown as it has or coped with the holiday crowds. The huge water tower is a conspicuous landmark on Denge Beach. Its purpose is to store at a sufficient elevation enough water, several hundred thousand gallons, to supply the area if and when the pumps stop working.

But to return to the flowers. There are the foxgloves mingled with viper's bugloss, with broom, yellow-horned poppies, henbane and valerian. There are drifts of sea pink, sea campion, and mustard patches of starry stonecrop. What used to be considered an uncommon plant, the Nottingham catchfly, has established itself and is everywhere abundant. But that much greater rarity, the sea holly, a native of the beachlands, is unfortunately becoming more and more scarce, and one is fortunate to be shown where it occurs or doubly lucky to stumble across it oneself. It is a stiff, shrubby plant about a foot high. Its leaves are strongly veined, stiff and prickly, and the roundish flower heads are blue. A garden variety of it is fairly commonly grown in herbaceous borders, but that seems an odd place to me after seeing it out there on the blazing shingle.

There are a number of other rare and curious flowers on the beachlands to which Mr Francis Rose has drawn my attention; and I would like to say how much I am indebted to him for expert information and identification. His *Flora of Kent* will be a book that every lover of flowers will find to be a "must". He has pointed out to me the little crucifer *Teesdalea nudicaulis*, which is particularly luxuriant on places where the beach is more consolidated; it also occurs on the shingle at Hythe, but nowhere else in Kent. Mr Rose has shown me the extremely rare stinking hawksbeard, *Crepis fœtida*, which is only known in two other places in Britain. He has pointed out also how some rare mosses are growing as epiphytes on the woody stems of stunted blackthorn, including a remarkable sub-alpine species, *Antitrichia curtipendula*, and has shown me also the ramping fumitory which occurs in these thickets.

Mr Rose has also drawn my attention to the fact that on Lydd Common, nearly three miles from the sea, marram grass and sand sedge survive, as relics of a sea shore, probably pre-Roman, when ancient sand dunes overlay very early shingle beds.

And on Romney Warren, which is a continuation of the same ancient sand dunes, there are many rare clovers, especially *Trifolium glomeratum*, *subterraneum* and *suffocatum*, various medicks and the spring vetch. The whole locality is indeed a remarkable one for small leguminous plants, and rivals some of the dunes of South-west England in this respect. In some of the dune hollows the pyramid orchis is still frequent, and the white knotted pearl-wort and the dwarf pink centaury are still to be found. In spite of bungalows and other buildings there is still a thicket or two of sea buckthorn glorious with orange berries in autumn, and on the broken ground near Littlestone that extraordinary plant the stinking goosefoot with an odour of rotten fish.

Between Littlestone and Greatstone the promenade forms a causeway across the former inlet which was the ancient estuary of the Rother, and in this damp, low-lying area there are some relics of the old salt marsh. Here there are sea aster, sea bullrush, salt-water crowfoot and another rare goosefoot, *Chenopodium botryodes*. The lovely little pink-flowered sea heath used to occur here, but now it only survives in two similar places farther west on Dungeness.

The whole ecology of plant life on the shingle beachlands is a most fascinating and absorbing study. Even to the amateur, and by that I mean the ordinary lover of wild flowers, the way in which differing plant communities colonise both recent and ancient shingle is extraordinarily interesting. We can also follow the progression from the most recent storm shelf, where the sea spray reaches, to those shingle beds which must have accumulated more than fifteen hundred years ago and are now three miles from the high-tide mark.

On the most recent full, the storm shelf, there are sea purslane and sea beet. In its lee or on the second full there is sea kale, with its big glaucous leaves and compact masses of white flowers. Then the yellow-horned poppy, sea dock, sea campion and the rarer sea pea. One plant I noticed in particular, which was abundant on the bare shingle, within a hundred yards of the sea, was the little geranium herb-robert. Then a few varieties of grasses succeed, such as sea meadow grass and false oat grass. There are sea plantains and sea spurrey, milkwort, thrift, convolvulus, and a little farther back still, yellow ragwort, hound's-tongue, pungent rest-harrow, bird's-foot trefoil and clover.

One might have thought that if plants such as these have succeeded in living on shingle which has only been in existence from ten to a hundred years, then farther back on the ancient shingle the whole would have long since been completely covered by vegetation. But such is not the case; there is a great deal of beach as bare as ever it was when first cast up by the storm waves of so long ago.

We can follow the stages in the development of plant colonies. First we start with the naked shingle. This is windswept, exposed to intense light, the surface layers hold no moisture, become excessively hot in summer but hold no heat and rapidly chill. It seems impossible that vegetation should ever succeed on such utterly barren terrain. Such indeed is the case in many parts. But elsewhere, what at first appear as bare or discoloured pebbles are found on closer inspection to be part-covered and patched with a very close-growing lichen. This is stage two. Why it should take centuries to achieve is not easy to explain, though the combined causes appear to be minute pitting of the surface of the shingle due to the erosive action of sun and frost, expansion and contraction; position in relation to wind and weather; and that little extra or prolonged condensation due to depth, size and density of the shingle.

The lichen spreads, decays, and the fragments fall among the interstices of the pebbles and are carried down by rain. This, together with dust and sand and other wind-blown debris, both organic and inorganic, will in time begin to choke the drainage. Where the pebbles are large and the drainage "perfect" this will take countless years, but where the shingle is smaller, more compact, more intermixed with sand or silt this choking up occurs more rapidly. In places it is possible to excavate beach and find it almost as clean four feet down as it is at the surface. In other places one has only to dig a foot deep to disclose "dirty" shingle.

Wind eddies have much to do with this effect, which leads to stage three. Most of Denge Beach on the west side was requisitioned by the War Office for military training, and much of it is pitted with the small craters produced by mortar bombs and other missiles. These craters are about a foot deep and two to three feet wide. Naturally, each explosion exposed virgin shingle, and they were all made between 1940 and 1945. Thus each crater started from scratch, so to speak, in acquiring blown debris and a possible plant community.

Their study reveals great diversity. A large number of the craters are as naked as upon the day the bomb exploded: there is not a vestige of rubbish or plant life in them. Other holes showed small accumulations of dried plant fragments and pieces of lichen. A few craters more favourably situated as regards wind eddies and currents had collected quite a floor of debris in which a large grey lichen was common, and sheep's-bit scabious, cinquefoil, trefoil, thyme and other small plants had found a foothold.

In a few craters I examined, nearly the whole of the interior was overgrown: there was bedstraw, wood sage, cranesbill, catchfly and numerous others already mentioned, sometimes all roped and strangled with dodder. This might be regarded as stage four and it is remarkable that it could be reached in twelve years.

Stage five can of course only be observed on the undisturbed shingle. This is where plants have matted together over considerable areas and where shrubs sometimes succeed in obtaining a footing, bramble, gorse, elder, blackthorn, sallow and holly, with honeysuckle, woody nightshade and traveller's-joy rambling over them.

The holly is probably the most interesting shrub that has succeeded on the beachlands. On one of the very old shingle beds south-west of Lydd there is a remarkable "forest" of holly, known as the Holmstone or Holly Stone, which has been in existence for at least twelve hundred years. Almost by a stroke of luck it was mentioned in the Saxon charter, in which the King of Kent granted certain privileges and land to the Monastery of Lyminge in A.D. 740. It indicated that cattle might be pastured "next to the marsh which is called Bishopswic as far as the wood called Ripp". The word Ripp, Rype or Ripe is still in common use about Lydd. The West Ripe, in which the Holmstone or Ripp Wood occurs, unfortunately lies within the territory permanently occupied by the military camp and can only be visited on obtaining a permit from the commandant, and then only when firing practice is not in progress.

It is a grievous pity in many ways that this military camp was ever established on Dungeness. One might, however, say that wherever a military camp is situated it brings many undesirable things in its train. No doubt the desolation of Dungeness appeared the ideal spot for an artillery range some sixty years ago. What was already a "barren waste" could not be rendered any more barren to anyone's disadvantage. But the War Department took no heed of the fact that Dungeness was unique, neither did it show much foresight in the matter of guns, for in a few years the increased range of guns far outstripped the four-thousand-yard ranges available on the West Ripe. The artillerymen for whom the camp was established had to go to Salisbury Plain. The War Department, however, did not relinquish its hold on the land, and it soon became a station for the Tank Corps.

During World War II the War Department requisitioned almost the whole of the beachlands, and flora and fauna and some buildings suffered considerably thereby. In time of war and dire need this was understandable and inevitable, but as not infrequently has happened once a Government department has taken a hold on a particular area heaven and earth may be moved but it proves well-nigh impossible to dislodge it. There has been the greatest danger that we might lose altogether all the beachland that was requisitioned, and it is something of a coincidence that at the very moment I am writing these pages about the rare charm and unusual interest of Dungeness I have heard that the battle is being won and that the War Department has relinquished its hold on some of the beachland.

For this we have to be thankful to one man, a man who has devoted more than twenty years of his life, his capital, his very pension to secure for nature lovers everywhere and for all time this unique reserve, with its peculiar geographical interest, its lovely flora and its wonderful birds; Mr R. B. Burrowes, who first saw Dungeness in 1901, who went to live there when he retired in 1930 and who from then on fought a lone battle against bungalow development, the speculative builder and the War Department. Of this bitter struggle and the lovely and rare birds for which he sought sanctuary, more in another chapter. But let us pay tribute here to this gallant gentleman for the preservation of the land alone; it is as precious in its own way as any mere, as any lakeland mountain.

It is an ill wind that blows no good, and it must not be thought that the military camp is condemned out of hand. It is not too large, there are rarely more than one thousand troops stationed there; but nevertheless it employs quite a large number of civilians and it has certainly brought prosperity to Lydd. While it controls a great deal of the oldest beachlands, including three unusual sheets of water known as The Midrips, The Wicks and The South Brooks, it does nevertheless form a most effective barrier to development and intrusion from the west. There is now not a single inhabited building from the Coast Guard Station where the coast road from Camber Sands turns inland, to the Coast Guard Station at Dungeness—six miles of unspoiled shore (except for the targets behind part of it). One has but to see the shambles and jerry-building and ugliness of Camber Sands to appreciate at least this. True the area is almost a prohibited area and much of its original flora and fauna has been destroyed or driven away by tanks, concrete roads, military works and explosives. Nevertheless a great deal of it is still there, and one day, who knows, military training may be no longer necessary and we shall get the whole of the beachlands back again, and future generations will be thankful to an obsolete War Department!

★   ★   ★   ★   ★

But we were, I believe, taking an early-morning walk down

the road past this camp to the derelict site of the British Sailor, an inn that was one time built on the beach so that the Rye fisherman, or the Hastings or Brighton fisherman for that matter, might put ashore there for a quick one while passing to and fro on their lawful occasions. If the walk is too far, about three miles, cycle down. On a fine almost windless morning cycling is a real delight across the levels, so little exertion is needed, one speeds along so silently, and there are no hedges across the beachlands— one can see everything. If June and July have not been too scorching even early August can be delightful. I once spent the first week in August at Lydd, and every day I went cycling or walking across the levels. One morning I went on this very road to the British Sailor, and after taking my dip I came back past the ruins of the inn and some buildings near the beach and attempted to cycle along a narrow embankment called Green Bank which hereabouts runs some three or more miles dead straight, east and west. It must have been an old sea-wall or coastal defence embankment, for the shingle on the landward side is in places eight to ten feet below the top of it, while on the seaward side it is only four to six feet below.

This embankment is thickly grass grown, but it is just possible to cycle cautiously along the undulating top of it. A postman, the only man I met all that morning, told me he used it fairly regularly to reach the next road-end at the Hope and Anchor. Unfortunately, before it reaches that ruined inn the embankment peters out in the shingle, and the postman has to push his machine across nearly a mile of beach. He seemed to think it was worth it rather than go back four miles, but I have a suspicion he does it because he loves the beachlands.

I rode along carefully, but oh how carefree! The butterflies rise from my wheel in clouds, blues, small coppers, hedge browns, gatekeepers, meadow browns, skippers and large whites. There are swarms of grasshoppers, and countless humble bees crowding on the sage and the bugloss. At last I stop, not because like the page I could go no longer, but because I must stop to take it all in, to see and to breathe.

My bicycle slips down the bank among the flowers and the

butterflies, and I just stand and stare across this wilderness, so wild
and so desolate a stretch of terrain. No, there is no place like it
anywhere in Britain, nowhere in the world. In front, behind,
east and west, thousands of acres of beachland; some absolutely
bare, some with the lightest discoloration of lichen, some thin
grass, and some with patches of vegetation varying in size and
texture according to the plant colonisation.

The air is so clear that the mile I have come seems but a hundred yards; and that air is intoxicating, sweet, surcharged with
the fragrance of flowers—yellow bedstraw, wild parsnip, wood
sage, thyme, clover and a score of others. It makes one breathe
long and deep.

Beyond the storm beaches I can see the narrow blue ribbon of
the Channel and the steamers so close in that they seem to glide
along the beach. Across the levels the landmarks of the lighthouse,
the water tower and the tower of Lydd church form an arc to
the east and north, while to the west are the dunes of Camber,
with Fairlight far beyond and the outlines of Rye and Playden. I
sit down among the grasshoppers and the meadow browns, and
getting out my notebook try to put down on paper what I see
and feel. But again and again my pen dries in the warm sun
before I have written a word. How can I convey the sense of
spaciousness, the oceanic blue, the immense uninterrupted horizon? How can pen and ink carry the fragrance of countless
flowers borne on the sea breeze? (A grasshopper has just plopped
on my paper and I am loath to disturb him. . . . He leaps away and
the wheezy chirruping of his thousand merry companions makes
me day-dream.) I wish I could dip my pen in the tremulous heat
haze that now ripples like water over the beachlands; perhaps
then their magic might creep into these pages.

It is bank holiday weekend, but there is not a soul in sight.
The butterflies flip gaily by, a great black-backed gull drifts
overhead, faintly from the shore comes the piping of a little
party of waders—and then along the embankment comes a hare;
it wasn't wearing white kid gloves, but it certainly had black
velvet-tipped ears, and I fancy it stood up on its hind legs and,
taking a large turnip-shaped watch from its pocket, said perfectly

clearly: "I shall be late at Lydd, I shall be late at Lydd." And as a matter of fact I was.

★   ★   ★   ★   ★

If you take the other road from Lydd, the one that leads to the Hope and Anchor, you will have the opportunity of seeing one other feature of the flora of the shingle, that is the flowers of the sewer. This does not sound very pleasant because most people associate the word sewer with house drains. But in The Marsh the word is commonly used to describe any large drainage channel which conveys water to the sea or to the Royal Military Canal, such as the White Kemp Sewer, Jury's Gut Sewer and the Denge Marsh Sewer. Far from being unpleasant, these waterways have many charming reaches and at times exceedingly lovely flowers, and are always of absorbing interest to the flower lover.

The Denge Marsh Sewer is perhaps the best of them all. It has such variety. It commences, if one can say a sewer begins anywhere, near New Romney and runs in a southerly direction skirting the shingle of the East Beach; it then passes through Denge Marsh south of Lydd, and at Dengemarsh Farm turns south-east and passes through the shingle of the West Beach to reach the sea by the sluice-gates at Pen Bars, near the Hope and Anchor.

The lowest reaches of this sewer are beautiful. I have seen it in June when its sheltered banks are aglow with masses of spring flowers, beds of wild yellow iris standing in the water, foxgloves, valerian, henbane and bugloss mixed with sea kale, thrift, stonecrop, and horned poppy on the banks. And again in August when the sewer is choked with gay masses of yellow loosestrife, clumps of purple loosestrife, jungles of reeds and reed mace, great water plantain and great water dock, and all the flowers of the shingle run riot within easy reach of water.

Out in the centre of the beachlands are a remarkable series of pools or pits in which the water is quite fresh. Some of these, the Hoppen Pits, developed naturally owing to changes in direction of the shingle ridge formation, which left lens-shaped spaces between successive ridges. This is well seen from the air. There are others,

114

created very recently, caused by the excavation of shingle, the grading and processing of which is a growing and important industry.

In all these, interesting marsh or fen vegetation has developed such as the pondweeds, including the rare *Potamogeton trichoides*. The buckbean or bogbean occurs commonly, and is not only one of the loveliest of our water plants but also one of the most difficult to describe, for there seems to be no word to describe a petal which is "bearded"; Francis Rose gets over it by describing them as "furry petals". The great spearwort is well established, and there is the marsh fern, the marsh cinquefoil and several rare sedges for the specialist.

What I have written about the charm of Dungeness will, I hope, encourage many to visit it. But there is one snag, which I did mention at the beginning of this chapter but have not so far dealt with. This is the problem of walking on the shingle. If you have plenty of time and thick-soled boots this may not worry you overmuch. But, ladies, don't attempt it with your narrow shoes and slender heels, it's purgatory; and, gents, in thin-soled shoes it's no fun to go any distance. Wear boots if you are going to explore the beachlands properly—if not, wear back-stays.

I said this once to a lady of my acquaintance, and she looked at me very "old-fashioned" as they say in Sussex. I had to hasten to explain that back-stays (far from being anything she might have imagined) were pieces of tough board worn underfoot, like skis or snowshoes. Each stay is about five inches wide and a foot or so in length. It has a leather loop or strap screwed just forward of the centre, under which the toe of the boot can be slipped fairly tightly. There is no other fastening. One walks or half slides, but one's heel leaves the board before the back-stay leaves the shingle, the board then coming up with a sharp clatter against the heel. This is most disconcerting when you first learn to use them, because the whole thing seems much too loose on the boots. But having once mastered the art you will realise that this very looseness leads to free and tireless travel. If the back-stay were secured firmly to the boot like a skate one would be for ever stumbling, for then the front edge of the board would dig into the shingle as the heel was raised. As it is, one so to speak puts down the board, walks on it and then picks it up again as the foot advances for the next step. Rather like the caterpillar vehicle, which puts down its own track to run on and, having passed over, picks it up behind.

Do not despise the back-stay on account of its simplicity. It is one of those primitive devices exactly suited to its job. It has grown up with the people of the beach from time immemorial, and in spite of roads and railways the back-stays are still in use. I had fun and entertainment in learning to use them. One must first learn to walk properly, but later one can employ a kind of glide, half-way between sliding and ski-ing, and as the beach is undulating there are possibilities for quite rapid movement. I don't pretend that back-staying will ever become a popular sport. Heaven forbid! But if you haven't altogether lost your love of fun and adventure, then don't forget to take your pair with you when you go exploring Dungeness.

Chapter VII

FARMING

It is a long time from the Neolithic Depression to the end of the twentieth century; probably some twelve thousand years have passed since the first deposition of that silt which was to be the foundation of The Marsh. But although the area has been up and down, above and below sea level many times, the net result has been that the alluvium steadily increased and today, with the whole Marsh consolidated, its depth may be anything from forty to sixty feet above the original sea bed.

As we have seen, the deposition of river and marine silt was neither steady nor even. So much depended upon the position and efficacy of the natural shore defences—the beaches, the beds and spits of shingle. Where these successfully held off the sea and the scour of tidal currents, quiet waters and lagoons would lie behind, and here the silt deposited would be the finest sediment. Furthermore, in such backwaters, first marine and then salt-marsh vegetation would flourish, and hence there would be a considerable admixture of organic material to the inorganic silt.

Elsewhere the defences would be breached or unformed, and continuous tidal movements of a large volume of water would only allow the deposition of much heavier material, or where the rivers cut their way through, there would be none at all. As the shingle spits and bars were continuously changing, building up in one place and wearing thin and giving way in others, and as the rivers too were frequently changing course it will be seen that although alluvium was always steadily keeping pace with the sinking of the land, the way in which it was deposited, its quality and its mixture were subject to continuous variation. Thus while the whole of the soil of The Marsh, with the exception of the beachlands of Dungeness, can be described quite correctly as alluvial, and to the uninitiated it all appears much of a muchness, its composition does nevertheless vary enormously, and the effect of these differences, particularly upon pasture, is striking.

While it can be deduced from ancient records that from the very earliest times a certain amount of cultivation has always been carried on wherever land was reclaimed on The Marsh, it was not that which made the place famous. It was the pastures. These grasslands, beyond their level and breezy character, do not appear to have anything remarkable about them at all. The fields are large, averaging about twenty acres, but there being few trees and the fact that the fields are often separated one from another only by narrow dykes and watercourses make them appear much larger than they really are. They look continuous. In Guldeford Marsh and parts of Romney Marsh where trees are very scarce one gets the impression when walking across them, far away from roads and buildings, that one is walking on the grassy uplands of the South Downs—rolled out flat. There is a wonderful spaciousness, and an edge to the clean north-east breeze. There is no gorse, but there are blackthorn bushes hugging the dykes and here and there a willow, bowing and flashing as its leaves turn away from the wind. There are the songs of larks and the cry of the peewit, and here and there and everywhere the bleat of sheep, and lambs far and lambs near.

That is the secret of The Marsh—the reason for its fame. It is its grass, the quality of its pasture, what the grazier knows as its fatting quality, its amazing stock-carrying capacity, but at the same time its tantalising variability.

For there are pastures which can carry and fatten from six to ten sheep per acre in the summer. On the most famous fields ten to fourteen sheep can be found. This perhaps will not mean much to the layman, but if he compares these remarkable figures with those of such rough pastures as the South Downs, which can only carry two sheep or less per acre in the summer, or with some of the world's famous sheep farms, as in Argentina or Australia, where so many acres are counted for one sheep, he will begin to understand the force of the figures. Furthermore the point about these famous Marsh pastures is that they are not merely keeping sheep in a growing condition, but they are fattening them. They are not folded on any crop, no extra food is given them, they eat the grass only, and such is its amazing quality that it fattens ten sheep to the acre.

The tantalising thing about these most productive soils is that they are not common to the whole of The Marsh. If they were they would most undoubtedly be the most famous, the most productive pastures in the world. But there is, so to speak, a catch in it. Here is a famous field fattening ten sheep to the acre, and right alongside it, separated from it by no more than a ditch or a fence, is another field which will do no more than keep two or three sheep in a growing condition. Here is a good field supporting six sheep to the acre, while on the other side of the lane there is a poor pasture scarcely able to carry two. In fact, out of a total area of grassland of 27,000 acres less than 8,000 acres may be properly described as fattening pastures. The sheep farmer recognises four grades.

One would have thought that the reason for one field being so much better than another would be due to the varieties of grass and plants which grew upon it. But the mystery of The Marsh pastures is that except in extreme cases there appears to be little or no difference. An enormous amount of study and research has been devoted to the subject, both as to the composition of the soil and the plants which grow upon it. In a Report for the Board of Agriculture and Fisheries (1911) on the Agriculture and Soils of Kent, Surrey and Sussex, A. D. Hall and E. J. Russell gave special attention to The Marsh and made interesting and thorough botanical and mechanical analyses. For the former a portion of a fatting field and of a non-fatting field were fenced off and allowed to run to hay. It was then possible to determine what the grasses were. The result was as follows:

	Fatting %	Non-Fatting %
Perennial rye grass	50·6	56·6
Bent grass	20·2	2·6
Crested dogtail grass	15·4	15·1
Yellow oat grass	4·3	11·8
Meadow barley grass	0·2	4·6
Timothy grass	0·4	2·0

	Fatting	Non-Fatting
Rough-stalked meadow grass	2·1	1·2
Yorkshire fog grass	0·9	—
Cocksfoot grass	—	0·1
Sheep's fescue grass	0·1	0·3
White clover	2·1	0·9
Buttercup	3·6	3·7
Various weeds	0·1	1·1

This was an attempt to find out if the difference in the feeding value of the two fields "could be correlated with the botanical character of the herbage". That this was not so even the novice can see after a glance at the figures. In both cases fifty per cent or more of the grasses was perennial rye grass, and in both cases less than six per cent was made up of clover and weeds. The only really noticeable difference is the greater quantity of bent in the fatting land, replaced by more yellow oat and meadow barley. But, as Hall and Russell say, bent grass "has never been regarded as specially valuable".

As the botanical analysis made it clear that type of vegetation was not the cause for a good or a poor pasture, the experts were forced to the conclusion that it was the quality of the vegetation that really mattered. Further careful study did indeed show that the grasses of the fatting field were more leafy, while those of the non-fatting field were more stemmy.

"There was a little less fibre and a little more nutrient material in the grass from the fatting pasture. Now the more fibre a food contains the more work the animal has to do in order to digest the food until a point is reached when the energy an animal derives from the digested part of the food is all used up in the work of digestion and nothing is left over for other work, nor is there any surplus out of which to make flesh or fat."

This might seem a satisfactory conclusion, but it is not the solution of the mystery. For what makes the same grass more leafy, more nutrient in one place than in another where it is more stemmy, more fibrous? Hall and Russell went to enormous trouble to make mechanical analyses of the soil, to a depth in some cases of seven feet, in some nine different fields. It would perhaps be tedious to reproduce here their elaborate tables of results; readers particularly interested in the subject can refer to them in the works mentioned above and below. It is sufficient here to say that foot by foot the two experts analysed every spit of the soil into fine gravel, coarse sand, fine sand, silt, fine silt, clay, stones, calcium carbonate and water. In almost every series and at almost every depth fine sand preponderated, as high as seventy-five per cent in some cases.

The experts were also struck by sudden changes in strata:

"Though the surface soil resembles the underlying layer very closely, yet not infrequently a complete and sudden change in composition may set in not far below the surface ... at Midley, somewhere between the second and third foot, the whole surface material gives place to a soil composed almost wholly of fine sand. At Orgarswick no change was found down to a depth of seven feet when a bed of peat was encountered; similarly at Hope-all-Saints the heavy soil persists to a depth of six feet, while at Lydd a bed of shingle occurs at no great depth."

But though the two experts completed a difficult and exacting task and, apart from anything else, confirmed beyond doubt the extraordinarily variable way in which the alluvium had been deposited, they had to admit the mystery was not solved:

"The mechanical analyses of The Marsh soils ... fail to throw any light on the superiority of one field over its neighbour; not only do the soils from the rich fields in different places show no similarity, but if the best soil at Lydd be compared with its medium and poor neighbours no significant differences can be found. Similarly the Orgarswick rich land, being only a trifle heavier."

What then could the answer be? It is not surprising that since the work of Hall and Russell many other scientists and agriculturalists have tried to solve the mystery, notably Furneaux, Brade-Birks, and Cole and Dubey. Dr J. K. Dubey of Wye College is now pretty certain that he has the answer. It is not the sort of vegetation. One farmer told me how he had let a part of one of his best fatting pastures run to seed, how he had assiduously collected all the seed and re-sown it in place of a poor pasture, and that it *did not produce a fatting pasture*; and incidentally the good pasture was considerably degraded by being allowed to run to seed.

It is not the mechanical constituents of the soil, as Hall and Russell have so conclusively shown. Dr Dubey is convinced that it is the arrangement of the constituents that matters, i.e. he has "related pasture performance and fertility to the soil profile." Something like nine different soils series have been established in The Marsh. It is interesting to note that the different strata are classified as: sand, shingle, loamy sand, sandy loam, silt loam, loam and silty loam, silty clay loam, clay loam, peat. To the layman this may seem somewhat technical, and he will probably be intrigued by the difference between sandy loam and loamy sand.

Nevertheless the fact that it is possible to distinguish so many different strata in the alluvium of The Marsh emphasises two important points. First it shows how different is alluvial soil from sedentary soil. Sedentary soil has been formed *in situ* and, on account of the comparatively long time taken for its formation, the coarsest material is generally at the surface because all finer material has been washed away or washed down. In an alluvial soil, the materials of which have been sorted by running water, the deposition is much more uniform, and often the finest material is found at or near the surface.

Secondly the varying strata show the extraordinary complexity and diversity of the river, tidal and marine movements which brought about the deposition and mixture and sortation of the silt and sand which form the soil of The Marsh.

G. H. Garrad, O.B.E., formerly County Agricultural Organiser for Kent, commenting on Dubey's researches says:

"It was found that practically all the fatting pastures are on a soil formation where the surface layer to a depth of 10–20 inches is loam or silty loam, the texture becomes heavier with increasing depth but is never very heavy and at 2–3 feet (occasionally 4 feet) it becomes lighter again. The high fertility of these soils is very largely due to the fact that their texture facilitates a perfect natural drainage."

There are fatting pastures in nearly all the fourteen parishes wholly within The Marsh, and the soil profile varies considerably in each. The famous Finn Series, according to Cole and Dubey, reads, starting from the surface: 1st foot, loam and silty loam; 2nd foot, silt loam; 3rd foot, silty clay loam; 4th foot, silt loam; 5th foot, loamy sand; 6th foot, loamy sand; 7th, 8th and 9th foot, sand.

It is worth comparing this with the soil profile of a breeding but a non-fatting pasture, say the Ivychurch Series: 1st, 2nd and 3rd foot, silty clay loam; 4th foot, clay loam, then silty loam; 5th and 6th foot, loamy sand; 7th, 8th and 9th foot, sand. And it will be observed that the breeding pasture has a heavier soil at the surface. Thus water will drain through with difficulty; hence the pasture will tend to be wet. The Finn Series is "a well drained and well aerated soil reputed to retain sufficient water in the summer to maintain vigorous growth". (Agricultural Land Commission, 1947.)

Whether this is the last word on the mystery of The Marsh pastures I should very much doubt, but being no expert on the subject I naturally hesitate to suggest along what lines further research will proceed. But it does appear from recent work in agricultural chemistry that normal plant growth is controlled by extremely small quantities of chemical substances. Professor R. L. Wain, D.Sc., of the University of London has shown how certain substances, in such minute proportions as one in fifty million, are capable of profound effect in the regulation of plant growth. He has also shown how too much of it has an opposite effect or creates distortions or freakish growth.

Professor T. Wallace has been carrying out systematic research on the subject of mineral deficiencies in farm crops. Such deficiencies may be iron, manganese, potassium, magnesium, phosphorus and boron. And it is of particular interest that it has been conclusively proved that Romney Marsh is deficient in manganese. He says this "has proved a very serious problem in cereals, especially oats and wheat, in cropping many calcareous soils, especially in low-lying areas where the water table is high, such as . . . the Kent Marshes . . . and various alluvial soils. Many cases of failure or of poor yields in oats and wheat have been recorded from soils of high grazing repute due to this deficiency." More recently, in 1968, an extremely interesting and authoritative work has been published. This was Bulletin No. 4 of the *Soil Survey of Great Britain* and is entitled 'Soils of Romney Marsh' by R. D. Green of the Rothamsted Experimental Station. An absorbing study, but whether it is the last word on the subject, who can say?

*   *   *   *   *

Whatever may be the secret of these famous pastures we must not lose sight of the fact that they are famous only on account of the sheep that are bred, nourished and fattened upon them. William Cobbett visited The Marsh in September 1823 and of his ride from Appledore to Old Romney he wrote:

"In quitting this Appledore I crossed a canal (The Royal Military) and entered on Romney Marsh. This was grass-land on both sides of me to a great distance. The flocks and herds immense. The sheep are of a breed that takes its name from the Marsh. They are called Romney Marsh sheep. Very pretty and large. . . . The cattle appear to be all of the Sussex breed. . . . With cattle of this kind and with sheep such as I have spoken of before this Marsh abounds in every part of it; and the sight is most beautiful."

The sight of many sheep does I think appeal to almost every one. Whether it is the herd instinct in us or the atavistic instinct for flocks and herds, or whether it is on account of the profound part sheep have played in the life of man and Aryan civilisation; or again whether it is because ever since David sheep have been a symbol in religion for man himself, culminating in the Good Shepherd as the cherished ideal of Our Lord Himself, no one can really say. On the green pastures and beside the still waters of The Marsh one can see many sheep, and when they are rounded up for shearing or dipping, for the market or for agisting, then the hundreds run into thousands and one can feast one's eyes on the milling, surging, hurrying throngs to the full.

In 1939, on an area of about forty thousand acres, there were 178,176 sheep. This vast number has only been exceeded once before, in 1891, since agricultural returns were first collected nearly a hundred years ago. There have of course been sheep on The Marsh since "times out of mind", probably from those earliest days when the Marisci, the men of the marsh, first settled there. But to begin with, tillage was probably more important than grazing. In fact it has been suggested that up to the middle of the fourteenth century the population of Romney Marsh proper was considerably higher than it has ever been since. This would allow for many more hands to be at work on the land.

The Black Death in 1349 is said to have so reduced the population that it was no longer possible to keep large areas under the plough. This sounds plausible, but whether it is strictly true is difficult to ascertain. There is no doubt that from the end of the fourteenth century wool was becoming England's most important export. If there was a shortage of labour then it would be the natural thing to use the land for pastoral purposes, for where one man can mind sheep on fifty acres it would require a dozen men to till them. Furthermore the Ports were still at their prime, and the volume of merchandise carried by their vessels was greater than that of any other port bar London. As we have seen, Winchelsea was one of the ports on the South Coast which received the royal mandate for the regulation of the wool trade. Lydd became a great wool market. Thus wealth came to the sheep farmers, and from that time to the present day sheep have always been the most important charge of the Marshmen. The wealth they brought spurred men on to the reclamation of all the marshland, and when finally in the nineteenth century the whole was consolidated and every port left high and dry, sheep might safely graze where bloody battles were fought and where ships and men had been locked in deadly conflict.

The Marsh is one of the most exposed sheep runs in Britain.

It might be thought that mountain sheep, as in Wales, West-morland or the hills of Scotland, had a harder time; but it is generally true to say that it is nearly always possible for mountain sheep to find shelter in the lee of hills, ridges, crags or even walls, not to mention descending to the valleys in severe weather. On The Marsh there is no shelter: there are no natural defences, no walls, no hedges, few trees. The black north-easter comes howling through the Straits, direct, it feels, from Siberia. Like a scythe blade it sweeps across the levels bitter and sharp. Once you have experienced it you will never forget it. The sheep endure it.

From the sou'wester also there is no protection. The bleak deserts of Dungeness subtract nothing from its fury. The gales which roar up the Channel storm across The Marsh, and to see the ragged rain curtains, each greyer than the last, torn and drenching, lashed across the levels, makes one thankful to be within the walls of Rye. The sheep endure it.

To live, thrive and breed in such conditions has called forth the hardiest of animals. The origin of the Kent or Romney Marsh Sheep is a little doubtful, but the breed is probably of Flemish origin. As we have seen, the Ports did much trade and were often linked in alliance with Flanders, and it is said that as the result of that intercourse cherries, hops and this breed of sheep came to Kent. Hall and Russell say that

> "there is no record of the original introduction of this sheep into Romney Marsh; its Flemish origin can only be surmised from its resemblance to the sheep in Flanders and its unlikeness to the down and heath sheep by which it is surrounded. . . . At any rate when it first emerged into distinct notice towards the close of the 18th century it was a coarse, hardy, long-woolled sheep, well esteemed by the butchers despite the inferior quality of the mutton."

During the last one hundred and fifty years much has been done to improve the stock, both by careful selection and by cross-breeding. Wall of Ashford, Gourd of Sittingbourne, Rigden of Lyminge, Powell of Lenham, and the Kent Farm Institute are some of those whose work has been of importance. The

Romney Marsh sheep today is "white-faced, with a broad head furnished with a forelock and a pronounced Roman nose, a thick neck, and a close fleece of long semi-lustre wool . . . a long heavy sheep with powerful bone and strong constitution. The typical sheep have black noses." But the sheep farmer is faced with many problems, and fluctuating markets for wool, markets for meat, markets for pure-bred rams complicate them. It is a curious fact that the pure-bred Romney is not the ideal sheep for The Marsh farmer, not as a flock, unless of course he is a breeder of thorough-bred stock. The average sheep farmer is not so much concerned with the breed as he is with the market for his produce. The most important demand is meat, and if he is to get a good price he must produce the kind of joint the butcher, and ultimately the customer, wants. Fashions, and rations, are always changing, but for some twenty-five years the tendency has been for "smaller-framed, more compact and particularly earlier-maturing sheep, with better legs" (G. H. Garrad).

The pure-bred Romney is therefore unsuitable for the meat market, yet its hardiness is essential to stand the rigours of The Marsh. Hence cross-bred sheep are common on all the levels. A number of experiments have been tried with very varying success, and Romneys have been crossed with Southdowns, Dorsetdowns, Oxfords and Suffolks. The most popular and probably the most successful cross is that of the Romney ewe with the Southdown ram. The Southdowns are the smallest of the Down breeds and are renowned for their mutton and thick, well-developed hind quarters. The result of the cross is a sheep combining the better qualities of both, a smallish, well-fleshed body, a medium-length wool of demi-lustre quality, but at the same time a hardy animal which can stand up to the exposure of both winter and summer.

This might seem to solve one of the sheep farmer's problems, but a moment's thought will show that it does not do so. In the second or third year he would be master of a flock of cross-breds, and as Garrad says: "The first cross ewe is often an excellent sheep, and if one cross breeds her the cross-bred lamb—which is the second cross—may be a good sheep, but the crossing should stop there. It is undesirable . . . to breed from ewes which are beyond the second cross." So we see on The Marsh among nearly all the large sheep farmers, two flocks running side by side, one pure-bred Romney and the other Southdown × Kent half-breeds.

Some sheep masters, as for example Mr H. J. Blacklock of Lydd, specialise in pedigree flocks. Their task is not merely to supply The Marsh but the world. For it is true to say that the world does indeed regard Great Britain as the stud farm from which can be obtained thorough-bred specimens of many breeds of sheep that have been developed in this country. Romneys have been sent all over the world, to Argentina, Chile, Falkland Islands, Patagonia, Brazil, South Africa, North America, Russia; while Australia and New Zealand have of course hundreds of thousands of them. They are an important export, some twenty-two thousand rams going abroad every year.

The fact that the pastures, however good they may be, cannot carry the same number of sheep in winter as in summer means that the farmer has to reduce his flock every autumn. He usually sells his fat sheep and some of his lambs, while the other superfluous animals are sent away to winter on upland farms in Sussex, Kent and Surrey. In recent years these keep sheep have not been very popular with upland farmers, so unless the marsh farmer possesses such an inland hill farm of his own he is often hard put to it to dispose of his sheep other than to the butcher.

What complicates the problem still further for him is the fact that in the following May, when the summer flush of grass commences, he needs all his sheep on the pastures to cope with the growth. He frequently has to buy sheep for the purpose, for it is imperative that the grazier should not allow his best pastures to get out of hand. It is said that you should be able to throw a sixpence as far as you can on one of these pastures and then walk on to it and pick it up. If you cannot find it it means that the grass is not being grazed hard enough. I have tried this on a bowling green and have had no difficulty whatever in finding the coin, but I must admit I have lost a sixpence or two on the ordinary house lawns until the mower went over them. Having a trace of the Scot in me, I have not yet flung a sixpence as far as I could on Romney Marsh. All of which goes to prove how exceptionally close the grass is cropped. Failure to keep it grazed close means that it runs to stem, with which sheep cannot cope. In any case, as Mr Cooke of East Guldeford said, "Sheep like the grass which grew yesterday, not last week".

One of the most controversial questions on The Marsh is whether or not these famous pastures should be ploughed up. The land is exceptionally fertile and is capable of producing astonishing crops. When William Cobbett continued his ride in the direction of New Romney he wrote:

> "The next village, which was two miles further on, was Old Romney, and along here I had, for great part of the way corn-fields on one side of me and grass-land on the other. I asked what the amount of the crop of wheat would be. They told me better than five quarters to the acre. . . . I never saw corn like this before."

That was in 1823, but both before and on two or three occasions since, in times of dire need when bread was more important than meat, quite a considerable portion of The Marsh was under the plough. Agricultural returns have only been collected since 1866, but in this connection some of the figures make interesting reading:

Year	Tillage Acres	Permanent Grass Acres	Total Acres	Cattle	Sheep
1866	5,776	31,606	38,093	1,104	77,168
1891	7,819	33,739	43,012	2,838	179,633
1918	8,018	30,600	43,084	3,431	137,196
1931	2,824	32,917	39,476	3,849	160,057
1939	3,892	35,178	43,602	3,739	178,176
1944	14,141	21,085	38,374	3,509	99,990

The increase in tillage and reduction in the numbers of sheep during the First World War is clear. But the effect of World War II is striking, for it will be observed that the tillage acreage is increased fivefold over the years of the great depression and the number of sheep nearly halved.

Allowance must be made for the fact that under the threat of invasion in 1940 the Government decided to remove from The Marsh as many herds and flocks as could be accommodated elsewhere. This immense and urgent task, which did indeed have priority over the evacuation of civilians, was accomplished; "sheep-train specials" moved eighty-five thousand sheep, some going as far as Yorkshire, and for over two years the movement of animals into The Marsh was prohibited. It is true to say that few if any of these evacuees ever returned, and by 1948 the number of sheep on The Marsh was the lowest on record for ninety years, only ninety-eight thousand seven hundred and thirteen.

While this reduction is in part due to war dispersal and to length of time it takes to build up a new flock (the Romney ewe as a rule has only one lamb), it is mainly due to the tremendous change which has occurred in the system of farming on The Marsh. This was at first forced upon the farmers by the exigencies of war and the urgencies of the nation's food supply. But now, many years after the cessation of hostilities, forty per cent. of The Marsh is still under the plough and there is no move to change back to what was essentially a pastoral economy.

Though the farmer still hesitates to plough up the most famous of the fatting fields, about which there is sharp difference of opinion, for many graziers contend that to do so will mean it will never be a fatting pasture again, he has nevertheless broken land which has been pasture for as long as man can remember. There is a saying that "to break a pasture will make a man and to make a pasture will break a man", and there is no doubt that this highly fertile soil has yielded and is yielding astonishing crops. But the vexed question is, can it be returned to grass, as it must be under a system of ley farming, and become again a fatting pasture?

The old graziers still say no, but G. H. Garrad in his booklet *The Romney Marsh Problem* says:

"Modern knowledge of cultivations, seeds mixtures, artificial manures, etc., have made the old proverb out of date. Some marsh farmers have laid down new pastures with conspicuous success and have found that sheep will fatten more quickly on them than on their very best old pasture."

If this proves true over The Marsh as a whole it may well mean that the new system of farming has come to stay—unless gross overcropping ruins the land.

*　　*　　*　　*　　*

In 1948 the Minister of Agriculture and Fisheries directed that the Agricultural Land Commission should investigate into the agricultural use of Romney. He did so under Section 84 of the Agriculture Act, 1947, which gave him the power, if full and efficient use of the land was not being made, to acquire that land by compulsory purchase or by hiring. This was the first area in Britain to be so investigated and it caused a sensation!

There is an amusing story going round The Marsh about the appointment of this Commission. It was said that as the Government of the day were beginning to lose face it was high time someone did something to restore their prestige. What could be done? What had other great dictators done to win fame? Some thought of Adolf Hitler, some thought of Mussolini. Wasn't it Benito who had done something to the Pontine Marshes? Hadn't he drained malarial swamps and reclaimed thousands of acres of good land? Surely there was some marsh in Britain awaiting the hand of a great government to transform it into prosperous farms. The story continues that one of the high-ups, turning the pages of a gazetteer, under the word Marsh discovered Romney Marsh. What a heaven-sent opportunity! Here was 50,000 acres on the shores of Kent, only seventy miles from London, under their very noses, a vast marsh awaiting reclamation—nobody had thought of it. Benito's act should be repeated. With a flourish of trumpets the investigation was ordered.

The Marsh farmers enjoyed their joke, and had it been true how much they would have enjoyed the look of dismay and consternation on the faces of the commissioners when they discovered that Romney Marsh was not marshland, was no reeking malarial swamp, but a great well-drained prairie consisting of 17,000 acres of arable cultivation and 30,000 acres of good pasture. But The Marsh farmers were also annoyed, and justly, for on the face of it this investigation seemed to cast a slur both on them and their farming methods. Furthermore it could only be regarded as a threat, to dispossess them "by compulsory purchase" if the commissioners were satisfied that "full and efficient use of the land for agriculture" was not being made. This was all the harder to bear after the magnificent effort the farmers had made during the war. The commissioners themselves in their Draft Report wrote the following:

"The increase in arable acreage (during the war) is an indication of the resource and courage of the agricultural community of Romney Marsh. The geographical location of the area necessarily meant that throughout the whole of the war agricultural operations were carried out under considerable difficulties, starting with the threat of invasion of the country in the early part of the war, followed by almost continuous air raids and culminating in the flying bomb menace. Damage was caused to houses, buildings and land. In addition the activities of the Service Departments in a front-line area like Romney Marsh inevitably rendered farming operations more difficult. In spite of these difficulties and uncertainties, the agricultural community continued to farm the land and in fact succeeded in increasing the arable acreage more than fourfold."

In the restrained language of the Report this is a fine tribute to The Marsh farmers; and it is only just to say at this point that the Commissioners carried out their investigation in a masterly and at the same time a scrupulously fair, thorough and considerate manner. The real truth of the matter, and what indeed was not generally known at the time, was that at a conference convened by the Kent County Council, at which representatives of the Kent Agricultural Executive Committee, the Kent Rivers Catchment Board, the Lydd and New Romney Borough Councils, and the Romney Marsh, East Ashford, and Tenterden Rural District Councils and the National Farmers' Union were present, the following resolution was submitted to the Minister of Agriculture:

"That this conference is of the opinion that, provided a

reasonable future for the farming industry is assured, it is in the best national and other interests that the agricultural development of Romney Marsh should be directed to the provision and maintenance of upwards of 20,000 acres under arable cultivation."

The Minister, "although unwilling . . . to commit himself . . . expressed his agreement in principle . . ." and "He intimated that Romney Marsh was essentially the kind of area which should be investigated by the Agricultural Land Commission."

So it turned out, much to everyone's astonishment, that the farmers' leaders themselves were ultimately responsible for the investigation! Queer things happen officially, and one can only assume that the rank and file were so engrossed in their work, the production of food, that they were out of touch with the committees and councils that were deciding how their work should be done.

And how did it all end? Well, the commissioners did a thorough job of work; they at least knew what they were doing and what they were looking for. Their report was full of valuable and interesting facts, sound common sense and genuine efforts to understand work on The Marsh. They considered a number of farming systems which could be adopted on Romney Marsh, of which the principal were: (i) Sheep Farming; (ii) Dairy Farming; (iii) Arable Farming, including Market Gardening; and (iv) Ley Farming. They came to the conclusion that ley farming "was best suited to the needs of the Marsh as a whole to ensure its full and efficient use for agriculture. Not only is it a logical development of the change-over effected during the war years from the predominating system of sheep farming to a system of crops and stock, *but it is in fact already being practised by a number of Marsh farmers.*" (The italics are mine.)

This was the principal recommendation, and it was supported by a number of minor recommendations, such as new houses for an increased labour force, numerous implement and store sheds, four miles of new road, extension of electricity and water services, and so on, all things which almost every farming community could do with. And their conclusion with regard to Section 84?

" . . . we consider that all the recommendations we have put forward for work to be carried out and fixed equipment to be provided for the full and efficient use of the land can reasonably be expected to be put into effect by the owners, lessees and occupiers in Romney Marsh, and we do not consider it is necessary for the Minister to exercise his powers of compulsory purchase or hiring under Sub-section 7 of Section 84 of the Agriculture Act 1947.

"We have the honour to be, etc.

"Agricultural Land Commission."

★   ★   ★   ★   ★

While the investigation did little more than vindicate The Marsh farmers and recommend that the great changes they had made during the previous nine years in their farming methods should be continued, it was nevertheless a milestone in the story of The Marsh. It underlines the fact that The Marsh has taken on a new look. If you had seen it in the early thirties you might have thought tillage was unknown there. Looking for a ploughed field was like looking for a marble on Dungeness. Today it is completely changed. Nearly half is or has been under the plough. The suitability of the soil permits a wide range of crops—wheat, oats, beans, linseed, potatoes, sugar beet, maize and various roots being a few of the farm crops. The Marsh is also peculiarly suited for the growing of crops for seed. This is partly due to its peninsular character, which is a protection from severe frost, partly to the exceptional fertility of the soil and partly due to its somewhat isolated position, which reduces the risk of cross-pollination. For many years turnip seed has been a speciality of The Marsh, but now one can see runner beans, spinach, beet, mangolds, red clover, wild white clover, cress, carrots, peas, beans and various grasses, all for seed crops.

Great care is taken to prevent cross-fertilisation between allied crops, as for examples mangolds and beet. The allocation of seed is strictly controlled and The Marsh is zoned. For example beet for seed can only be sown south-west of the Appledore–New Romney road, while mangolds may only be grown to the north-east of this dividing line.

Market gardening too is gaining some ground, and besides the usual vegetables for the table there is some soft-fruit growing, and one sees raspberries and strawberries. A recent innovation has been the growing of bulbs, such as daffodils and tulips. Two Lincolnshire farmers, Messrs Clifton Bros., of Dymchurch and Appledore, have found the soil of The Marsh very suitable. Its stoneless nature allows the bulbs to form a good shape, and its generally light, somewhat sandy character permits the grown bulbs to be lifted cleanly with a good unsoiled skin. These bulb farms are always a delight to the eye, but I do not think The Marsh will ever completely take on this aspect of Holland, although in so many other ways it has features reminiscent of that country.

There is indeed a limiting factor which controls all farming operations on The Marsh and that is labour. Not only is there an increasing shortage of experienced agricultural labourers, and a general tendency for the countryman to drift to the towns and to industry, but The Marsh suffers from the peculiar disadvantage that, having for so many years been almost wholly pastoral, its scanty population is both inadequate and inexperienced for other farming systems. It is almost impossible to attract new labour to the district, and in any case it would not yet be possible to house the hands required. During the war, and since, it has been a common practice during harvests to employ casual labour, establish harvest camps, encourage townfolk, schoolboys and so on to help.

For this reason it might appear best for The Marsh to remain largely pastoral. But the sheep farmer has his own special labour problem too. There can be no sheep without a shepherd, and it must be remembered that in nine cases out of ten the sheep farmer is not his own shepherd. On The Marsh a shepherd is called the looker—and this designation must not be misunderstood, for in some parts of the country the term means little more than a "minder" or a "watcher". But on The Marsh the looker is in very fact the shepherd. Sheep are his life's work; he learnt his skill from his father, and he from his father before that. His skill, his profession, if you like, is hereditary.

The work of the looker never ends. It is a seven-day-a-week-fifty-two-week-a-year job. He rarely takes, let alone asks for, a holiday. He has his own dog and he has his own cow, which the farmer provides for him and which is one of the few compensations for a life of almost ceaseless toil. He is a grand fellow, but of his type the numbers get less and less. In what other trade or profession should we find such a worker, who has no half days, no week-ends, no holidays?

It is so easy to say let someone else do the job or the farmer himself, so that his looker can get a break. But the problem is complicated because the good shepherd knows his sheep, and the trained sheep-dog will work for him alone. It would take a long time for a stranger to familiarise himself with the flock and its varied and individual needs, and he would have to bring his own trained dog. Even the farmer himself cannot use or get the looker's dog to work sheep with him; he too would have to have his own dog and to have spent endless time in its training. Compared with the gathering of sheep off the fells and bringing them down over scree and crag to the dale the movement of sheep across the dead levels of The Marsh must seem an easy task. True, it is much less strenuous, but it is tricky. There is not the room to manœuvre, for while many pastures are wide they are almost without exception bounded by water. Sewer and ditch, dyke and canal are the only fences. The crossings and bridges are narrow and few and the route from place to place often as "ravelly as witch-yarn on the spindles". There is little doubt that one of the most serious problems in the near future will be the gradual disappearance of the hereditary shepherd. Sheep cannot be tended by a forty-eight-hour-a-week man—unless you have three of them. I just cannot imagine what would happen to agriculture in this country if every farm labourer knocked off when the hooter sounded.

It is fitting to pay tribute to those who work on the land and in particular to those who mind flocks and herds. Can they strike? Would they strike? Does the good shepherd desert his sheep? To me, the lineage of a hereditary shepherd is as noble as any in the land. I doff my cap to the looker.

CHAPTER IX

WILD BIRDS

How well I recollect with what great expectations I first went down to The Marsh to see its birds. I expected to see wild duck and waders, terns and stone curlew, all those fascinating birds of the marsh and the shore line, of reedy dyke and shallow mere. Yet it was none of these that first compelled my attention. As I came down on to the levels of the Brede between Winchelsea and Rye, with the old tree-grown sea cliffs behind me and the wide green pastures in front, it was not the cry of a plover or a gull that greeted me, but the ringing, laughing cry of the green woodpecker. I saw him leave the level, swoop in undulating flight across the narrow lane—red head and canary rump were brilliant in the sunshine—and up into an old ash tree above me; and there the merry cry rang out again.

Nothing remarkable in seeing the green woodpecker here, I thought; after all, it was but the fringe of The Marsh, and it was a common enough bird throughout the thirty miles of woodland Sussex through which I had just passed. But it was the shadow before. An hour or two later while walking along the Royal Military Canal near the Kent Ditch I saw a pair. These I accounted for because the scores of old elm trees which line the canal would provide admirable nesting sites. But beyond Appledore where a section of the canal belongs to the National Trust I saw three. On the breezy expanse of Guldeford Marsh there was a green woodpecker mocking my attempts to photograph that quaintest of all barn-like churches, St Mary's. And at Brenzett, where one or two fine old trees cluster about the church, a pair undoubtedly had a nest. But what really astonished me was to see and hear green woodpeckers on the beachlands of Dungeness. Far out on the shingle between the Half-way bush and the Hoppen Pits I could hardly believe my ears when I heard its voice coming from a clump of stunted shrubs.

The presence of a woodland bird on the wide, almost treeless levels of The Marsh would be inexplicable were it not for a curious trait of behaviour which the green woodpecker has developed within quite recent times. Normally, as its name implies, it finds most of its food on the bark and trunks of trees, rotten or infested with the larvæ of insects. It has evolved special equipment for this awkward task—paired toes, stiff tail, powerful beak—and can work its way up a vertical trunk or overhanging branch with ease. It is obviously a bird most ill-adapted to move about on the ground. But ants have become a most important item in its food supply; ants it is determined to find, and everywhere on lawns, pastures and even on Dungeness it goes in search of them.

Ants abound on The Marsh. It is one of the odd jobs of the looker to spud the emmett casts—ant hills—wherever they begin to form and disfigure the sheep pastures. It is because the green woodpecker has discovered this abundant supply of its favourite food that it has become one of the commonest birds of the levels. The elms along the canal and the few trees commonly seen near the churches afford it some nesting sites; but there have been instances of telegraph poles being bored by this hard-working bird to provide it with a nesting hole. Here and there wooden fences border the narrow roads that wind and twist across The Marsh, and while cycling quietly along beside them it is well worth keeping a sharp eye on the posts. On several occasions I have passed literally within arm's length of a green woodpecker clinging there and never attempting to fly until I stopped.

Bird watchers and ornithologists will say it is all wrong to start this chapter on birds of The Marsh with these references to the woodpecker. How right they are! It was only because this interloper forced himself upon my attention from the first day that I have forced him upon yours. The glory of this unique area is in its shore birds, its waders, its ducks, and in its enormous potentialities as a nature reserve where some of our choicest and rarest birds might breed.

More than three-quarters of The Marsh is pasture or arable land and there is nothing particularly interesting to be observed upon it. But everywhere it is intersected by waterlets and sewers and bounded by the Royal Military Canal, and in just one or two places there are marshy low-lying areas. These form the first areas of interest. The beachlands of Dungeness together with the pits and meres are the next zone of outstanding importance; and the shore, particularly the West Beach together with Pett Level and the pits and open water close to the shore, constitute the third zone. The sea, inshore, might be regarded as the fourth.

It is difficult to know where to begin, but I think the story of Pett Level is one of the most exciting and fascinating events that have ever happened among British birds. Pett Level is the last extremity of The Marsh westward. It lies south of the low ridge upon the eastern end of which Winchelsea stands. It ends abruptly below the heights which lead up to Fairlight. Pett Level for the most part lies below high-water mark. It is protected, or was protected, from the sea by an old shingle bank. This shingle bank has steadily been wearing thinner and thinner, and the sea broke through in 1926 and caused serious flooding. The breach was temporarily repaired, and since the war a fine new sea-wall of unusual design has been built, and the Level should be safe from another inundation for a long time to come.

It was during the war, however, that the amazing thing happened. Under the threat of invasion it was decided among other defence measures to flood Pett Level. Why this area should have been chosen has not been disclosed, and it is difficult to see why Hitler should have had his baleful eye on this particular level rather than any other along the South-East Coast. However, someone knew something, and during the summer of 1940 with very little difficulty the sea was let in by breaching the old sea-wall. About 1,000 acres were flooded. The depth of the water varied considerably, being rarely more than six feet, but the whole area was dotted with islands. These islands were no other than the higher ground and the tops of ditch banks. With fluctuations of tide and rainfall considerable muddy flats were often exposed. To complete the picture it must be remembered that the whole flood area was only separated from the open sea by the top of the old sea-wall.

Thus by a most extraordinary chance the green pastures of Pett

Level were transformed into a vast lagoon which must have resembled in an astonishing manner the appearance of the bay before ever The Marsh was consolidated. It's an ill wind that blows no one any good, and while we can sympathise with many who suffered on account of the flooding, what a stroke of luck this was for one man and through him for all bird lovers and ornithologists!

The flooded level was a prohibited area. It was for some reason so "special" that not even the military were allowed into it. The only man who had the right to enter or cross it was Mr Reginald Cooke, who was in charge of the coast-guard post at Pett Level. If the man in charge had been any other than a lover of birds the events on the level might never have been recorded and the thrilling pages in *British Birds*, Vol. XLI, never have been written. But by good chance Reg. Cooke was there, and not only is he a bird lover but he knows his birds, and he took the trouble to record many of the things he saw. I have had the great pleasure of meeting him, and he gave me a first-hand account of the affair.

All the first autumn and winter numbers of duck and waders began congregating there and, being completely unmolested, must have found it the perfect sanctuary. It is safe to say there had been nothing like it on the South-East Coast for centuries. Reg. Cooke noticed the steadily increasing number of birds, and by March 1941 he realised that there was an excellent chance that some of them might breed there. There was a good deal of vegetation on the islands and he was thrilled to find the first mallard's nest on April 3rd. As there were sheld-duck, shoveler, widgeon, teal, pintail, tufted duck, besides lapwing, redshank, coot and moorhen, all in considerable numbers, his hopes rose high that some would nest.

But he admitted that he never even dreamed of what actually happened. Fortunately he was able to secure a flat-bottomed boat and during his brief spells off duty he was able to explore parts of the huge island-studded lagoon. I quote from his paper in *British Birds*:

"On the 25th I found eleven Mallards' nests, one Shoveler's (the first so far as I know ever found on Pett Level), and many Coots', Moorhens', Lapwings' and Redshanks'. Almost every tuft of grass held a Redshank's nest, while some had made nests like that of a Lapwing, on dried mud. . . . The next visit on May 6th was a very interesting one. On one small island, not more than a quarter of an acre in extent, there were five Shovelers' nests, five Mallards', three Lapwings' and five Redshanks'. . . . I saw about twenty nests with eggs of the Black-headed Gull and seven nests with eggs of the Herring Gull. . . . On the same day I found the first Garganey's nest. . . . Many Ringed Plover had nests on the dried up mud where the water had fallen away from the islands by evaporation. In every case their nests were lined with small shells, which must have been brought from the sea-shore.

"About May 16th I made another visit, this time more than anything to get some idea of the numbers of Black-headed and Herring Gulls and Terns that were breeding. I estimated that there were 250 pairs of Black-headed Gulls, 20 pairs of Herring Gulls, 100 pairs of Common and 50 pairs of Little Tern."

When one realises that all this was happening barely nine months after the flooding of the Level, it not only makes one's eyes open in wonder but it emphasises the immediate response that birds make to the ideal and completely protected area. Yet it was only a beginning. Rarities came: black terns, bar-tailed godwits and, later in the year, when the great migratory movement south began, there were ruff and greenshank, spotted redshanks and hen and montagu harriers.

"By early October I calculated that about 5,000 ducks were on the waters, including Mallard, Widgeon, Teal, Shoveler, Sheld-Duck, Tufted Duck and Pochard, while Pintail had returned in numbers. Waders seen were Redshanks, Knot, Dunlin, and Purple Sandpipers. . . . Pochard, Scaup, and Brent Geese were also numerous. . . . Other ducks seen were Goosanders, one or two on every visit I paid to the flood, and on December 28th seven were seen together."

So the astonishing story goes on for three years. It is enough to make every bird watcher's mouth water, though I doubt if many of them would have cared to change places with Mr Cooke at the time, for his was front-line work with a vengeance. This was "Bomb Alley", air raids day and night, with the threat of invasion uncomfortably imminent. It is reassuring to know that there were odd times when he could turn his telescope towards his beloved birds.

"On June 2nd whilst on duty at the coast-guard hut I saw a Spoonbill. It was fishing the pools at half tide and feeding mainly on small crabs. This was the first occasion I had seen one, and I watched it through the large telescope for over an hour—and it was still fishing when I went off duty."

He had his heart-aches too, for one day some troops stationed in the area found his boat and "made an expedition to many of the islands, stealing all the eggs they could find. It was a great pity and a blow to me as most of the eggs were on the point of hatching." Another time the flooded level became the target for artillery and mortar fire, with the result that the water was contaminated and many hundreds of bottom-feeding birds died. And then at last in February 1944 the water was drained off, the danger had passed away; but so too had this wonderful sanctuary. "It seems like a dream, now," Reg. Cooke told me. "People say I'm romancing. But it's true, every word of it. See, there are my notes, and it would all happen again if we had the like conditions."

*   *   *   *   *

"If we had the like conditions." What a challenge that is to bird lovers everywhere! Not that I am suggesting that Pett Level should be permanently flooded and much excellent land wasted. But what a challenge it is that some such reserve should not be created to attract and hold many of our loveliest and most interesting birds.

So I thought in the year 1950. And then a remarkable thing happened. It has already been mentioned how thin the old sea-wall had been wearing. It had been broken through once; now there was grave danger of the sea breaking in again, so the Kent River Board, who are responsible for coastal defence, planned a great new sea-wall. And they have carried through their plan. A wall, rivalling the Dymchurch Wall itself, now protects the whole length of the Pett Level, from near the cliff end leading up to Fairlight until it loses itself in Winchelsea Beach. It is a sea defence of unusual design, and no doubt the experience gained at Dymchurch has influenced the engineers in its shaping.

A temporary wooden sea-wall was constructed along the shore of Pett Level in 1934. But such a structure could not last long, and soon after the war ended work was begun on the new sea-wall. This was in seven sections altogether nearly five miles long. Some of it is clay wall, some 10,000 feet of it is groyning, but the main sea-wall, 8,400 feet long, is of special interest and of unusual form. The work has been carried out to the design and the supervision of Mr C. H. Dobbie, M.I.C.E., chief engineer of the Rother and Jury's Gut Catchment Board.

In principle this is a clay wall protected by sheet steel piling, concrete blocks and asphalt. The *Muck Shifter* describes its construction as follows:

"On the seaward side against the beach there is first a line of 10 feet deep sheet steel piling by Appleby Frodingham, surmounted by 9 in. by 14 in. reinforced concrete coping. Then comes the front of the (lower) wall sloping about 20 degrees and about 16 feet wide faced with precast concrete blocks 2 ft. by 2 ft. by 8 in., with 1½ in. bituminous joints."

Next comes what is known as the berm. (The meaning of this technical term can be grasped at once from the photograph, but is not easy to describe.) What it really amounts to is an asphalt flat linking the top of the lower wall with the foot of the upper wall. The upper wall is set back, staggered, so to speak, from the lower wall by the width of the berm. It is almost like a fine asphalt roadway between the two concrete-block-faced walls. It will indeed make a most attractive promenade, but the berm was not employed in the construction with that idea in mind.

In a paper presented to the International Navigation Congress at Lisbon in 1949 Mr C. H. Dobbie said:

"The new wall under construction in Rye Bay has a berm 7·6 metres wide at highest tide level. By this means the first impact of the wave is met by the bottom front of the wall backed by its entire mass. The troublesome top of the wave dissipates its energy on the berm and is finally excluded from the land by the high wall of light construction."

The upper wall is like the lower, only faced with concrete blocks of smaller size. It has a pre-cast concrete coping, and the top of the wall is a six-foot flat with paving slabs. The longer and steeper slope on the landward side is grass planted to hold the surface of the bank. A very good road has now been completed at the foot of the embankment, and thus Pett is now linked with Winchelsea and Rye by a fast level road, and every point on the new sea-wall will be easily and speedily accessible. Flights of steps have been made over the wall to give easy access to the beach from this road, and these should prevent damage to the grass bank by encouraging people not to scramble up and down the landward side.

To reduce expense, material for the embankment was taken from the level as near to the working as possible. An enormous quantity of earth was needed, with the result that four huge shallow "pits" were left in the level. About six feet deep, these pits soon filled with water and thus became four lakes or meres with a surface area of some thirty acres. Immediately, before ever the work on the wall was finished, birds came. Here in fact was a miniature of the wartime floods. True the water was fresh and not salt, and was not subject to tidal variations. But to a number of birds these are advantages. Birds came, birds that had rejoiced in the floods came, waterfowl, ducks, waders and seabirds. That summer in 1951 when the work was just being completed I saw the meres for the first time. I was returning from a visit to Reg. Cooke at Pett and was cycling along the rough low road that ran along the landward side of the embankment. Upon drawing level with the water I left my bicycle on the bank and walked across the ditch to inspect the pits. Reg. Cooke had told me I might see something, but it is hard to describe my astonishment when on reaching the edge of the mere I saw three sheld-duck leave the water under my very nose. There were other duck and a number of waders, and as I stumbled along the rough banking dividing two pits, all my eyes on the water, I almost fell over a man lying full length in the rough grass, his eye glued to a telescope.

A bird watcher if ever there was one, and I, like a clumsy loon, had blundered in and driven away the birds he was studying. I tried to apologise for such carelessness, it was inexcusable. But he did not seem to mind, in fact his eye did not leave his telescope, and I realised he was not looking at the ducks; sheld-duck were small beer to him.

"Over there, on the other side of the water."

I looked, and discerned on a little muddy island three waders, medium size, but too far away to distinguish the species.

"What are they?" I asked, now talking in a whisper.

For answer he beckoned me to the telescope. I lay flat and looked for a long time. It was a powerful glass and now the three waders looked near enough to touch. They were elegant, lovely; they were absolutely new to me. I could see every detail. They were quite unalarmed, my intrusion and the noisy departure of the sheld-ducks had not made them uneasy. I stared, holding my breath.

"What," I whispered again, "what, in the name of James Fisher, are they?"

"Spotted redshank," he exulted. "Spotted redshank, man, and I've been watching them for half an hour."

Every bird-watching enthusiast will understand his excitement and my delight. The first time one sees a new species is always a red-letter day. It is not that it just adds one more name to one's Life List, as the Americans call it. It's much more than that. It's a new experience, a revelation of a new expression of life. A new species is like a fine landmark which one reaches unexpectedly and then looks back upon with delight.

If any shadow of doubt had ever crossed my mind that Reg.

Cooke's account of the birds of Pett floods was a trifle exaggerated it vanished. I knew then that all he had recorded had indeed happened, and that given like conditions it could happen again. It is happening again. The Kent River Board is aware of the potentialities of these four pits as a unique bird sanctuary. A memorial to Colonel J. Body has been erected on the new sea-wall at this point, and at the time of writing there is every chance that the pits will be developed as a Nature Reserve facing this memorial. In fact, from 1978 the water-level in one of the pools has been controlled so that during the late summer months it is reduced to a depth of only a few inches. The result has been astonishing. The muddy pool becomes crowded with migrant waders—Godwit, Little Stint, Dunlin, Greenshank, Purple Sandpiper, Spotted Redshank, together with Curlew, Shelduck, Little and Common Terns. The last time I was there, an Arctic Skua flew overhead.

This Pett pool is only small and a great variety of bird life is concentrated in easy view. But it must not, however, be thought that this is all there is for bird lovers on The Marsh. The Royal Society for the Protection of Birds owns thirteen hundred acres of the beachlands of Dungeness. Something like a sanctuary! Or should be, for this is a unique terrain, with its vast shingle, its meres and pits, its delightful flora, its peninsular character and its background of The Marsh. Yet it has been in dire trouble. Time and again it has been in peril and we have been in danger of losing it all. And by we I mean you and me, all who love birds and wild flowers, wild and desolate country, unspoiled seaboard.

Neither the interest nor the resources of the R.S.P.B. would have been of any avail had it not been for one man. Professor R. B. Burrowes first saw Dungeness in 1901. He was so captivated by its unique character and wonderful bird life that although he had travelled to many parts of the world it was to Lydd that he retired in 1930 to begin his long battle for the birds. He has had to fight the speculative builder, bungalow growth, the wild fowler, egg thief, and the War Office.

The R.S.P.B. was interested in the idea of acquiring part of

Dungeness as a bird reserve. But it is only fair to say that the Society had not the initiative and drive in those days, for it had not the resources or the backing of a strong public opinion which it enjoys today. It was out of touch with the risks which threatened the area. Mr Burrowes was on the spot; he not only knew the dangers, but whenever a sale of land was in the air or cautiously put on the market he heard of it. And if that sale was a part or threatened a part of the great reserve he had in mind he forestalled it. He bought it. On one occasion it is true to say he made his offer almost overnight. No time to confer with the Committee, no time even to consult his own pocket. Time only to purchase, and that without any personal consideration as to whether he would ever be repaid. Mr Burrowes spent his entire capital, Mr Burrowes mortgaged even his pension, that the land might be saved.

In the summer of 1951 I had the privilege of staying with Mr Burrowes at Lydd. He was in his eighty-first year, yet he was as enthusiastic as he had ever been fifty years before. What impressed me most about this grand old man was not so much his determination to win the battle of Dungeness but his devotion to the interests of wild life everywhere. He was no specialist just for the avocet or the Kentish plover or the stone curlew. It was in his heart that wild life, birds and beasts, whether in Britain or Bechuanaland, should have their chance, should enjoy their lives, should be respected and enjoyed by human beings.

He saw that Dungeness could be one of Britain's most interesting nature reserves. Even when he first knew it, half of it had gone. If only he had been born sooner it is conceivable that the whole might have been saved. But the War Office were there first; a permanent camp and artillery ranges covered half the beachlands. But most of the remainder would still make a wonderful sanctuary, and, as I have pointed out earlier, the occupation by the military of a large part of the western beachlands was a mixed blessing in so far as it put an impassable barrier and acted as a protection to the proposed reserve on the west and made access to the shore for beach huts, bungalows or building estates impossible.

Although continuous gunfire, exploding shells and beach-lands swept by rifle fire are no encouragement to wild life, Mr Burrowes felt that his right flank was secure. The danger was from the north and east. As the roads improved so did the builder see his opportunity. Furthermore, the craze for a beach hut, a bungalow, a railway carriage, anything on or near the sea shore that could make a holiday residence, was at its height between the wars. Greatstone's arrested development took a new lease of life, and houses and bungalows and holiday camps rapidly grew up and stretched out along the East Beach towards Dungeness Lighthouse.

It would perhaps be tedious to record all the problems, dis-appointments and discouragements which Mr Burrowes experi-enced. "The trouble was", as he writes in a letter to me, "that neither the R.S.P.B. nor anyone else did anything in the matter, leaving it all to me and letting things slide, and though, of course, no harm to me was intended that did not lessen my anxiety and loss of money." This does not mean of course that the attitude of the Society was unfriendly—quite the reverse; and it is a fact that without the Society's aid the beach could not have been held. Nevertheless, the strain was very great, both financially and in anxiety over the constant threat of losing the terrain. It led, too, to misunderstanding and loss of money over the various transac-tions, and in the end the Society was out of pocket about the same as himself, namely £4,000.

However unsatisfactory this may seem, it must be regarded by bird lovers everywhere as the purchase tax. Four distinct but con-tiguous areas had finally been purchased and these are Boulder-wall Farm, Walkers Outlands, The Hoppen Pits and the West Beach, amounting in all to some thirteen hundred acres. Boards were erected, and the whole area became a protected reserve. Watchers kept an eye on it during the breeding season, and gulls, tern, Kentish plover, stone curlew, ring plover and other species nested there. The area was in no way fenced, and there was trouble with egg thieves, both local and stranger, and predatory birds and beasts.

But the fascination of Dungeness is not only in its breeding

species but in the vast numbers of birds which pass to and fro
over the area during migration and which winter there. The
ducks, geese and swans which visit the pits and pass to and fro
between the pastures and the sewers and the sea shore. The
enormous numbers of seabirds which gather offshore and visit
the fresh-water meres, the arable and the grasslands. The great
companies of waders.

Just when there seemed every chance that the reserve would
become a success and that the R.S.P.B. would exploit the possibilities of this unique terrain and take sterner measures for its
protection the war came. This meant not only bombs day and
night, aerial combats, invasion precautions and flying bombs, it
meant that the whole of the reserve was requisitioned by the War
Office. Suddenly it was as though the camp at Lydd knew no
bounds, tanks and mobile guns churned the beachlands, shells
and mortar bombs pitted the shingle, rifle and machine-gun fire
swept the shores and whined out to sea.

With the end of the war the land was not derequisitioned. It
became a no-man's-land where an unexploded bomb might burst
underfoot, where anyone might venture if he dared to shoot duck
or rob nests, where several concrete roads led hither and thither
and along which at any time an army convoy might deploy and
a mock battle rage. No wonder that six years later scarcely a pair
of Kentish plovers could be found there, the plaintive cry of the
stone curlew rarely heard, the gulls unsuccessfully trying to re-
establish their gullery, the ducks avoiding the pits, and the terns
gone to a pit on the west side of the mouth of the Rother. Foxes,
taking advantage of the derelict state of affairs, took their toll of
what life still struggled there, while magpies and crows, un-
checked by any keeper, multiplied to become a menace to bird
life over the whole Marsh.

No wonder Mr Burrowes despaired! He had met his toughest
opponent; and his gravest concern was that the Society, feeling
the iron grip of the War Office was never to be relaxed, began to
consider the prospect of relinquishing their ownership. They
could do no good there, and it seemed the money might be spent
better elsewhere—after the manner of the enormous success of

their experiment with Havergate Island and the avocet. They sent a representative down to make a thorough examination and report on the whole area. He spent more than six weeks on the spot.

I had the good fortune of meeting Mr R. A. W. Reynolds just before he completed his work. If ever there was a thorough ornithologist who was at the same time a tremendous enthusiast, this was he. The day we spent together was unforgettable. He met me at Rye, and after a snack at The Mermaid we went on a whirlwind tour of all The Marsh that was of direct interest. I say whirlwind, for he drove an open sports car, and to me, a pedestrian, at a breakneck speed along the winding lanes and narrow concrete roads. Being hatless, it was days before I got my hair disentangled and weeks before the notes I tried to write as we sped from place to place were deciphered.

We visited the four pits at Pett, burst in upon the clerk in charge of the works on the wall and discussed with him the prospects of making the pits a nature reserve. I remember Reynolds describing in some detail how a kind of floating but anchored island could be made to encourage the black tern to nest there. (Reg. Cooke had seen black terns during the Pett floods, and they still lingered.) The young man in charge was a trifle bewildered, and although he struggled with the unfamiliar technicalities of making nesting sites for black terns I very much doubt if the Kent River Board ever received an account of the suggestions.

After examining the pits and the new sea-wall which will make such a magnificent grandstand when the reserve is developed, we raced along the rough road below it towards Winchelsea Beach and the mouth of the Rother. He drew up just when there seemed no bones left in my body and pointed out the gravel pit where the ternery was. He lent me his powerful glasses, and I must say I saw through them one of the loveliest sights I have ever seen of nesting birds. All along the beach edging the pit was a carpet and fringe of sea pink. You know how good prismatics make objects stereoscopic; well, there was this lovely fringe of thrift picked out in the finest detail against the blue waters of the pit. In the pit was a sort of island and spit of shingle and all over it were the terns, common terns, sitting, flying, alighting, swimming on the water and feeding the first newly hatched young. Terns are the most graceful of all birds, so elegant, swallow- almost butterfly-like, white and blue-grey, with black caps and scarlet bills. It was a wonderful sight, and behind them were the shingly banks of the pit, more thrift and horned poppy, mistily out of focus, and beyond, the hazy green of the unending levels.

We were going to cross the Rother by the ferry at Rye Harbour so that I might see the dunes and the new sand-bank developing in the lee of the river mouth. But the ferryman was at lunch, so I had to leave that for another day. We raced back to Rye and then along the Royal Military Canal towards the Isle of Oxney. We had just passed the county boundary stone at the Kent Ditch when Reynolds slowed down and cautiously stopped. Quietly we scrambled out, climbed the bank and crept down to the reed-choked canal under the overhanging elms. But here I was to be disappointed, for the bird we had come to see, the great reed warbler, had either departed or was skulking silently out of sight. Reynolds was extremely proud of having spotted this bird a fortnight earlier (and who wouldn't be?), for it was only the twelfth time this bird had ever been recorded in Britain. He told me how he had brought an eminent ornithologist to confirm his record. The old gentleman, rather hard of hearing, crawled about on all fours, with his hand frequently to his ear and ever and again whispering loudly "Can you hear him?" Suddenly the great reed warbler burst into song (and it is a strong song) so obligingly near that the old gentleman couldn't fail to hear it. The look of rapture that spread over his face, Reynolds said, was something he would never forget. Once again it was the enthusiast hearing and seeing for the first time in a long life-time a new bird.

Although I never saw it, I felt at least the next best thing, contact with the man who had, and the place where it may even then have been. And I was proud to think that such a rarity had enriched the records of The Marsh at the very time that I was writing this book.

Our next port of call was a haystack on the top of the Isle of
Oxney. This was one of those haystacks built up with baled hay.
As rectangular masses cannot be fitted into a triangular shape, it
meant that there were interstices between the bales under the
thatch of the stack. It was here that a sheld-duck had gained
entrance and built her nest and laid her eggs. It was really a very
remarkable site, for normally sheld-ducks made their nest in the
ground, rabbit-burrows and such like. Reg. Cooke reported
many pairs nesting during the Pett floods in the high banks
bordering the north side and in rabbit-holes.

The incident emphasises the way in which many birds are able
to improvise when their normal nesting sites are not available.
Lack of normal sites is characteristic of The Marsh and Dungeness, and Reynolds told me of and showed me a number of
other quaint improvisations. As we made our hectic way back to
Camber Sands and then to The Midrips he told me of tree-
sparrows which were nesting in sheds and derelict buildings. I
photographed the nest of a carrion crow in, or should I say on, a
telegraph pole. Magpies were nesting in such low, stunted bushes
on the shingle that in one instance I was able to get a picture of
a couple of young magpies in the nest without having to climb
on so much as an empty petrol can.

Talking of tins reminds me of another quaint aspect of bird
life on the shingle. As might be expected, the wheatear is a bird
which is very common all along the shore from Fairlight to
Hythe. It is one of the four birds which Reg. Cooke listed for
me as most characteristic of the whole Marsh—the lapwing, the
meadow pipit, the mallard and the wheatear. The wheatear
nests in holes and crevices usually in or near the ground. But in
shingle there are no holes and no cracks or crannies ever develop,
hence the birds are very hard put to it to find a home anywhere
near their haunts. But discarded tins, that extraordinary by-
product of the twentieth century, have come to their aid; for
wherever along the shingle tins have been dumped (and what
corner of the kingdom escapes them?) there one can be certain
the wheatear will be nesting. Even out of the nesting season one
can see the birds keeping guard or look-out over their favourite

petrol can just as they do from a favourite rock on the fellside.

When houses and bungalows had to be evacuated during the war many birds made use of the buildings, and it is on record how a pair of black redstarts built their nest behind a picture that was hanging on the wall of a sitting-room. Another was built in a tool-shed and yet a third in a bathing-hut. This was in 1943 and 1944 and was at about the same time that the black redstarts, ordinarily a very rare bird in Britain, made their sensational appearance among the bomb-ruined buildings of London. Most readers will remember how one bird haunted Broadcasting House and had its song both recorded and broadcast from the building.

Many people have been under the impression that the black redstarts only came with the bombs. But Reg. Cooke's records show that, while never common, the bird has been almost continuously observed by him on Pett Level ever since May 1909, when he found a nest in an old sheep hut. There was a five-year break between 1918 and 1923, but otherwise it has been a breeding species there for some forty years, quite unbeknown in ornithological circles.

But I am forgetting my whirlwind tour. We talked of these things as we raced along to Lydd, and then in quick succession Reynolds took me down the three roads to the West Beach—to the British Sailor, The Hope and Anchor and The Pilot. This was largely R.S.P.B. property and he told me that if his report to that Society was satisfactory there was every hope that when the War Office derequisitioned the area a really big effort was going to be made to exploit the possibilities of the beachlands as a nature reserve and bird sanctuary. There were big problems, and the co-operation of neighbouring landowners was of the greatest importance. As he had noted elsewhere, it is no good encouraging birds to a choice spot if it is only to provide a duck-shoot for unscrupulous neighbours.

Several firms have large beach-crushing and grading plant on the shingle. As the demand for their products increases—and it is increasing at a great rate—so do their excavations attain

considerable dimensions. Extensive pits are created and, there being water beneath the whole of the Dungeness shingle at a depth of
six to eight feet, it means that these pits invariably fill with fresh
water if excavation is carried deep enough. Originally the pits
were not deep and there was only shallow water in them in winter
when the water table was high, and they dried out in summer.
But modern excavating tools and methods, some employing
suction, make it possible to go much deeper, to the full depth of
the shingle in fact, and thus deep pits are created and become
permanent bodies of water which are most attractive to birds.
In the shallows one sees waders; the deeper water attracts ducks,
geese and swans; and the margins, particularly when vegetation
has had time to get a hold, are most attractive to warblers.

Several of these gravel pits lie on the margins of the R.S.P.B.
property and it would be important that the birds attracted to
them should have a measure of protection. Neither Reynolds
nor I think there would be any difficulty in this direction; in
fact when I was having a chat with the manager of the British
Quarrying Company at Lydd, not about birds at all but about his
works and products, it was he himself who introduced the subject
of birds and how astonished and fascinated he had been by the
great numbers of birds, particularly geese, which at certain seasons
gather on his pits.

A certain amount of shooting is inevitable and in the opinion of
some necessary. The Marshmen have always been wildfowlers and
their legitimate sport need not be interfered with. But that is a very
different thing from the strangers who come into the area and
shoot everything, who have butts put up and conduct a massacre.

Egg stealing is another menace and no Act of Parliament
seems capable of checking it. Only alert and vigilant watchers
can protect a given area, and when that area is large and difficult
to traverse, as the shingle is, and with boundaries ill-defined, if
at all, the task is complicated and expensive. Two kinds of egg
thief are recognised, the specialist, or his minions, who is after the
rarities and is never satisfied without the full clutch; and the
wholesale poachers, who take everything to sell in the market as
plovers' eggs or ducks' eggs. During the war and post-war years

I've no doubt almost any kind of egg was welcome to an egg-starved population, but one could wish the public knew its wild birds' eggs better and could recognise a gull's egg or a tern's from the lapwing's egg it was supposed to have bought.

Besides the human thief there are both bird and animal thieves. Magpies and crows have been reaping a rich harvest, and until the R.S.P.B. and neighbouring landowners take a firm hand, all other nesting species are going to have a bad time. If the good and rare things are to survive at all it is not sufficient merely to provide them with a reserve; predators must be destroyed. Well-meaning people get very muddle-headed over this, and Mr Burrowes told me how one year he became so exasperated by the shocking depredations of the magpies that he took his gun out and did his best to lessen the number of the thieves. With the result that someone promptly reported to the R.S.P.B. that he was on their property shooting birds. He, of all people, received a stinging letter from the Society demanding explanation.

A more recent menace is the increasing number of foxes. Reynolds told me that when he first came down to the area Mr Burrowes had told him of this trouble, but though he had a great respect for the old man he did not believe there was much in it. But six weeks later, when I met him, he was just as convinced as Mr Burrowes. He told me how one morning he had been out early across the beachlands and two foxes had got up under his very nose, and on at least three other occasions he caught glimpses of these animals moving over the shingle. Five foxes in six weeks is pretty fair proof of their numbers and activity. Mr K. A. Ashby, famous sheep-farmer of Dean Court, Brookland, told me that foxes are very little trouble over The Marsh proper, and it seems to me that either the foxes come down from the wooded high ground to the north or live and maybe breed on the shingle. I should imagine the hares attract them as much as the bird life.

None of these observers on the spot mentioned weasels, yet curiously enough when I was first exploring the beachlands in the spring and summer of 1951 I saw more weasels than all the foxes put together. These will be a more serious menace and much more difficult to stamp out or keep out. A six-foot steel-mesh fence will keep out foxes and most human beings, but it will not keep out weasels.

On arrival at Dungeness we proposed climbing the lighthouse and interrogating the keepers on migrant birds. For once in a while the lighthouse was closed and the only keeper we met was a new man unfamiliar with the subject. Since then I have discovered that the Foreland is a most important arrival point for bird migrants coming in across the Channel. Mr N. H. Joy, who for many years lived at Dungeness, has been good enough to write to me on the subject. He describes how he

"spent whole nights up at the lighthouse, where I learnt a lot of new facts that have not yet been published. Very little is known about night migrants—and remember that all the Warblers migrate at night. I took a bird one night on its way to Greenland. Migrants always face the wind when travelling. They often 'crab', i.e. they go more or less sideways. Look out for this. They never go straight down wind."

One of the peculiarities of the birds arriving at the Foreland is that they do not come in from the south, but from the east or east-south-east, almost in line with the West Beach. For a long time there was talk of establishing a bird observatory and ringing station there. And now this has happened. From the very beginning, in 1952, it has been run by an independent committee, but it has been backed by the Kent Ornithological Society, the London Natural History Society, and the Hastings and East Sussex Natural History Society, and has "owed its very existence to the generosity of Mr Gordon T. Paine, owner of the Dungeness Estate, on whose land most of the observatory work is carried out". The Nature Conservancy, by arrangement with the R.S.P.B., arrange for a warden to run the observatory and to warden the Reserve. The list of birds that have been recorded as passing by there would astound even Reg. Cooke.

I know no more thrilling sound in nature than the cries of birds as in utter darkness they pass unseen overhead. No ride of the Valkyries could ever inspire me as this does. There is a faint cry away in the stormy sky, and as one strains to hear it repeated it comes again with startling clearness overhead, and then again and again from east and west. It tugs the heart to hear that forlorn cry far out on the relentless sea. Bear up, brave traveller. The shores of Kent are near! There is no such thing as courage, we are told, in the make-up of a bird. It responds to an urge which it cannot resist. Yet there is a steadfastness of purpose in its tremendous effort which cannot fail to evoke in our hearts a sense of wonder and admiration. Thousands fail and fall into the sea. How many no one can ever say; but the startling fall in numbers that not infrequently occurs among migrant birds which come to breed in Britain is some indication of the magnitude of the disasters which occur out there—out there where the beam of Dungeness lighthouse is no more than a faint spark of hope to be quenched in the flying spume.

They arrive in hundreds, thousands, in tens of thousands. Some pass straight on, their journey far from accomplished. Others rest, crowding about the lighthouse which has been their guide, on every ledge and rail, some slithering down its smooth sides to the ground, more continually arriving. In the half-light of the grey dawn their multitudes can be seen on the beaches, on the roads, on buildings. Soon they are restless, moving, and before ever the east colours they melt away, spreading inland to water, pastures, greening woods, or preparing for yet another stage in their great journey.

For not all birds arriving at this favoured spot on our southern shore are those that come to breed in England. Very far from all, for vast numbers of birds which make their landfall at Dungeness are passage migrants whose journey's end is not yet. They are going on, to the far north, Scotland, the Faroes, Iceland. (Did not N. H. Joy take a bird that was bound for Greenland?) Some to Scandinavia, Spitzbergen and Novaya Zemblya. Little wonder that Reynolds and I talked of a bird observation station where birds might be caught, ringed and released, and information gathered and a census made of the winged travellers that pass through this Castel Benito, this Charing Cross of the bird world.

We talked enthusiastically. Reynolds did not like things done by halves. This was unique terrain with a unique position; it could be *made* the most interesting reserve in Southern England. To own the property and put up boards and do nothing else is worse than useless. It must be exploited, that is its attractiveness to birds enhanced, and it must be completely protected. Then that bird which takes its name from the only county where it breeds, the Kentish plover, will succeed and increase and not put us to perpetual shame by the sad records of but a single pair seen at the Midrips in this year or that. Then the common gull, which despite its name has only one nesting colony south of the Border, may establish itself on Dungeness and a new gullery enrich the area. The stone curlew, that quaint but fast disappearing bird from British haunts, will hold its own and never again dwindle to the skimpy half-dozen pairs which struggle to survive on the shingle. The terns, of which there were about sixty-five pairs nesting in the pits near the mouth of the Rother, will no longer have to battle against incessant pilfering, but will be able to return to the protected area, and a great ternery, amongst all the exquisite flowers of the beachlands, will be the result. We have had the object-lesson of the Pett floods and what could happen there so swiftly, and there surely is conclusive proof of the success that would attend a fully protected reserve only a few miles to the east.

I had to say goodbye to Reynolds with no time to visit Cheyne Court. It had been a wonderful day, quite unforgettable, for not only had he told me so much that was both interesting and stimulating, but by careful planning and speed of movement he had been able to give me a complete picture of the area, its present condition, its future possibilities. He very much wanted me to see Cheyne Court, but as this was no longer owned by the Society he felt it was not so important as what we had already seen. In any case, we had no time. After a sensational race across The Marsh by way of those fantastic elbow turns we rocketed into Rye with less than fifteen seconds to spare to catch my train.

A few weeks later it was Mr Burrowes, in his eightieth year, who set off on bicycle from Lydd to show me Cheyne Court. This was a good six miles across the long levels of Walland Marsh, and what had been the reserve was quite a distance from the lane and some two miles to encompass. The area, about 137 acres, was bounded by dykes a yard or two wide, with moderately high banks to the east and south. It was just a wide pasture in the middle of Walland Marsh, open to every wind that blew and without a single tree. I never saw a place look less like a bird sanctuary. Quite frankly I wondered what there was to see. The air was grand, it was like walking on the top of the South Downs; there was a feeling of spaciousness, there was so much sky and nothing to shut it out, one caught something of the personality of The Marsh; there were sheep, but there were no birds, only a few magpies, a green woodpecker, and a few moorhens in the dyke.

When we reached the south end, however, I saw how the level of the area was changing. It became very low, so much so that the dyke broadened out into a wide pool bordered by a muddy swamp. The bank along which we were walking must have been twelve or fifteen feet above the level of the water. It was plain that in winter this low-lying area would be completely flooded, and right out there in the middle of those wide open spaces a shallow lake several acres in extent would gleam among the pastures. The attractiveness of the place to wildfowl was immediately apparent, and indeed as we crept cautiously round under the bank to reach a goodview point, we were rewarded on topping the rise by seeing six sheld-duck, some teal, mallard, redshank, lapwing and numerous small waders, and this was the first week in August. I realised what a wonderful spot this would be in late autumn or early spring, and then with a shock that I find difficult to describe I observed five shooting butts lined up along the edge of the water.

Well, that is the scandalous kind of thing that happens when either the neighbours of a bird sanctuary will not co-operate or when a reserve to which birds have been encouraged is sold or changes hands. The birds are attracted to a place only for the unscrupulous to slaughter them as they leave it. What has happened at Cheyne Court? It has been bought and sold. The Royal Society for the Protection of Birds acquired it as a sanctuary for wildfowl. It was a remarkable spot, not unique as Dungeness is but in juxtaposition to the beachlands it possessed exceptional possibilities. Its misfortune was that the low-lying part was on its margin and afforded, as I have described, a duck-shoot for neighbouring landowners. Unfortunately nothing was done or could be done to remedy this, though it appears the greatest pity that a shallow pool could not have been excavated in the centre of the area, protected by distance from its boundaries, so that duck might pitch into it with safety and upon leaving be able to rise above range before crossing its confines.

With nothing done, those responsible were naturally disappointed with the place as a whole. It is probably fair to say that there was no popular appeal about it. It was neither a Minsmere nor a Havergate Island. It was not secluded; there was no cover. No special bird bred there. So it was sold. The present owner is interested in birds, but he is a farmer and naturally the farm comes first.

We had nearly completed our circuit of the ground when we saw towards the centre of it the bobbing heads of a number of duck. There were several score, but a little too far away for us to ascertain the number or the species, for duck have a disturbing way of thrusting their heads up to look and then of dodging down below the herbage to hide. Except for a few mallard we flushed in the dyke, they did not take flight.

In our scrambles across gates and dykes I had dropped my fountain pen, and did not discover the loss till some hours later. I went back, alone, retracing my steps with care, searching at every crossing. It was late evening, the sun had set behind the rim of low hills away to the north-west. The Marsh was darkening, but the fleecy backs of slowly moving sheep were palely outlined by the bright bands of light across the sky. The water in the dykes glinted and rippled in the cold little breeze that whispered across the levels. It was strange and lonely, not eerie perhaps, but the touch of The Marsh of which I had been dimly conscious that afternoon was now a grip. I understood how of old the Marsh folk believed in the Pharisees. I could have believed in them myself that evening, and if I had met a troupe of the little folk bearing aloft my pen in mischievous prank I should not have been surprised. Sometimes I think they did get hold of it, for it does not always write what I expect, and then just when I want to get on it runs dry. . . . There, would you believe it, the thing has run dry even as I write these words. Puck, you imp, you've had a hand in this!

I found the pen under a barway. I couldn't see it, but as I felt about in the long grass my fingers touched its smooth barrel. There was a thrill in discovering it like that. Did that knavish sprite put it into my hand to tease me with it ever after? If I could see "farther into a millstone than most" I might know, but for all its pranks this pen is something I would never wish to lose. The Marsh took it and The Marsh gave it back.

As I hurried warm-hearted homewards across the bedewed and dusky levels the duck took flight from Cheyne Court. Their voices and the sound of wings came to me from the rising mists, and then I saw them rising high against the last glow of the evening sky. In triumphant V-formations they passed overhead and disappeared into the steely firmament seawards.

CHAPTER X

THE TOWNS AND VILLAGES TODAY

No visitor can fail to enjoy Rye. Whether he is interested in history or golf, archaeology or architecture, Romney Marsh or just an unusual and pleasant holiday, there is everything to please him here. I find Rye delightful, it is so compact. Sometimes I almost wish the walls were still standing to complete that feeling of exclusiveness, of bold defiant independence. When I stay in Rye it is not that I do what Rye does, but that I feel like a Ryer. I have that feeling of living on the top of the hill, of belonging to a community that knows its own mind and goes its own way. Although it is no longer literally possible, I feel I have the power to shut the gates and exclude the alien, the stranger and the enemy.

There is only one gate standing today, the Land Gate, so called because it guarded the main approach to the town on the land-ward side. To enter Rye by this imposing gateway is to feel flattered. You feel welcomed—surely it would be shut against you were you a nobody? Queen Elizabeth entered by this gate when in 1573 she visited the town and honoured it with the title "Rye Royal". When it was first built, in the fourteenth century, the gateway was defended by both portcullis and drawbridge. These have long since disappeared, but otherwise the gate-house is still in good repair. It contains a hall and living quarters, and the entrance to each tower is defended by a shaft, called a meurtrière, through which stones and other missiles could be hurled upon the enemy.

The gate forms part of the town walls which were built in the reign of Edward III. As we have seen, Rye suffered attacks and raids by the French on several occasions, and it was not until after the disastrous sacking and burning of 1370 that the town petitioned the king. The grim old fortress known as the Ypres

Tower on the south side of the town was built more than a hundred years before, and while no doubt it was strong enough to resist all the French could bring against it, it could not protect the town. When the king gave permission for the walls to be built the Ypres tower was included in the circuit, but this was not known for certain until, in the Second World War, a house built against the tower was demolished in an air-raid. Then a small section of the wall was disclosed, and although the rest of it had long since disappeared, due to the erosion of the cliffs on the east by the sea, it was clear that Ypres Tower and the Land Gate were linked by the wall protecting the town on the east side.

On the north the town wall ran from the Land Gate to the Strand Gate. Some of this section can be seen behind the houses in Cinque Port Street. I was fortunate in discovering an old print by G. H. Grimm, in the possession of Mr F. White, dated 1784, showing the South or Strand Gate and some of the town wall adjoining. Mr White very kindly permitted me to take the photograph of the print, which is reproduced here. It will be seen how substantial the walls were and their somewhat unusual construction. The Strand Gate itself, which gave access to the quay, the ancient Strand, was pulled down in 1815, and all that remains of it, a stone bearing the arms of the Cinque Ports, can be seen built into the wall of a house in Mermaid Street.

The town wall continued round the west cliff and completed the circuit by once again linking up with the Ypres Tower, but before we explore that grim old fortress let us walk up Mermaid Street. Was there ever street so delightfully named, that at the same time lived up to its name? Surely there is no other street like this anywhere in South-eastern England. It is cobbled and rises fairly steeply from the Strand to the top of the hill. But while there have been alterations and restorations, there is still enough sixteenth- and seventeenth-century work and style to transport one in a flash to the Elizabethan era. There is the fine building of the Old Hospital, home of the Jeake family, and opposite to it the store house which Samuel Jeakes built, bearing upon a stone in the wall the date June 13, 1689. Being an astrologer he was mighty particular about the heavenly bodies being favourably disposed before he undertook this venture. The symbols of the horoscope are visible on the stone, and we must regard them as having been propitious, for not only has the house stood when many others have fallen into decay, but the date too remains for us to mark the time.

Then there is the Mermaid Inn. It bears road signs and is a little disfigured, but I find it very charming with its timber, its lattice windows, its old roping wistaria. One quiet Sunday morning in April I stood at the top of the hill looking down this street, half in shadow, half in sunshine, hoping to get a photograph that was not too hackneyed. There was a car halfway down the hill, and a small group of people, but neither would move, and then seemingly out of nowhere an old fellow came shuffling up the street. He wore a loose and tattered old coat, a staff was in his left hand, an old bag on a bit of rope was slung over his right shoulder. He was swearing aloud, cursing the whole world, as indeed it seemed to have damned him. He came on; none appeared to notice him but me. Could he have been a ghost? Had he walked straight out of the past? There was no time for thought, only instant action. As he passed The Mermaid, thumping with his stick and pouring out his lurid oaths, I pressed the shutter. He might well have heard the click and turned upon me as a suitable object for his maledictions, but he passed me by as though it were I who was the ghost. He thumped on round the corner by Lamb House, where once lived Henry James and later Rumer Godden, the authoress, whose many delightful stories in and about Rye have charmed countless readers.

Being an enthusiastic amateur photographer I thought I had got the "picture of the year"—we get these extravagant ideas—but later on I began seriously to wonder if the whole incident had not been a figment of my imagination. Naturally I became extremely impatient to see what was on the negative and could scarcely wait until I returned home to develop the film. Now I wish I could turn this into a true ghost story and say that there was nothing on the film. But I must disappoint you. The old fellow was on the negative exactly as I saw him passing The Mermaid.

This does not prove anything, of course, except that the picture has not been acclaimed at The Royal yet.

Watchbell Street where it looks on to Church Square runs Mermaid Street pretty close. There are some fascinating houses in the row; one displays a massive beam which was the centre piece of an old post windmill, and the quaintest of all is the Old Stone House, said to be the house which was occupied by the Friars of the Sack, one of only three such houses where monks and nuns lived together in the same building. It was not surprising to learn that such an Order was abolished by a Pope many hundreds of years ago. The Old Stone House was the home of Mr Leo Vidler, a one-time Mayor of Rye whose knowledge of the town and all its antiquaries was second to none. His son, the eminent theologian Dr Alec Vidler, now resides there.

The great church of St Mary's stands squarely on the top of the hill. It is rather jostled by buildings on the north side, but on the south and west there is a spacious yard which gives it dignity. It has suffered many vicissitudes. There are numerous marks of fire on the older Norman and early English stonework, restorations in various styles have been carried out, and many puzzling features still await elucidation. There is a Burne-Jones window, the Adoration of the Magi, in the north aisle of the nave; and both Archbishop Benson and A. C. Benson are commemorated in stained-glass windows. But it is not the purpose of this book to describe any building in detail; to do so would be never to finish. Besides, it has been done before and more competently than I could ever do it. I must therefore be content with mentioning some of the things which await you to come and find them.

The Quay, which occupies the ancient and historic site of the Strand on the banks of the Tillingham, is on the levels below the west cliff. Some quaint old warehouses, black and looking shrunken in their desuetude, still stand; but not much merchandise, I fear, is ever stored there now. It would do one good to see, as of yore, a hundred tunnes of Spanish wine therein. There were days when not only the spoils of war were piled upon the Strand, but much goods. There were iron and timber, salt and charcoal, wool and "billets" of wood, there was pottery, and always there was fish. When after the sixteenth century Rye had declined to a fifth-rate port and its mayor and jurats in 1618 were complaining "now is our harbour so decayed that all trade has forsaken us"; even then its trade just survived and struggled desperately on till the twentieth century.

Within living memory ketch-rigged barges and other vessels have sailed up to Rye with their cargoes of timber from the Baltic and coal from the Tyne. But, as we have seen, the volume of water was for ever decreasing and the mouth of the Rother becoming ever more attenuated. The Salts of Rye were inned—the last innings for the whole of The Marsh—in 1825. The last barge to move along the Royal Military Canal, which connected Hythe and Rye, did so, according to Mr Leo Vidler, whose family was for years in local shipping, in 1880. Nowadays, apart from fishing vessels, a cargo rarely indeed comes up the Rother. As an old salt told me down the Harbour, "It be a nine days' wunder to see 'un."

It was intriguing, however, to see not so long ago a vessel of some 260 tons tied up to the quay, bearing a painted notice-board on her deck announcing that she was going in search of Captain Kidd's treasure and advertising for a crew to join her on this adventure to the South China Seas. At the foot of the board it read, "Phone Rye ——". I could not help thinking that this was not the way Long John Silver would have gone about the task! However, the spirit of adventure was not dead yet in Rye, and I was only too glad to wish them well on their romantic voyage. Captain Kidd, who was executed on the scaffold at Execution Dock near Tilbury in 1701, had declared at his trial for piracy that his treasure was worth some £120,000. Those who had planned the voyage were said to have in their possession certain maps which had been found in an old sea-chest which had once belonged to Captain Kidd. As in all good treasure-hunt stories, these maps had been marked, whether with an X or with skull and crossbones has not been disclosed, where the stuff was buried. Two hundred and fifty years is a long time, but the whole adventure was based on the belief that the maps were genuine.

I wish I could report success for this inspiriting expedition, but

Rye's grim old fortress, Ypres Tower

The miniature railway

A magnificent "Pacific" engine

The Royal Military Canal, a defence against Napoleon and Hitler

A derelict church where sheep now graze

The "Marsh" frog

A tern from a beachland colony

The great church of St Thomas, Winchelsea

St Mary's, East Guldeford, like a barn on Guldeford Marsh

"Steeples settin' beside churches" - Brookland Church

Dungeness's two nuclear power stations

"Port of Stranded Pride" - Rye from the air

the sequel was grievous. The vessel was caught in furious November gales in the Channel, enormous waves pounded her and dismasted her. She had sent out distress signals, and a frigate took her in tow. But the tow parted. Two lifeboats and a tug went to her assistance; night fell, oil was poured on the water, searchlights trained on the wreck; a collision occurred between the treasure ship and the frigate. At last the crew was taken off and the vessel abandoned. She was driven ashore later, badly damaged and with much valuable gear ruined. One cannot help hoping this will not be the end of the quest; such adventures in these prosaic days capture our imagination, and in any case it is high time the old pirate's hoard was brought to the light of day.

Rye has always been the nurse of adventure. One can well imagine the Portsmen of nearly a thousand years earlier setting sail on their warlike expeditions from this cliff-girt peninsula and under the shadow of the Ypres Tower. True, the tower was not built until after 1249, by Henry III, but it is a curious thing that although this is more than seven centuries ago, one gets the feeling after studying the great story of the Portsmen and of The Marsh that it is a comparatively recent event in their history!

Do not expect too much of the Ypres Tower. Over and over again one overhears visitors declare, "How small it is". This may partly be due to the massiveness of the Land Gate, which leads them to expect something big in the way of a fortress—if that was the size of the gateway. Gaunt, four-square, it is a rugged old pile and full of interest, and bears on its west side stone machicoulis projecting from the battlements. This is a very early example of such defensive device, which did not come generally into use until two centuries later. Towards the end of the eighteenth century it was put to use as a gaol, and the guide who conducts visitors over the tower seems to concentrate more on this unhappy part of its history than the earlier. The old fortress was still good enough to stand up to modern aerial bombardment when houses built against it were demolished in the Second World War.

The tower itself was damaged, but the Rye authorities in conjunction with the Ministry of Works have restored and re-roofed it and it is now an award-winning museum.

There is a charming little terrace beneath its walls on the south side. It is the old Gun Garden, where a cannon battery was established to defend the approaches to the port until the end of the nineteenth century. But in the twentieth century, in 1980, what a joyous event took place here. Queen Elizabeth the Queen Mother had recently been installed as Lord Warden of the Cinque Ports, and of course in accordance with her 'duties' she visited each of the famous ports. The Mayor of Rye, Cllr Mrs J. Kirkham, had most urgently to think in what way she could mark this illustrious visit and at the same time give Her Majesty an eightieth birthday present. She thought of the Gun Garden. The Mayor raised, by public subscription, sufficient funds to have three cannon replaced, remounted in authentic gun carriages and in position ready for the Queen Mother's visit. She presented them to the Lord Warden as a birthday gift. Need I attempt to describe how that Gracious Lady, accepting them with that wonderful smile, said that she had never before received a present of cannon.

*   *   *   *   *

A mile or so down river from Rye is the small and not very prepossessing village of Rye Harbour. There are one or two big and busy works, but for the tripper it is a disappointing place, for the mouth of the river is still a mile farther on, and the Rother is narrow and the boats coming in and out are few. For those who are interested in birds and wild flowers there is a miniature Dungeness to the south to be explored. This is Nook Beach and the more recent accumulation of shingle that has piled up against the mouth of the Rother, and it is one of the pits in a depression between the two that the terns have been using as a breeding ground. A new well-made road now links the village of Winchelsea Beach with Pett, and all the way along this shore the bird life is full of interest, especially in winter. Seabirds, divers, grebes, ducks and geese often gather in considerable numbers. It may be rather an unhappy way to draw attention to their number and variety, but Mr R. Cooke has drawn my attention to the appalling numbers of birds killed by oil that he has found along this beach. During five years in which he has kept records he has found more than ten thousand birds washed up on the beach, dead or dying. This on only a three-and-a-half-mile-stretch of shore; and even these which he has seen can only be a fraction of those that reach the beach. It is a scandalous thing that this discharge of oil waste from ships should continue. Theoretically it should not be done in narrow waters or within a certain mileage of the coast. But who can see and who can enforce? The damnable practice continues, the oil floats on the surface, and any bird unlucky enough to encounter it is doomed.

It might be thought that birds would recognise the filthy stuff and be wise to the danger. As a matter of fact they are, and no bird either swims into it or alights upon an oily patch deliberately. As Reg. Cooke has pointed out, it is the divers which suffer the worst. What happens is that these birds spend considerable time under the surface in pursuit of fish, sometimes as long as a minute. During this period they can travel considerable distances and when they surface they may be forty or fifty yards from the point where they dived. Hence while they may dive where the surface is clean they may emerge in the midst of an oil patch. The oil will cover head, breast and back, and is so wickedly glutinous and tenacious that no bird can remove it from its plumage. It cannot fly, it can no longer dive; it starves, rolling on the surface at the mercy of the waves until drowned or cast ashore.

It is a shocking and shameful thing to see these fine birds, common and velvet scoter, guillemot, razorbill, red-throated diver, great crested and Slavonian grebe, eider duck, to name but a few, writhing, gasping, helpless, dying in their ghastly distress upon our beaches. Reg. Cooke told me, and there was a note of anguish in his voice as he did so, that in one awful period of ten days between the 7th and 18th of March he found no less than four hundred and fifty birds along Pett beach. In one pitiful group there was every grebe on the British list.

The agonising thing is that for most of the birds that come ashore in this way nothing can be done. They are too near dead, too exhausted, too bedevilled with oil to be cleansed or cared for. In those few cases where the oiling is not too extensive and the bird not too distressed it is possible with care and patience to clean it. But it is a long job. Reg. Cooke told me of five eider duck, all moderately oiled but helpless, which he gathered and penned and attempted to cleanse. It took from two to three weeks before the birds could fly and care for themselves, and all that time they had to be fed—on herrings mostly. Four out of the five survived and went safely out to sea. Blessings on their rescuer. But who shall cope with two thousand a year? And what are four out of the tens of thousands around our coasts year after year?

★   ★   ★   ★   ★

Fishing has been a means of livelihood from time immemorial, and we have seen how the first men who came to settle on the shores of the bay and upon its islands and shingle spits were not only fishermen and responsible for a considerable portion of England's food supply, but that the very pursuit of their trade eventually made the Portsmen the power that they and their confederation became in the land. Time and again they fought for the king, and their fishing vessels put on their castles and became men-of-war. Time and again they turned pirate and plundered the king's enemies—and his friends on occasion—and brought the spoils back to the ports. But always the Portsmen were fishermen, managing affairs at Yarmouth, superintending the herring fishery and sending gifts of porpoise to please or appease high officers of state.

We have seen how the demand for ever bigger ships for the king's navy, coupled with the desertion of the sea, took all power from the Cinque Ports. One after another they became little inland towns with neither bay nor harbour. Apart from Dover and Hastings, which are outside our area, only Rye with the Rother remained an active though small port, and even today fishing vessels still come up the narrow, winding river to the town. Their numbers are steadily growing less. This is not because there are no fish in the sea or because there is no demand for the fish, but because there are neither the men to man the ships nor the financial return to encourage men to run them.

Compared to the marshman the fisherman has always had hold

of the uncomfortable end of the stick. True, in their heyday the Barons of the Ports were second to none in the land. Their royal charters and honours and privileges seem at first sight completely to overshadow the Level and the Liberty of Romney Marsh. But when the smoke of battle has cleared and the sound of the trumpets died away, the fisherman still has to catch fish, he still has to face and to overcome all the uncertainties of the sea, and he still has for the most part to sell or dispose of his catch while it is still in a condition fit to eat.

The marshman, who is the farmer today, has not these difficulties to contend with. At first he certainly had great problems. His struggle to inn, to drain and to defend against the sea took centuries of effort. The life was unhealthy; ague abounded, and it was not until all drainage was thorough and complete at the end of the nineteenth century that The Marsh became a healthy place in which to live. But even so, such troubles were not those of the seafarer, and, more important still, the farmer has the product of his lands and the work of his hands continuously under his eye. He is subject to the vagaries of the weather, just as the fisherman is, and he is sometimes troubled by pests, as the fisherman is by the whims and failings of the shoals. When all is said and done, however, the farmer can store his products, he can keep his flocks and herds alive, he can hold his goods not for one or two days, but for weeks or months, and sell as it pleases or is convenient to him. His lands remain, permanent and real, with his home in the midst. For the fisherman, however well appointed his home in the port, his real home is his ship. And as the sea is his domain he is inevitably a seafarer, a wanderer, something of a rolling stone, and there are no stores in his barns.

As The Marsh has triumphed over the sea, so has the farmer consolidated his position to the ever-increasing disadvantage of the seafarer. Yet in spite of all, the fisherman lives on, and although he has no proper harbours and no sheltered waters in which to tie up his craft he still goes about his business from the very beach itself.

This is one of the most remarkable and interesting things about the fishing craft of the South and South-east Coasts during the past two centuries. The will to go to sea was still there, but the means to do it were not, for the old-style ships of the past were no longer suitable nor serviceable for the new conditions. From Hastings to Hythe, indeed one might go much wider and say from Shoreham to Dover, the only suitable shores for landing fishing vessels of any size were beach. To stand the heavy strain of being hauled up a steep and bouldery beach, and to be launched from it again every time the vessel went to sea, called for a much stouter craft than of yore. So a heavier, stouter, more beamy vessel began to be made. By the eighteenth century the old square sail at last gave place to the lugsail, which is really a fore-and-aft sail, and not only was the appearance altered but the handling of the vessels made much easier, their sailing closer to the wind enhanced and their speed considerably increased.

Thus by the nineteenth century the fishermen all along the Sussex and Kent Channel coast were using two- or three-masted luggers. All had the high transom stern, and later the "lute" stern, or beaching-counter as it was called, to prevent as far as possible the vessel shipping water when she was beached or launched in a seaway. Nearly all these vessels, except the few coming up the Rother, worked directly from the beach, and the method of fishing then in general practice was the drift-net. This was a line of nets suspended vertically in the water from floats, such as is employed for catching herring or other fish near the surface.

By 1850 another change, this time in fishing methods, struck a blow at those using the traditional drift-net. The trawl-net, which is towed along the sea-bottom, came into use, and by it rich new harvests were reaped from fishing grounds, of which Rye Bay was certainly not the least, and which hitherto had been almost untouched. For trawling, bigger and more powerful craft were necessary, and as such could not be either conveniently or safely beached on the open seaway it meant that these vessels came from distant ports and harbours and thus the fishing industry declined for more than fifty years.

It was the oil-driven engine of the twentieth century that brought opportunity back, and had it not been for two world wars, competing and more "attractive" vocations for young men, high costs, and, let it be said, changing behaviour on the part of the herring, it might well have restored the ancient fishing industry to some prosperity. I wonder! The old salt down at Rye Harbour thought differently. He told of the days, fifty years ago, when he was skipper of the *Industry*, as sound a lugger as ever set sail from Rye. Two men and a boy were the crew and "them was the days, sure". But one day as they were lying becalmed five miles south-east of Dungeness, with a good catch aboard and anxious for the market, what should they see but another lugger making speed for Rye Harbour with never a sail set.

"We stared, guv'nor," said the old salt, chewing his tobacco and spitting into the Rother. "We stared fit to bust. An' as she come nigh enough I hails 'er: 'What the devil?' An' the laughter of the —— devil comes from 'er, sure enough, an' a voice bawls out: 'Ye're old fashioned, ha, ha, ye're behind the times, Skipper!' An' she goes by, pup-pup-puppin', with one of they —— new-fangled moters fitted in 'er, an' she makes Rye twenty-four hours afore we gets in."

I wish I could tell it all in his amusing and forceful language. But as the original would be unprintable I must briefly summarise. Being a young and enterprising young man—he was skipper of his own lugger at eighteen—it was not long before he too was pup-pup-puppin' along, and doing well. What was the sense of slaving and hauling on the nets when the motor could do it for you? Why be idle, becalmed, when the motor could get you to port? Why let the other fellow get his catch to the market first? And why indeed pay for a boy when there was no longer any need for a third member of the crew? Why, indeed? Competition and costs drove them to it. Even if any one of those skippers could have foreseen the future, circumstances would have been too strong for them.

What happened? The boys were no longer wanted, the luggers sailed with a crew of two men. There was no longer any apprentice learning seamanship and the ways of fish and fishing. And if you don't go to sea young, when will you go? The petrol engine, boon as it may have been in the first two decades of the twentieth century, was the curse of the fishing industry, as it has been the curse of our modern civilisation. It dispensed with the very material that would have been shaped into first-rate seamen. It is men that are wanted. While we most of us like to retain some of the colourful customs and pageantry of the past it is a little uncomfortable to suffer puff and blah about Barons and privileges, Seals and Cinque Ports when there are not men enough even to man the luggers.

There will of course always be the few to man some of the little ships. There would have been no miracle of Dunkirk without them. The glory of that heroic episode will in a thousand years glow as undimmed as the triumph of the Portsmen in the battle of Les Espagnols-sur-Mer of nearly a thousand years agone. And Rye still makes luggers. They are built of local oak and elm, their spars and masts are of fir. They still carry sails, but all are now fitted with petrol engines. The largest are 27 feet long on the keel and have a burden of 16 tons. Some go to Hastings, some to Eastbourne, Newhaven and Brighton, some still come up the Rother, and some still beach on Dungeness.

*　　*　　*　　*　　*

A method of fishing which was common along the shore from Pett to Hythe, and occasionally seen today, is by "keddle nets". The Kent River Board has jurisdiction over the foreshore, and it is that authority which nowadays grants permission to erect the nets. Actually the right of certain Corporations to grant leases of the Kiddell or fishing grounds dates back to remote times, but only a few fishermen avail themselves of the opportunity to apply. A good deal of work is attached to it and being controlled by the tides the time to attend to the catch is often mighty inconvenient.

To describe the keddle net is simple in a diagram, but in so many words it is not easy. Imagine a net hanging vertical in the water, running out to sea at right angles to the shore some thirty to fifty yards. Around the seaward end of this is another net arranged in an open circle like a broken hoop or the handle of an iron kettle. The ends of this net, called the "bythe", just overlap the end of the straight net, but are not joined to it. In times gone by posts were driven into the sand to carry these nets upright, and smaller pegs were driven in all the way round to hold the nets in position hard down on the sand. Except off the foreland of Dungeness all the shores of Rye Bay and St Mary's Bay are shallow, sandy and very gently shelving. It was therefore possible to do this construction work at long low tide. The supporting posts were left permanently in position, though of course they needed constant re-erection and replacement every season. Today, while the nets are still pegged down to the sandy bottom, posts are not used, and floats are employed to hold the nets upright in the water; thus the nets rise and fall with the tide.

Fish moving along close inshore at high tide meet the straight net and turn seaward. Travelling close to the net they pass from its end into the "bythe", and, being fish, few discover the way to escape is by the way they came in. Fish alarmed instinctively turn towards deeper water, and that of course is into the net. Sometimes, where the shelve of the shore allows, a second straight net projects seaward beyond the bythe of the first net and at its extremity is a second bythe. On rare occasions there is a third. Such an arrangement might reach more than two hundred yards seawards from high-water mark, and it will be seen that the catching potential of keddle nets is very considerable. Furthermore, whether the fish are moving east to west or west to east, the nets are just as effective. Between Pett and Dungeness there were at one time as many as fifty keddle nets in operation; today there are not more than five.

The fish of course can only be collected at low tide, and spring tides only permit the far-reaching nets to be visited. The catch must be collected as the tide recedes from the nets; to wait until the fish are left high and dry would lead to damage and loss. Care must be taken not to handle the "wyvers" or "weavers", most unpleasant stinging fish, and one must work fast if two or more nets have to be worked. Mackerel are the usual and most important catch, but quite a variety of fish is taken and occasionally salmon are found in the nets—a $15\frac{1}{2}$-pounder on one occasion recently. Fishing by keddle nets begins at the end of April or beginning of May, and it is when the "mack'rel birds", the terns, are active that the keddle-net fishermen expect to be busy.

One thing I saw being used along these sandy shores which I've not seen elsewhere were chained spades. These are two short-handled narrow-bladed spades linked together by a short length of chain. Two men use them, facing each other, and of course rhythmically and simultaneously, as that is the purpose of the chaining. By this means wet caving sand can be excavated with great speed in the search for bait and for other purposes.

Just before leaving Rye Harbour there is one other odd job that ought to be mentioned. Ever since the reign of Queen Anne "boulders", sea-worn blue flints, have been collected by hand from the foreshore. This used to be quite a lucrative job, and at one time nearly the whole population of Rye Harbour village used to go bouldering. The Potteries, who use the flints, paid as much as £1 a ton thirty or forty years ago; but the price has fallen since, and now I believe George and Arthur Mills are the only boulderers left. The heaps they gather together are collected by lorry and travel by rail, but they used to go by sea and canal to the Midlands. Bouldering, like herb harvesting, is one of those old, simple but hard-slogging occupations fast disappearing. It's heavy work and heavy going on the shingle; if you gathered a ton a day you would be mighty industrious, and if you got £3 a week for them you'd be lucky.

*   *   *   *   *

On the west side of the Rother's mouth it is all shingle and blue boulders, piling up against the river's outflow, a miniature Dungeness, but on the east side there is scarcely a pebble to be seen—it is all sand. The contrast is striking, all the more so when we know that two miles farther on the shingle begins again and piles up in that monstrosity, the Foreland. Inshore it is very shallow here, and at low tides sometimes more than half a mile of sand is exposed. Little wonder that to our sun-sea-and-sand-loving population Camber Sands have become a popular holiday resort. And shame too that at such a delightful spot authority allowed before the war such appalling shacks, beach-huts, cabins, fun-fairs and other horrors of mushroom and hideous growth to fester there in untidy, higgledy-piggledy shoddiness. No one can complain of sightly buildings which give good service to holiday-makers, or of neat, tasteful holiday houses by the sea, though even these should fit into a plan that allows for proper access to the sea and not be permitted to become a barrier of backyards with owners who fancy they have a right over all the foreshore down to the low-tide mark. But why, oh, why must the seaside holiday-maker be catered for with bumper cars and penny-in-the-slot machines and *fun*-fairs and cheap-jack trumperiness?

The onset of the Second World War struck the fungus of Camber Sands like a blight. The village had to be evacuated, and some four or more years of utter and enforced neglect played havoc with the jerry building. It was a sorry sight in 1945, yet when one found a way through the blown sand and the ruins and the neglected "roads", and in spite of the line of dilapidated beach and bathing huts behind one, the deserted sands were exquisitely lovely. Miles and miles of firm clean sand in a broad sweep to the piers of the Rother's mouth, with the high ground of Fairlight Head some six miles beyond; and away to the east, gradually narrowing toward the beaches of the Holmstone and Dungeness, it appeared to stretch to the lighthouse some seven miles distant. And the dark-blue riband of the sea, looking so narrow and so far away, bounded a delightful natural playground. Here and there pools of water or still-wet sand reflected the cirrus-and-blue of August skies, and yet never a soul ran on the sands or danced like David before the Lord. It made one realise how beautiful our shores and beaches had been and might have been.

This expanse of sand, some of which is exposed by every tide twice a day, is exhibiting a new feature in the formation of The Marsh. It is blowing. It is a curious thing that in all the long history of the uplifts and depressions out of which, as we have seen, The Marsh evolved this has only happened once before, in pre-Roman times. This was because although much marine sand was brought into the great bay by tidal waters, it was always mixed more or less with river silt. This naturally tended to make it "muddy", which would either not dry or only cake during the few hours of exposure at low tide. Camber Sands are not muddy. Under the influence of wind and sun they dry quickly, the compact surface loosens and very soon individual grains are free to drift along in the wind.

As the prevailing wind is south-west and as almost invariably a sea breeze blows on the warmest, sunniest days, the wind-blown sand drifts landward. Wherever there is an eddy the movement of the sand grains is halted. Hence, wherever there is an obstruction, some object which checks the steady flow of the breeze, be it a pebble or a house, there the sand stops and accumulates. It is absorbingly interesting to watch this happening. At first you may not be aware the sand is drifting, but soon you notice little smoke-like wisps scurrying along the surface. If the sand is drying rapidly and the wind strong, these wisps become streamers, or a moving haze inches deep, or even clouds on gusty days. If the last, the sands are best avoided, but if it is moving delicately, all you have to do is to drop some object on the sand, a shoe or a book, or yourself if need be, and if the sand is blowing steadily the effect is immediate. You can see the sand whirl into eddies on the leeward side and come to a stop. More follows and piles on the top. Now and again a stronger gust whips up the loose sand into a miniature whirlwind, but the accumulation steadily goes on, and in quite a short time an elongated heap as high as the obstruction has piled up in its lee. A change of wind will, of course, rapidly remove the loose drift and begin piling up another in a new position. But it will be seen that the bigger the object the bigger the drift, and if this drift has time to consolidate it will itself become an obstruction and bring about a fresh accumulation in its own lee.

In this manner big drifts, and then sand dunes, develop. If the obstructions are permanent, such as an embankment or wall or buildings, if the resulting dunes become consolidated, particularly by the growth of marram grass and other dune-loving plants, and if these vast accumulations occur above or beyond high-water mark, where tidal erosion cannot wear them away, then the dunes reach considerable dimensions. All these conditions are fulfilled at Camber, and the effect is really quite extraordinary.

Dunes, in some places nearly forty feet high, stretch for almost a mile and a half from the East Pier to Camber. After the long miles of the level Marsh these hummocky sand-hills look quite queer. They rear up higher than anything The Marsh has ever known for more than two thousand years, and yet they have scarcely themselves been a hundred years in the making. They are a new feature in the landscape, but that they constitute a threat seems unlikely, for the sand appears to be held and is not yet seriously creeping upon the land behind.

During the five years of evacuation the drifting sand certainly piled in among the buildings. Some small houses were three-quarters buried and soon would be again were it not for the ceaseless labours of the occupiers to keep their dwellings clear. Fortunately there is sufficient marram grass to hold most of the sand-hills together, and although more sand is continually piling up on top of it, this wonderful grass, coarse and sharp though it is, always manages to win through, and protects Guldeford Marsh from becoming a desert.

In the lee of the dunes and just level with the ferry, which comes across from Rye Harbour, is the famous golf links. This delightful course with its fast greens has provided sport for almost every great name in the golfing world. Every links has of course its own peculiar character, but there is something about Rye especially keen and inspiring. It is probably best known for the Oxford and Cambridge match which is played here, and it was on this course that Hugh Neilson, Cambridge golfing blue, drove off from the 13th tee and killed a lark which rose from the ground thirty yards in front of him. It was one of those very rare accidents that occur on the links. The ball's flight was scarcely affected, but Neilson, who was then all square, lost that hole and the next to go two down.

Before leaving Camber Sands there is one sport I must mention, and that is the sand- or land-yachting which can be enjoyed there. The prevailing wind is ideal, and the surface as good as anywhere I know, and there is length for a superb run, besides space for manœuvre. The only difficulty is getting the yacht down on to the sands, what with dunes, beach-huts, narrow roads and high embankments. But the enthusiast will know how to overcome these things. Sand-yachting is to my thinking the most delightful and exciting seaside sport there is. With a good yacht, well-cut sail and efficient wheels and steering it is possible in a good breeze to reach forty miles per hour, or should I say knots?

On pneumatic tyres the yacht runs absolutely silently, and lying so low to the sands she seems to skim like a sea swallow. But I should explain perhaps to those who do not know, that a sand yacht is no more than a platform slung low on four wheels with a mast stepped for'd. The front axle should be wide, 7 to 10 feet, the back axle is only half this and turns on a pivot, so that the yacht may be steered either with a tiller or a steering wheel, according to the nautical or mechanical skill of the builder. The mast must be well stepped and efficiently stayed and braced, and the front wheels must be very strong, for the ride thrust is terrific, especially when tacking. I once made what I thought was a light, fast model and used bicycle wheels. While I sailed her fairly successfully, the very first time I rather foolishly let an inexperienced fellow sail her—he was mad to have a try—he buckled both wheels on the very first turn!

There has been sand-yacht racing on Camber Sands, and I hope there will be again. But to get a good home-made yacht from the home town to the seaside and back again is not easy, or else very expensive. I shall never forget my experience when after a summer holiday's fun I decided to *sail* my yacht home. I had to make a very early start, in the grey dawn of a Sunday morning in fact, as only by so doing could I hope to have the roads clear for four or five hours, which I estimated I needed to see me home. I hoisted sail in a cold light breeze, with the first light steeling the sea and only the long wash of the incoming tide to bid me *bon voyage*.

Patience V—that was her name—made pretty sailing across the levels. What would have happened had I met a vehicle on those narrow roads I cannot imagine, for not only was there no room to pass, but beyond a wooden skid she had no brakes. But all went well till we came to a level-crossing. I had forgotten this, and as there was no means of opening the gates I had to ring a bell.

I was very loath to do this, as four o'clock on a sabbath morning was no time to rouse the custodian. I anticipated his displeasure, but I am afraid I had not taken into account the effect of Patience V. I had rung twice—it was enough to wake the dead from the dreamy sleep of the Levels—when the cottage window opened and a tousled head pushed through the curtains uttering terrible oaths. Suddenly, as his eyes became accustomed to the light, he saw what must have appeared to him a yacht in full sail trying to force a passage through the narrows.

The language stopped dead. His eyes literally bulged and his jaw dropped. I feared either a fit or a slamming of the window to shut out the sight of something worse than pink elephants.

"Good morning," I called out, trying not to be too bright but to sound as natural as possible. "So sorry, but this is the only time I can safely sail her home."

Slowly the mouth shut. "My Gawd," in an awed voice, and then the curtain dropped and all was still.

I fretted and fumed. Not only was I worried about delay, but I honestly felt some concern for the keeper of the gates, wondering how on earth one treated apoplexy or shock, or both, and whether I ought to go to his aid, or turn ship about and set course elsewhere. I was in something of a dilemma, for a pretty brisk wind was rising, and Patience V was bucking like a race-horse, and I had much ado to stop her ramming the gates or capsizing. I had just decided to lower sail so that I might go to the cottage to ascertain all was well when the front door opened.

He was too tough a fellow to be knocked out by a sand-yacht and too good a chap to leave me there aground. The silence was accounted for by the fact that he had come down in his stockinged feet. He had slipped his boots on and now walked to the gates.

"Most awfully sorry," I apologised again. "Rotten to have to drag you out at this time in the morning. But I just can't get her home when there's traffic on the roads."

He said nothing. The gates clanged open and automatically I tautened sail. Like a thoroughbred when the starter raises the gate at Epsom, Patience V sprang forward. She swerved violently as she hit the rails with her starboard wheel and just missed the keeper. He put out his hand to protect himself from the boom, but she recovered and in a split second I pushed into his hand the last bit of folded paper I had left in my pocket. He deserved it. What he thought or said or did I have no idea. Patience with the bit between her teeth was flying down the lane almost out of control, and I had no leisure so much as to look round. Tiller steering on a narrow carriageway is very exacting.

It was impossible to avoid passing through one or two villages on the way home, and they were part of the trip I least looked forward to. This was partly because I did not know what obstructions I might meet or how much foot-slogging might be necessary (of course one had to get out and push in built-up areas or uphill) and partly because I did not know the law with regard to sand-yachts on the public highway, or any special relaxations or otherwise laid down on their behalf in the highway code. I was not anxious to argue my rights or wrongs with a village constable.

All went well, however, except in one small market town where I discovered two things: that milkmen deliver milk very early on Sunday mornings and that they still do so in the remoter parts of Kent and Sussex by horse and cart. These facts have no significance in themselves; it is the attitude taken up by the horses to sand-yachts which is disturbing. They don't like sand-yachts, in fact the mere sight of one sends them off into tantrums. The first meeting took everyone by surprise, horse, milkman, milk and myself. There it was, a quiet little grey thing with drooping mien and knocking knees on its perpetual and uneventful sabbath round, and suddenly all was changed—it saw Patience.

Now Patience and I were coming along the High Street at about three knots. There was scarcely any air, the sail was idly flapping and I had one foot over the side, punting her silently along. I happened to be watching the horse when suddenly it threw up its head and in spite of blinkers and tousled fetlock it saw Patience, and as clear as I see this page I saw its lips move as it said to itself, "Sand-yacht".

As the milkman came out of a gate things happened with

electrifying rapidity. The horse snorted, seemed to rear on its hind legs and veer towards the pavement all in the same movement. A large, almost empty can on the tail of the cart fell out on to the road with a startling clash. Evidently thinking that Patience had fired a broadside into it, the horse bolted. The milkman, resourceful fellow, put down his crate and with a run and a flying leap gained the tailboard in the nick of time and, seizing the reins, went down the High Street as no charioteer had done since Roman times. It was a stirring sight; a second can fell out and milk spurted like a bursting bomb. I could have enjoyed it had I not felt guilty of all the trouble, and was mighty glad to turn up North Street and get away from it all.

But ill fortune dogged me, for believe it or not a second milk cart with its brown mare was jogging slowly towards me. I halted instantly and struggled to turn Patience about so that I might withdraw unseen to the shambles of the High Street. It was no use, she had already seen me. Horse sense or horse telepathy had put her on the *qui vive*. The pattern of behaviour was similar, only the mare wouldn't pass me. She swung round with that lively precision that would have done credit to the Royal Horse Artillery, and with a clatter of hooves made speed for home and happiness completely regardless of bit, rein, language or master.

It was exceedingly disconcerting to think that not less than two milk floats, with horses and drivers, were careering about in that market town so early on a Sunday morning. Whether they met or how that chariot race ended I never made any attempt to ascertain. Like Brer Rabbit, I lay low. It would be better for the milkmen to believe that a ghost yacht with Old Nick himself at the helm had passed that way than to disillusion them. It was a relief to reach the open country and a freshening breeze and to put many silent miles between me and the spilt milk.

★   ★   ★   ★   ★

I have digressed somewhat, but only to underline this most excellent sport of sand-yachting which can be had on Camber Sands. On second thoughts perhaps I should never have described my experience on the roads. But take it as a caution not to attempt it. It is far better to make your yacht in portions easily assembled and easily transportable. The authorities would frown, I am sure, on fleets of sand-yachts converging on Rye, for most of the streets are narrow and one-way. Ryans have been familiar with ships since before the Conquest, but such a half-breed in their streets would scarcely please them.

There is another magnificent stretch of sand on the other side of Dungeness, St Mary's Bay; and at low tide the Romney Sands sweep in a grand semicircle from Lydd-on-Sea past Greatstone and Littlestone to Dymchurch and beyond. This is not so satisfactory for sand-yachting as Camber and Broomhill sands because at high tide the sand is completely covered, right up to the Wall, and there is no draw-off, no parking place. But for ordinary seaside holiday-making, for sun, sea, sand and space, this is a truly wonderful playground. It is not surprising that holiday towns and holiday homes have sprung up all along the bay. True they suffer from arrested development, particularly Littlestone, with its big hotels and houses which halt abruptly as if all its architects and builders had suddenly gone on strike or emigrated to Australia, never to return.

But this is the era of holiday camps. The rage for holiday-making in sociable crowds is no new thing; the Brightons and Blackpools are monstrous witness of its popularity. The latest craze, and it seems scarcely a decade old, is not so much to forgather in the same resort, but to become part of a compact and specially catered-for community. Everything is on tap; from the delightful little chalet which for a week or fortnight you can call your own to the organised games on the sand or the entertainment in the concert hall in which you take a part, everything is arranged. You have no anxieties for the morrow—food, children, amusements; all will be in capable and experienced hands. You shed responsibilities; everything will run like clockwork. All you have to do is to enjoy yourself.

In the distracting and harassing days in which we live it is therefore no wonder that the holiday camp makes a strong and successful appeal. And when it is well sited, and with a sea frontage almost its own, with long clean sands, such as Maddiesons near Littlestone or Beachlands at Dymchurch, or Pontin at Camber, that success seems assured.

For those who still like to retain their independence while living in a holiday community the caravan holiday has certainly not yet reached the peak of its popularity. But it grows rapidly, and throughout the country one sees areas allotted to the caravaners. However, I have never seen anywhere else such arrangements made as on a site near Dymchurch. This was a big ground with literally hundreds of caravans, not haphazardly out-spanning, but drawn up in straight orderly rows, with "roads", "avenues" and "streets" separating them. There were shops, post office, proper sanitary arrangements and visiting tradesmen. Such regimentation and urbanisation apparently are necessities when numbers are great and popular sites few, but I cannot help wondering if the caravaners have found what they were seeking. It was as remote from a gypsy life as a flat in Chelsea, and with less privacy than Oxford Circus.

Dymchurch is a small seaside resort which at first sight might appear as new as Littlestone, and the very first time I visited it I asked to be directed to the New Hall. We arrived at a new hall, quite recently erected almost on the "sea-front"—that is, on the level of the Wall, because Dymchurch has no sea-front except the Wall. But this was certainly not the New Hall, although a great many trippers and holiday-makers could direct us to nothing else. Eventually we found it a few hundred yards farther on, only to discover that the building was new in the fifteenth century, when it replaced a much older building which was partially destroyed by fire. Some of the old charred beams are actually built into the New Hall.

It was here that century after century the Court of the Lords, Bailiffs, and Jurats of Romney Marsh sat. For more than a thousand years the Lords of Romney Marsh were holders of twenty-three proud and ancient titles held on the gift of the King. Since the early-thirteenth century the Grand Lathe has been held in Whit-week so that the Lords might appoint a Bailiff and Jurats. But in 1951 the Lords of Blackmanstone, Bilsington, Burmarsh, Eastbridge, Honeychild, Orlestone, Snave,

Warehorne and Willop had assembled as of old and re-elected Major M. Teichman-Derville, Lord of Eastbridge, as Bailiff. It was a sad occasion, for the first duty of the Bailiff was to inform his brethren that the Bailiff of Romney Marsh had no longer any power as of old. By Act of Parliament they had been divested of their last privileges, and from October 1st the justices were to be appointed by the Lord Chancellor. No longer would one of their number hand to the King his cup on Whit Sunday, or be responsible for providing him with a sparrowhawk at Lammas. The Court sat for the last time on September 5th 1951, and thus came to an end the most ancient and most important body associated with The Marsh. For their first charge from the King was the care of the land, and it was they who were responsible for the provision and upkeep of walls and waterways. They preserved the new-found land and by protecting it made possible the reclamation of more. Thus they were both creators and protectors.

There are some interesting relics preserved in the New Hall: neolithic implements; a fifteenth-century chair in the Court Room; a seventeenth-century wine jar which was washed up on the coast; numerous coins, maps, a magnificent array of standard weights and measures in copper and brass, and the Romney Marsh Corporation Bowl of 1822. This bowl is rather lovely, with roses and scenes of coursing and ploughing. One of its couplets reads:

"He that by the plough would thrive
Himself must either hold or drive."

Perhaps nothing is better known than or makes so immediate an appeal to the holiday-maker as the miniature railway which runs between Hythe and Dungeness through Dymchurch and New Romney. It is pretty true to say there is nothing like it in the world, and it certainly claims to be the "World's Smallest Public Railway". It is popularly known as the "Line that Jack built" because originally the idea of building this railway was that of Captain J. E. P. Howey and his friend Count Zborowski. Both were world-famous as racing motorists, but privately they were miniature-railway enthusiasts, and they had determined that upon ending their racing careers they would lay down a public railway using a fifteen-inch gauge. In his last race at Turin Count Zborowski was killed, but Captain Howey carried out the idea alone.

It so happened that just at this time the Southern Railway, that was, were considering an extension of their line, from Apple-dore to New Romney, on to Hythe. It came about that Sir Herbert Walker, General Manager of S.R., offered the route to Captain Howey with a promise of full support and no opposition. It was a really wonderful bargain, for not only did it relieve the S.R. of the responsibility of running and the cost of this extension, but it gave to the miniature enthusiast a remarkable opportunity to build a line on almost dead-level country and at a place on the coast not only where there was a real need for transport but where novel means would be a special attraction to holiday-makers.

Eight miles of track were originally laid down between Hythe and New Romney, all done by labour hired on the spot. There were no real engineering feats except the crossing of innumerable dykes, though of course the canal was a big obstacle. This was bridged by a lattice girder structure which was actually built in six days! The rush was in order that it might be completed in time for King George VI, then Duke of York, who expressed a wish to drive a train over the railway while he was on a visit to the boys' camp at Dymchurch, a camp in which he took so great an interest. As the Guide published by Ian Allan proudly records: "The railway people saw to it that his wish was gratified, well before the opening of the line for general traffic." The bridge is still known as the Duke of York's bridge.

The line was opened in June 1927. But two years later it was extended to Dungeness and now the track is fourteen miles long and the number of passengers carried per annum is 325,000. No freight or mail are carried, and the railway only runs in the summer months from March to the end of September, but it has certainly justified its existence. During the war one of the loco-motives was armoured and, mounting an A.A. gun, patrolled this very important and vulnerable coastline. The little railway also played its part in assembling much of the apparatus and materials for the delivery end of "Pluto", which left the coast near Dungeness.

The railway is equipped with some really beautiful rolling stock. Originally passengers travelled in open four-wheel trucks, but now "Pullman" coaches, streamlined, sprung, well upholstered and with plate-glass windows, make travelling comfortable as well as novel. But of course what really appeals most to everyone and in particular to the miniature enthusiast are the engines. The company has ten steam locomotives and one petrol driven. They are mostly of the 4–6–2 type built between 1925 and 1931. Although the track gauge is approximately one-quarter standard gauge, the locomotives are built on a scale of four inches to the foot, or one-third full size. Five of them are scale models of the L.N.E.R. "Pacifics" and were built by Davey-Paxman Ltd, of Colchester. The engines and tenders weigh about 8 tons. Two others, "Winston Churchill" and "Doctor Syn", are modelled on the Canadian Pacific locomotives type 2–8–2, and were built by the Yorkshire Engine Company, of Sheffield.

Readers of the famous Dr Syn stories will be interested to know that the ship the *City of London* which figures largely in one of them was wrecked off Dymchurch, and its figurehead may still be seen in a yard just outside the village. And talking of ships reminds us of the long association which Dymchurch men have had with the sea, not only on their lawful occasions, but unlawfully. From very early times men along these coasts, being so near to France—only thirty miles or so—have engaged in illegal trade with the Continent. Their expert knowledge of the coast on both sides of the Channel, of the run of the tides and currents and their experienced seamanship enabled them both to run to and fro in their little ships with speed and cunning and to defy arrest with skill and daring.

The earliest form of organised smuggling was known as "owling" and concerned itself with the running of English wool to the Continent against the various restrictions and duties placed upon it. The fact that sheep-farming on The Marsh was rapidly expanding added impetus to the traffic, but it was probably the deep resentment felt against foreign speculators, to whom the customs were farmed, that drove English farmers, merchants and seamen into the "business". It was extremely galling to Englishmen to have to pay heavy dues while foreign merchants were granted exemptions and carried their goods, and ours, to and fro duty free. Dymchurch, Rye, Lydd and Winchelsea all experienced the aggravation of privileged foreigners in their midst.

Later, towards the end of the seventeenth century, with customs duties considerably increased on numerous imports, the smuggling of goods into the country started a much more unpleasant, ugly and dangerous traffic. All the coastlands of Kent and Sussex experienced its tyranny. It was in fact almost impossible for anyone living within a mile or two of the coast to escape becoming embroiled in the traffic. What the "Gentlemen" would do to gain their ends knew no limits. If the church or the barn, or your stable or your woodlump provided them with what they needed, it was utilised or commandeered. If you complained or obstructed them there was no end to the persecution you would experience. On the other hand, once you connived at their business your mouth was shut.

> "If you do as you've been told, 'likely there's a chance,
> You'll be given a dainty doll, all the way from France,
> With a cap of Valenciennes, and a velvet hood—
> A present from the Gentlemen, along o' being good!
>   Five and twenty ponies
>   Trotting through the dark—
>   Brandy for the Parson,
>   'Baccy for the Clerk;
>   Laces for a lady; letters for a spy,
> And watch the wall, my darling, while the Gentlemen
>   go by!"

Kipling in his Smuggler's Song tends, as so many writers have done, to romanticise the smuggler. Looking back over more than a century and a half it is easy to minimise, overlook or forget his cruelties, murders, dastardly retaliation and merciless tyranny.

His dash and daring, however, his cunning, his secret passages, his caves and caches, all create an aura of romance and adventure which capture, at least, a youthful imagination.

The coast from Hastings to Folkestone, with the desolate stretches of shingle and the wide, open spaces of The Marsh behind it, with its tortuous lanes and tracks, was the ideal terrain of the smuggler. No wonder Dymchurch and Lydd and New Romney and Rye, and indeed almost every village on The Marsh, are full of tales of their nefarious doings. And there are records too of the awful crimes they committed upon those who betrayed them. During the Napoleonic wars it is pretty true to say that the smugglers were "the mainstay of the French espionage system".

It was not easy to stamp out. While smugglers were commonly hanged if they forcibly resisted—until less than a hundred years ago a gibbet stood in Dymchurch where the war memorial now stands—the usual punishment was transportation or navy service. This, however, was rather like throwing Brer Rabbit into the bramble bush. For on the voyage out to the penal settlement the smuggler proved of such value as a seaman that it was no uncommon thing for him to be made use of on the return journey; thus he frequently gained his freedom and his home port. Similarly in the navy his skill in sail and his experienced seamanship rapidly brought him promotion above the average pressed man, and thus instead of punishment he gained distinction.

Out on The Marsh some of the lonely churches where contraband was not infrequently hidden still remain. Some of the great wine cellars which served the same purpose both in Rye and Winchelsea may still be inspected, and in Dymchurch the Smugglers' Inn, while not living up to its name, still does big business attracting visitors and tourists as much by its comfort and service as by its name, its stories and its legends.

Not far away are the last crumbling ruins of the church of Hope All Saints, one of the five churches New Romney possessed in pre-Reformation days. But it had long fallen into decay, and the smugglers found the lonely and deserted spot admirably suited them as a meeting place. But a story is told of how a Preventive

Officer, one tempestuous night, hiding himself by lying along the top of the ruined and weed-grown walls, overheard the plans for the running of contraband goods and thus successfully rounded up both gang and cargo.

Of all the five churches of New Romney only St Nicholas now stands. It was built in the late-eleventh century. To it the ships of the Cinque Port tied up. It withstood the hurricanes of the thirteenth century, and, as we have seen, so much debris was piled up around it that today its floor is still several feet below road level. In early days churches were commonly used for civic functions, and St Nicholas was no exception. The "election of the Mayor, the granting of the Freedom, the regular sessions of the Jurats and the Annual Cinque Port Meetings were usually held in it as the most convenient place for such gatherings". Major M. Teichman-Derville in his booklet "The Town and Port of New Romney" continues:

> "The use of our church for civil functions was not without its drawbacks to the officiating clergy, and in 1407 there is an entry of a receipt of a free gift of 3/4 from John Haccke, the vicar of Romene with a request 'that the Jurats in future shall not hold their session in his church, at the same time as Divine Service is being celebrated'."

It would require a complete volume to write all of what is known about New Romney, and that would not be half of its long history. As one of the original Cinque Ports it had the special advantage of being in their midst, for Hastings and the two Ancient Towns, Rye and Winchelsea, stood to the west, while Hythe, Dover and Sandwich lay to the east. It was natural therefore that many of the meetings of the Cinque Ports, the Brotherhood and the Guestling should be held there. Hence records and insignia, documents and banner, reposed there in the custody of the Mayor. As Teichman-Derville says:

> "No longer do the spires of three parish churches rise above New Romney, or its five windmills stand out against the sky; gone is our Market Cross, our old Town Hall, and all the pomp

and circumstance of our Cinque Port pageantry. But for all that we can still retain, and we ought to retain our pride in our old Town. . . . And let me remind you we have something else left to us besides our pride, something more tangible perhaps, but, unfortunately, more perishable. Though so much has disappeared, and the receding sea has rendered our once famous harbour but a memory, I would like to impress upon the people of Romney that they still have left to them what is probably one of the finest collections of records in existence, and to urge upon them their duty to take steps to preserve for future generations this unique heritage, almost the last remaining relic of our former greatness and our glorious past."

The iron chest made a century ago reposes in New Romney's Town Hall. It has two locks, and one key is held by the Mayor and the other by the Solicitors of the Ports. In it are kept many of the famous documents, the Black and the White Books which record the minutes of annual meetings of the Ports since the fourteenth century, and the forty-two diaries which record all matters relating to the Annual Herring Fair at Yarmouth. This chest also used to contain the original Cinque Ports banner, but the flag was discovered recently to be in such a dilapidated condition that it had to be restored, and it now hangs in the Cinque Port Hall at Dover. Teichman-Derville has been Mayor of New Romney times almost without number, and he has indeed played a conspicuous part in restoring and maintaining the dignity of this ancient town which has figured so bravely in English history. Yet in spite of all he has done it has been his unhappy lot to see Parliament sweep away the last vestiges of all the quaint, picturesque, honourable and historic rights, privileges and powers that were once vested in it. Let us hope that his impassioned plea for the preservation of that wonderful collection of records and documents may not fall on deaf ears.

Romney has had its own river, its own port, its own fleet. It was one of the original Cinque Ports. It has had its own Royal Charters, its incorporation, its seals, its own mint. It was granted its commission of sewers, sent two representatives to Parliament. Boasted five churches and five windmills. It had innumerable taverns, a ducking stool for "common scolds", a keeper of rabbits on the Warren, a dog whipper, a boy-bishop, its racecourse, a selected band called the New Romney Fencible Cavalry, and a law that any person caught for the third time cutting down a tree should be punished with death.

★   ★   ★   ★   ★

As we have seen, coastal defence and drainage of The Marsh have been the two fundamental tasks of the Marshmen. The new Pett wall, the defences east of Camber, and the Dymchurch wall are the present-day answer to the first; and there is no doubt whatever that never before in its history has The Marsh been so stoutly protected against the sea. Great storms can do terrible damage, even to concrete, as the heavy seas early in 1952 demonstrated alarmingly just east of Dymchurch. But the scotpayers—all those who occupy the low lands of the levels and pay wall scot—must feel satisfied and sleep easier than they have done for many centuries.

Drainage is a matter to which attention must continually be given. A well-constructed modern concrete wall can stand for many years with little or no attention; but a dyke, a channel, a sluice, a pump can rarely be left untended for long. Banks cave in, silt fills, debris blocks, and a man must be standing by to bring the pumps into action at a moment's notice. Almost the whole of The Marsh lies below high-water mark, but most of it is above low-water mark. Hence it is possible to drain water off the levels to the sea for five or six hours in every twelve, and automatically working sluices at several points along the coast perform this function. But the problem is complicated by the fact that The Marsh does not tilt towards the sea; instead the lowest levels are those most remote from the coast. The Dowels area, near Appledore, is so low that it is not possible to drain water from it by a natural fall, and until recent years this has always been the real marsh in The Marsh.

Little did Mr Pitt—I like this way in which a certain worthy in Rye described the great statesman as if he had known him all his life—little did Mr Pitt realise when he constructed his Royal Military Canal in 1804, as a defence measure against an invasion by Napoleon, that it would help to solve the drainage problem. The canal runs from Hythe to the Rother, a distance of some twenty-three miles. It was so constructed that artillery could be placed to cover every yard of it. No doubt if "Boney" had risked all and landed as anticipated between Fairlight and Folkestone the canal might have proved a very formidable obstacle. And Hitler too, had he dared, might have found his tanks badly bogged down in some of its deceptively shallow-looking reed-filled reaches. All was prepared for them, but neither corporal would or could take the plunge. So the Royal Military Canal served as the Martello towers and as the "humpies" and the block-houses of our own time served, only to stand and wait.

Before the railways were constructed the canal proved useful during the first half of the nineteenth century for the transport of coal and other heavy goods by barge between Hythe and Rye. It is not all reed-choked; some of it today is clear and very lovely, especially through and near Hythe—they hold a Venetian Carnival upon it every year—and at West Hythe near Stutfall Castle beneath the heights of Lympne. Part of it near Appledore is in National Trust, and it is said to be excellent for coarse angling. Yet in spite of these things it is its function in the system of drainage that has proved of greatest value.

The Kent Rivers Catchment Board has control over the whole of the canal from Hythe to Iden Lock where it joins the Rother, and with the three Internal Drainage Boards of Romney Marsh Level, Denge and Southbrooks, and the Level of New Romney is responsible for the whole extensive triangle of land east of the Rhee Wall. Its chief problem is the low-lying area of some 4,250 acres east of Appledore and mainly south of the canal. The Dowels, which comprises some 650 acres, would be a permanent lake without pumping, and after heavy rain most of the remaining 3,600 acres would be waterlogged for days. For many years there has been an old steam-driven centrifugal pump at Appledore, and while it did at least save the Dowels from becoming a lake it could neither cope adequately with the volume of water nor be brought into action at a moment's notice. But just before the war a modern installation was established at

Kenardington about two miles away. This comprised two horizontal screw-type Gwynne pumps, with Diesel engines generating some 130–150 horsepower each.

These pumps, in the charge of Mr C. J. King, are extremely efficient. They raise the water from drainage channels and deliver it into the Royal Military Canal at the astonishing rate of 8,500 gallons per minute per pump. They have the advantage in an emergency of being set in motion at a moment's notice. Little can go wrong with them, though one afternoon when I was inspecting they had had some trouble, for a piece of timber had floated up the sewer and by unlucky chance had passed through the steel grill protecting the intake and had damaged the flange. Eels are the only other things which caused a nuisance by slipping through the grill and being drawn to the intake.

The Kenardington Pumping Station has been so satisfactory both as regards drainage and the control it puts into the hands of the Catchment Board that it was decided after the war to replace the old steam pump at Appledore by a similar modern installation. I have seen this new pumping station and it certainly is a show piece. Mr R. F. Browing, who was originally in charge of the old pump, has transferred to the new as to a seventh heaven. The only trouble he had was the astounding quantity of water weed which, brought by the flow of water along the "rivers" and sewers, piled up on the grill before his intakes. This water weed was chiefly Canadian pondweed, potomageton and duckweed, but it accumulated in such masses as to prevent the proper flow of water to the pumps and had continuously to be removed by rake and pitchfork. Neither Browing nor King had ever experienced such quantity before 1951.

These two pumping stations, which are continuously manned, are capable when going all out of delivering to the Royal Military Canal some 35,000 gallons a minute, or two million gallons an hour, from the lowlands. This means really efficient drainage and has already transformed the marshy areas. All the water discharged into the canal, throughout its length, flows eastwards and enters the sea by a specially constructed waterway known as the Canal Cut near Hythe.

The canal, however, is more than a drainage channel. It has come to be regarded in recent years as a very important reservoir. A joint scheme has been carried out by the Catchment Board and the Romney Marsh Level Internal Drainage Board whereby early spring flood water can be impounded in the canal and later fed through pipes into the watercourses supplying The Marsh. This appears another paradox. Why feed water to the marshlands when every effort seems to have been made to drain it? But if you have borne with me so far you will understand the apparent contradiction. For in the first place, all The Marsh lies below high-water mark; if special efforts were not made to drain surplus water the whole would soon be a marsh and some of it permanent water. In the second, as the rainfall is light—only twenty-six inches, of which the loss from evaporation is twenty-one inches—it is essential, if the ground is not to dry out, to control the water level in the watercourses. Hence drainage and water level go hand in hand, and the twenty-three miles of Mr Pitt's canal function as a great sewer carrying flood water to the sea in impressive volume during winter and spring, but from April to August serve as a not inconsiderable reservoir supplying water to maintain an adequate level wherever it may be needed.

The whole complicated business of water-level control—I don't know how many hundreds of miles of waterlets there are in The Marsh—is under the most efficient and sensitive control. There are some seventy points of main control and a great many more operated by farmers on their own land. There is of course some difficulty when adjoining landowners may be using their land differently. For example if one is a grazier and the other an arable farmer the water-level requirements are different, for the arable farmer requires a lower level for his crops than the sheep-farmer does for his pastures. Thus there is a conflict of interests, and when the same channels supply both there can be complaints. Furthermore, if the water falls so low that the sewers and channels dry out, then the "wet fences" no longer function and the sheep stray and get among the crops. The grazier might regard this as poetic justice. But the Agricultural Land Commission in their Investigation declare: "In our view, however, it is too much to expect a drainage channel in all seasons to perform the dual role of drain and fence. In the interests of food production the grazier must, where necessary, provide fencing."

The Report goes on to make the following most interesting suggestion:

"Although the two Catchment Boards maintain a water level generally satisfactory to both the grazier and the arable farmer, this level has been determined empirically over a period of years. No attempt is made to vary it to suit a particular type of soil or a particular crop, and indeed there is little or no scientific evidence on which such variation could be made. We feel that in Romney Marsh where drainage is so much under man's control there are facilities for conducting experiments on the water level appropriate to different types of soils and crops. The information so gained would be of considerable scientific and practical value. Work on these lines has, we believe, already begun in Holland and we recommend that consideration should be given to the possibility of undertaking similar experimental work in Romney Marsh in which the drainage engineer, the scientist and the farmer could co-operate."

★　　★　　★　　★　　★

While on the subject of watercourses I must mention the matter of the frogs. One would expect that conditions would be ideal for them. So they are, but it is not the common frog that abounds there. It did, but it has been largely replaced in recent years by a new creature, the marsh frog, and as Major Maxwell Knight says: "The history of the introduction of the Marsh Frog into Kent is a striking illustration of what may happen when such experiments are undertaken."

It appears that in 1935 four pairs of this frog were brought to The Marsh and put in a garden pond. Whether the naturalist who did this had ideas of establishing the species there as a new species for Britain or as a local food supply I do not know. In fact there seems not a little controversy on the subject as to whether this frog, *Rana ridibunda*, is or is not a separate species or a variety of *Rana esculenta*, the edible frog. Whatever his intentions, the fact remains that the frogs soon made free of The Marsh. They must have found it amazingly to their liking, in two or three years people were complaining about the noise of their croaking, and today there is nowhere on The Marsh where the din of their chorus is not to be heard during the month of May.

It is a biggish frog and the male has inflatable vocal sacs. These "blow out" to about the size of an acorn and enable him to produce a croak that can be heard half a mile away on a still night. It is not easy to describe its colour, because it has the ability to change its colour to harmonise with its immediate surroundings. Thus it can be bright green at one time and dull browns and greys another. The squarish spots on the legs are characteristic, but it is by its behaviour that one can immediately recognise it. For it has the habit on sunny days of coming out of the water and squatting along the banks and dykes, never too far from the water. Immediately it is alarmed it leaps straight into the ditch with a loud plop.

The first time I met them was at East Guldeford. I had been looking at and photographing the quaint old double-barn-like church of St Mary's and had then taken a walk out across the grassy plains, so breezy and so like the South Downs. But inevitably my way ran along the edge of a watercourse, and to my growing astonishment I kept hearing a continuous plop, plop in front of me. At first I thought it was fish leaping or a water vole, and then, on more cautious walking and sharper observation, I saw that the noise was made by frogs leaping swiftly and cleanly straight from the bank into mid-channel. Plop, plop, plop. Once one knew what to look for it was fascinating to watch these creatures. There seemed to be an endless procession of them; all the time I kept walking so they leapt off the bank in front of me. They were most extraordinarily alert, and to try to approach one closely without it flying into the water was almost an impossibility. A long-handled butterfly net was needed to catch one.

The people of The Marsh don't like them. "Horrible things," said one farmer; "they're a curse." He could not really explain why, he just detested them, perhaps because they were strangers. It may be the noise too that adds to their dislike, for the males certainly do make an astonishing din at night during May. But there may be good reasons, not yet completely understood, which may prove their dislike not ill-founded. The marsh frog, unlike the common frog, remains very close to water. He never seems to wander "inland" beyond the banks of his watercourse and so he is not keeping down slugs and other pests which the common frog does with diligence. Furthermore, in the water the marsh frog is a voracious animal and includes in its enormous and varied menu the tadpoles of the common frog. Thus it neither does the good work of the common frog nor allows that frog to live. One good point in its favour is the fact that it consumes enormous numbers of mosquito larvæ. The diminution of this pest is already noticeable, but it will be some years yet before we know if the marsh frog is doing more harm than good.

★   ★   ★   ★   ★

The mention of a butterfly net which was necessary to capture a specimen of the marsh frog reminds me of the interesting fact that this part of the English coast has a special interest for the entomologist. Just as birds have made use of the Foreland as an arrival point when on their spring migrations to this country, so do immigrant butterflies often make their landfall between the cliffs of Fairlight and Folkestone. It comes as something of a surprise to many people that butterflies migrate at all, and although the fact was noted more than fifty years ago, it is only in the last decade or so that any real knowledge has been acquired. Quite a number of our butterflies and moths are migrant species, that is to say we should not see them at all were it not for their fairly regular arrival every spring. The painted lady, the clouded yellow and the red admiral immediately come to mind as immigrant butterflies. The time of their arrival varies considerably, as do their numbers, but the usual course is for a few of these butterflies to arrive in April or May. Most of these are mated females which soon lay their eggs and die. Thistle, clover and nettles are the common food plants, and thus we soon have a British-born-and-bred series of these butterflies. Except in the rarest instances few of these ever over-winter in Britain, and while there is a feeble effort at a return migration, most die here and we have to await new supplies the following spring.

199

These butterflies come from Mediterranean lands, chiefly North Africa. They breed continuously—there is not a long winter pause as in this country—often in enormous numbers, and it appears that in a very dry season or following a heat wave, there being little or no food plant left, the butterflies set out, occasionally in vast swarms, for fresh pastures. The movement is northward, sometimes the insects taking a mid-European route, sometimes taking a west-coast route via Spain and the Biscayan coast.

By the time they have crossed the Channel the swarms have usually tailed out, but there have been several notable occasions when the butterflies have arrived in a spectacular manner. During the war there was a sensational alert on board one of H.M. warships when a curious yellow cloud was observed moving over the sea. The alarm was sounded as it was believed to be a poison gas attack. One can imagine the anti-climax in the ward-room when the "gas" was discovered to be an enormous swarm of clouded yellow butterflies on migration. On another occasion the large cabbage white butterfly crossed from France in vast numbers and made their landfall at Bournemouth, where they came in like a snowstorm, sitting on everything and everybody, particularly the red coats of the bandsmen.

One of the most interesting butterfly invasions was that of the painted lady in 1952. This was unusual because it took place so early in the year, from February 21st to March 23rd. During all the time that records have been kept the total of all painted ladies seen in February is only ten, and the total for March is one hundred and nineteen. Yet in this remarkable invasion in 1952 more than nine hundred and fifty insects were reported, before a raging snowstorm brought the movement to a complete stand-still. The invasion was on a wide front, stretching from Bradwell-on-Sea in Essex to Bantry in County Cork, but the focal point was Pett Level. It was here that R. Cooke saw the first one on February 21st, and from then on for four weeks the butterflies continued to arrive, not en masse but in a steady stream. Some 270 records from East Sussex alone were received by Captain T. Dannreuther, who was then the Hon. Sec. of the Insect

Immigration Committee. When one remembers how few people take note of or identify a butterfly when they see one, and then again how few will take the trouble to fill in a report card and post it, it is fairly accurate to say that for every insect recorded at least a hundred passed by unobserved. This would put the invasion swarm at about 100,000 butterflies. Some observers rate this much too low and estimate that for every insect recorded a thousand pass unobserved. This would put the horde of invaders up to the million mark. Something between the two is probably correct.

I have been down on Dungeness during August and seen the large white or cabbage white butterfly coming in over the sea in a steady stream. It was surprising how close to the water they flew, but no doubt they quickly find, as birds do, that there is much less wind resistance at wave-top level. Butterflies are not dependent on the wind for their migratory flights, and in fact those that I saw coming in to the Foreland were travelling across wind. They did not seem very exhausted: some rested briefly on the shingle, but most kept on, travelling aslant the beach, and so inland. I counted an average of five a minute, three hundred an hour. If this was going on on such a narrow front as from Hythe to Pett alone, their numbers must have been hundreds of thousands every day. This particular migration went on for many weeks.

Quite a number of moths on the British list are also migrants, and while some are insignificant looking and of little interest except to the entomologist, several are magnificent insects. The death's head hawk and the convolvulus hawk, both some five inches across the wings and our largest moths, are migrants. The first arrives in early summer and eggs are laid on potato plants. The caterpillars hide during the day and are not often seen, but when the potatoes are lifted the pupæ are not infrequently found by the harvesters. The year 1950 was a good one and pupæ were found on many potato fields on The Marsh. None of these would ordinarily survive the winter, but they can be forced out if subjected to a high temperature. Larvæ of the convolvulus hawk are rarely found, but this moth is more often seen, especially in gardens where the sweet tobacco, nicotiana, is grown. The flowers of this plant open in the evening, and its nectar is secreted at the end of a very long tube. No ordinary moth has a tongue long enough to reach down to the nectar, but the proboscis of the convolvulus hawk is some three inches long, and thus it can do so with ease while hovering on rapidly beating wings before the blossom. As the moth is on the wing only at twilight it is the sole pollinator of the tobacco plant.

The best-known migrant moth is the little humming-bird hawk. No visitor to the beachlands where the viper's bugloss is in flower can fail to observe this fascinating insect as it darts from flower to flower, hovering before each and darting its long tongue into the blossoms. That of course is in a good year. Some years go by when scarcely an insect is reported, and then comes an outstanding year when immigrant moths come in vast swarms. The experts are kept busy explaining again and again that the little creature which flies in brilliant sunshine, which thrusts its slender "beak" into the flowers, which "hums" as it hovers, which has orange-coloured wings (the hind wings are amber coloured), is *not* a bird, but a moth which takes its name from the humming bird.

★　　★　　★　　★　　★

It is a far cry from moths to churches, and I may be justly censured for leaving all proper mention of the churches of The Marsh until my last pages. But, gentle reader, this is not really so, for from the first chapter to the last the great churches of The Marsh stand out, as in fact they actually do above the levels, as landmarks in time and space and history. It was the labours of the Church that showed the way and commenced the reclamation of The Marsh and the creation of new land. The monks of Canterbury and the Abbey of Fécamp worked diligently not only for the souls of men but for their material welfare. Where new land was won a church to the glory of God would be built. Thus all across The Marsh from Hythe through Romney Marsh, through Walland Marsh, through Guldeford Marsh to Rye and on to Winchelsea there are more churches than one might find in an equal area anywhere else in Britain.

The number of these churches, and the size of some of them, has given rise to the idea that The Marsh was much more heavily populated than it is today. Except for the Ports this is very unlikely, and it seems more probable that many of the churches which stand so lonely on the windy levels were erected not for the needs of a population but as an act of thanksgiving, or maybe as a gesture or under covenant to the Church by the new-land tenant.

The population of the Ports, at their prime, was much higher than today. Old Winchelsea must have had a population of nearly 5,000, Rye and New Romney about half this figure, and Hythe too, before the plague wiped out nearly half its inhabitants, was a good-sized port. In all these four towns, and Lydd makes a fifth, great churches, almost of cathedral size, were built. Old Winchelsea was destroyed, but the plan for the church of St Thomas on the new site was for a vast building. In the lay-out for the new town a central square of more than two acres was reserved for the church. According to many antiquarians it was never completed, but in the light of excavations that have been made it seems pretty certain that the foundations of the nave were laid. When some sixty years ago a grave was being dug near what would have been the west door of the nave, "portions of a pavement of tiles were discovered", and Mr J. D. H. Patch believed that "As one may safely presume that the floor would be the last thing to be done, this almost seems to prove that the nave did once exist." The fact that Winchelsea suffered so severely from attacks by the French might well account for the partial destruction of the building in 1380; on the other hand it has been suggested that the Black Death so completely wiped out the labourers that building was halted and that by the time the effects of this disaster had been made good the prosperity of Winchelsea was no more.

There used to be a detached campanile on the south-west of the church until 1790, but when this was dismantled it is said that "the stones and the foundations of the nave were sold for the repairs of Rye Harbour". All that now stands is the original chancel and its two side-chapels. On the south side is the Alard

Chantry, in which the centre monument was erected to the memory of Gervase Alard, who, as we have seen, was the first Englishman to bear the title of Admiral of the Fleet, and he was at the same time Warden of the Cinque Ports. The western monument is believed to be that of Stephen Alard, who was also Admiral and Warden during the reign of Edward II.

In the north aisle is the Farncombe Chantry, which contains three monuments. It is not certain whom they commemorate, but the figures are said "to be of a date anterior to the building of the church, and according to tradition were brought here from the Church of Old Winchelsea" (Patch). On the pillars of this aisle are crosses cut by Crusaders after their return from the Holy Land. However imposing, however beautiful, however merited the magnificent tombs in these two aisles, there is something about these Crusaders' crosses which catches the heart and fires the imagination. The tombs were built to the memory of the great, but these crosses were cut by the very hand of those who had fulfilled their vows, who had undertaken the arduous and dangerous journey, who had done their best to save the Holy Places and who had come back safely home to their own beloved land, to their kith and kin, and in the blessed peace of their own church had made their mark.

I have mentioned many times St Mary's, Rye, capping the hill with its battlemented tower and embodying in its structure many styles as the result of repeated repairs. In spite of damage and disaster, sacrilege and theft, it still stands complete, massive, majestic, dominating the Ancient Town, yet it is kindly, serenely mothering the clustering little houses which snuggle higgledy-piggledy around her ancient walls.

From the top of the old and sturdy battlements one can see away across the windy levels the great tower of All Saints, Lydd. This thirteenth-century church, more deservedly than any other, is known as the Cathedral of The Marsh. It is said to be the longest church in Kent, nearly 200 feet; and the tower, built in the fifteenth century by Wolsey when he was rector here and some years before he became Cardinal, is 132 feet high. It was the fate of this church to stand for seven hundred years amid all "this strange eventful history" and to come through almost unscathed, only, on the 15th October, 1940, to receive a direct hit from a German high-explosive bomb. It fell almost exactly upon the high altar, and the chancel was destroyed. Flying bombs, of which The Marsh had a terrible share, added to the damage. To reduce the cost of repairs a suggestion was made that the church might well be shortened, by approximately the length of the ruined chancel. But this was not at all to the liking of the people of Lydd. Their hearts were set upon the restoration of their great church in its entirety. The Borough of Lydd has about 3,000 inhabitants today, and they are no longer the wealthy wool merchants of Wolsey's day. For without doubt Lydd church was a "wool church", like many of those in the Cotswolds, having been built out of the fortunes of those who made money during the twelfth, thirteenth and fourteenth centuries when English wool had a limitless market. There is an old saying, "Romney for pride and Lydd for money". It is hardly true these days, for the people of Lydd have their pride, and what little money they have to spare they are determined shall rebuild the church—and they have succeeded.

Although Lydd suffered during the war and was often a target for enemy bombers it did nevertheless hit back, and in a most remarkable manner. When that extraordinary and ingenious idea of a pipe-line under the ocean, Pluto, became a reality it was from Dungeness that the pipe left the shores of England. Jerry, who undoubtedly knew that such an operation was afoot, was completely foxed about its position, and as far as can be ascertained was under the impression that our end of the pipe was in the Southampton neighbourhood. Little did he know that it was as near as Lydd, but this was due to the ingenuity and cunning of our planners and engineers. Huts, evacuated bungalows, a shingle works, housed the machinery and pumps; no new buildings attracted the eye of the enemy, no secret was better kept. Although there was a period when "the pipe" was leaking at the rate of thousands of gallons a day and a big area of the beachlands was saturated in petrol, no great harm was done, and Lydd eventually had the satisfaction of knowing that millions of gallons were pumped across to France to our invading armies, to hasten the liberation, to hasten the destruction of the doodle-bugs and rocket sites, to bring a speedy and glorious victory.

Lydd's great tower was undamaged by the bombing, and from its highest pinnacle one has an amazing view. There is the vista of the green Marsh stretching away to the hazy line of distant hills. There are the beachlands, a strange vast desert of shingle, arid and dreary under a midday sun or on a winter's day, but full of magical lights and colours on a June morning or a golden September evening. And there is the sea, a blue riband seeming to run halfway round the horizon. One can dream up here of days of long ago; for a moment one can enter the lives of those who crouched here against the screaming weather and peered out over the sea for sight of enemy sail. One catches Wolsey's pride when the work was finished and he stood here inspired, elated, ambitious. And the Time Machine works, and one travels back more than a thousand years, when a little Saxon church stood on this very spot, an island in a bay of mud-flats and shallows, beach and shingle spits, when the longships of the Danes came sliding up the creeks, and bloody battles were fought on the Holmstone and the Wicks.

St Nicholas church of New Romney has already figured largely in these pages, so let us take one glance at the fourth of the great churches of The Marsh, at Hythe. This remarkable edifice was originally built in 1100, but the magnificent chancel was added a century later. It might perhaps be described as a "herring church", built at the time the Cinque Ports were at their prime, though it is probable spoils of war brought as much wealth as the harvest of the sea. Unlike the other churches of the levels, this one is built on the hillside. Without one is struck by the fine buttresses and within by the remarkable difference in levels, which greatly enhances the high chancel. The thousand-odd skulls stacked tidily in the crypt are something of a puzzle. Because some of them are splintered or broken it has been suggested that they are the grisly remains of those who fell in battle. Other theories are that they were victims of the plague, buried in a common grave, which when unearthed were given resting place here. Alternatively they may be the remains of past generations, from a forgotten burial ground, and in fact there is said to be a very close resemblance to skulls found among Roman remains in London. Thus they might date to the days of the Roman occupation or the centuries immediately following.

Three miles to the west of Hythe are the ruins of the Roman fort which commanded the ancient port of Lemanis. It is known today as Stutfall Castle and lies on the slope of the hills which lead up steeply to their highest point where Lympne stands today. The ruins are not exactly impressive and they are not to be compared with the fine walls of Roman Pevensey. But they have an air of remoteness which is hard to define. Roman buildings, all over Britain and the Continent, are often striking on account of their everlastingness, their durability—monuments to people who built with never a thought for a decline and fall. Stutfall, the first perhaps of Roman forts ever to be built in Britain, was without doubt built with the same thoroughness as any other castra. What remains of the walls shows the same efficient use of brick, stone and mortar. But it is all awry. It is the site, not the masonry that has failed. There seem to have been landslides, as if the hill or terrace upon which the fort originally stood had slipped towards the levels, tearing the walls asunder and carrying them with it in crazy disorder. The ruins give the impression that the fort was built on a sloping hillside. How far the greatness of Rome seems away! What a vast bracket of time spans the days when these walls were built and today, when the jet planes leap from the airfield on the heights above!

Lympne airport has had an importance of its own. Many historic solo flights started from here: C. W. A. Scott to Darwin, Mollison to Cape Town, Jean Batten to Australia. It was bombed in 1940 and fell into desuetude. But recently it has become important and in 1969 the Rt. Hon. Edward Heath re-named it Ashford Airport.

But I have digressed. As if it were a stepping-stone between two thousand years, on the edge of the heights, stands Lympne church, of Norman origin. Behind it is the airfield, below it Stutfall Castle, and from the edge of its graveyard there is what I believe to be the most wonderful view of The Marsh to be seen anywhere. On the Isle of Oxney one is centrally placed, but here on the heights of Lympne one is nearly three times as high, and the whole expanse westwards reaches in fantastic mosaic to the horizon. And all across these long and windy levels are dotted the many other churches of The Marsh. What can I say about them that has not already been said a dozen times before? Of Ivey Church, where there is a priest's chamber above the south porch, a room where the visiting priest could spend the night. Of St Eanswythe, Brenzett, where the green woodpecker laughs all day, and near the entrance to which a little old tarred cottage, in a garden gay with flowers, hoists a television aerial. Of St Dunstans, Snargate, which in common with many other churches of the levels has plaques bearing texts to decorate its moulding walls, one plaque reading, "These sentences were erected in 1794 by Willm Bourne Junr. Churchwarden." Of Brookland, with its extraordinary bell tower of tarred oak, standing apart, detached from the church, and said to have fallen off in sheer astonishment on the day that a virgin came as a bride. Of St Mary's, East Guldeford, like a barn by the dyke, where the marsh frog croaks, with its blue comfrey and periwinkle, toadflax and mullein, strawberry and columbine springing from its cracking, crumbling walls. Of St Mary's, Stone-in-Oxney, which possesses a Roman altar which it has been suggested came originally from the fort at Lympne—Stutfall Castle. What impressed me was the likeness of this altar to one which I saw excavated on the site of a Roman fort at Bewcastle, four hundred miles across the kingdom on the Scottish borders of Cumbria.

But what can I say of these churches? Apart from the five great churches of the Ports I was saddened by them. Many were in a grievous state of decay. There were mould and mess, damp and mildew, chill and sadness. In one, which I will not name and which was in a particularly bad state, I came across a text-bearing plaque in the midst of bird droppings and mildew: "He was afraid and said how dreadful is this place. This is none other than the house of God and this is the gate of heaven."

Chapter XI

...AND TOMORROW

What does the future hold for The Marsh? He would indeed be a bold man who attempted to prophecy. Why even Puck failed me! Not a word did he say to me when I first took that adventurous journey by train to explore the Sixth Continent that twenty years afterwards some of the very line, the *permanent* way, over which I travelled would be ripped up, and gone for ever the delight of travelling from Appledore to New Romney—third class; that famed "Winchelsea", the station with its blue platform lamps, would be a crumbling dereliction; that no steam locomotive would ever more trail its long plume across the breezy levels. Trivial matters indeed—but to me like the handshake of a friend.

And why on earth didn't Puck warn me of the monstrous monstrosity that was going to arise from the lovely flower-decked beaches of Dungeness? A Nuclear Power Station! Ye Gods, surely this was in his line of business. Yet without warning there it stands today, colossal, fantastic, grotesque, towering, complex, glittering, roaring—words fail me. Let me quote from the official handout:

"Como todas las centrales britanicas . . ." Oh, I beg your pardon, I'm in the wrong column. I'll try again: "As in the case of all British stations in the nuclear power programmes planned up to 1962 Dungeness has two natural uranium, carbon dioxide gas cooled graphite moderated reactors. The heat produced by the splitting up of the uranium nuclei is carried away by the carbon dioxide gas passing through the channels in the graphite core which contain the fuel elements. Inside each reactor pressure vessel there are 2,170 tons of graphite, and in the 3,932 channels which run through it there are 294 tons of natural uranium."

Well now you know, or would it have made any difference if I had stuck to the column headed Espanol or Deutsch or Svensk? I'm not really making fun. I'm just knocked silly by the astonishing ingenuity, the complexity, the dazzling science, the intricate engineering of this triumph of British know how. How can I explain it to you? I am dazed by reactors, and carbon dioxide gas blowers, and biological shields, and graphite moderators, boron rods and turbo alternators, protons and neutrons. I dream of "neutrons emerging from the fissioning uranium nuclei at a speed of 10,000 miles a second. . . ." Thank you Central Electricity Generating Board, I loved it all. And gentle reader do not forget that you too can make arrangements for a visit and have the whole box of tricks shown and explained to you.

But was this really the place where I skidded over the shingle on back-stays? Where I heard the clap of a butterfly's wings? Why did it have to be put here? Well according to the C.E.G.B. it is cooling water that comes second after uranium, and the deep water off the Ness was the obvious place where some 21 million gallons *an hour* could be drawn—and discharged.

At first conservationists, marine biologists, ornithologists and environmental pollutionists were seriously concerned at what might be the result of this niagara of warm water. But after sundry alarms and much growth of seaweeds, nothing serious happened, and in fact the turbulence has undoubtedly attracted many seabirds.

But would not this huge edifice—and not only Station A but now also Station B (did I hear Puck whisper "and C")*—would not these acres of glass and steel and concrete, this forest of pylons and cables, interfere with migrating birds? Mr R. L. Scott, warden of the Bird Observatory and the R.S.P.B. Reserve, since 1960, says No. There are casualties of course at the pylons and cables as there are wherever these obstructions lie across the path of night-flying migrants. But the actual flow of birds in and out from the Ness, in their tens of thousands continues unabated and unobstructed.

Apparently the only thing that was obstructed by the Power

*I did indeed catch that whisper aright. The C.E.G.B. is now (1975) seeking permission from the Government to built a third Nuclear Power Station at Dungeness at an estimated cost of £500,000,000.

Station were the beams of the third lighthouse. This was partly the reason for the construction of No. 4—the elegant, ultra-modern, semi-automatic lighthouse standing half a mile to seaward.

And what of the birds? Since the Observatory was first established in 1952 under the wardenship of Bert Axell, and since 1960 under Bob Scott and others, the recording of migratory birds has gone from strength to strength. More than 105,000 migrants have been caught, measured, ringed and released. A Dungeness Robin was recovered in Portugal, a Blackbird in Finland, a Redwing in Moscow, a Lesser Whitethroat in the Lebanon, a Wheatear in Iceland.

But second to none as the work of the Observatory is, to my mind the real importance of what is going on in the Natural History of The Marsh is not only the firm establishment of Reserves, Sanctuaries, and Observation Station, but the remarkable co-operation among farmers and firms, societies and councils, boards and trusts, in a concerted endeavour to ensure a future for its wild life. Much of Walland and Guldeford Marshes have been declared an S.S.S.I., and it is good to know that the C.E.G.B. make a grant to the Observatory and co-operate with the warden, that the Amalgamated Roadstone Corporation, and indeed three other major gravel companies act on suggestions made by the warden and the Nature Conservancy so that their all-but-exhausted gravel pits contain islands and become superb wildfowl reserves.

On the east side of the road from Lydd to Dungeness, adjacent to it, and adjoining the A.R.C.'s works, is a fine example. One windy October day when visiting Bob Scott I watched the birds in this "pit", in reality a shallow mere of many acres and several islands. What an astounding sight! There were hundreds, indeed thousands, of duck of several species, there were at least three hundred oystercatchers, two score Canada geese, innumerable gulls, grebes . . . well it would be tedious to list them all, but how old Mr. Burrowes would have rejoiced in such success coming at last to the beachlands he believed in.

Nor is it only in Kent. On the Sussex side of the Rother, west of Rye Harbour, the old Nook Beach, some 219 hectares, have become an official Local Nature Reserve—the Rye Harbour Local Nature Reserve. Such things are not easy to establish, it takes literally years of effort, much goodwill, enthusiastic co-operation. Dr E. J. Harrison has been the mainspring, his indefatigable labours have brought together land owners, councils, County Council, Sussex Naturalists Trust (now The Sussex Trust for Nature Conservation), Sussex Ornithological Society, Rye Natural History Society, and the Nature Conservancy. Mrs B. Burt, well-known botanist, records some 37 plants of special botanical interest, and the Reserve's Annual Report records 28 migrant species of wader and 19 species of water fowl.

These things augur well. Dare I prophesy that there might yet come a time when the whole Marsh will be a reserve for wild life?

But what does the future hold for The Marsh? Perhaps it would be more meaningful to ask what does The Marsh hold for the future?

In the past we saw how sheep ousted ships, now sheaves oust sheep. The unthinkable has happened. Those world-celebrated sacred pastures are ploughed, more than 50 per cent of Romney Marsh proper is arable land. There are wheat and potatoes, strawberries and bulbs, where the Romneys grazed and grew fat. The Romney Marsh farmer has broken with tradition. The no-longer sacred pasture is sold (at a good price) as turf. Believe it or not the new precincts of St Paul's Cathedral were turfed by it. The land is ploughed, good crops result, it is re-seeded with indigenous rye grass and white clover, and again for a short time sheep are pastured. It pays says Mr H. Catt.

Sheep are still there, but their numbers reduced by a third. The Romneys are there, their fame untarnished. There are more Romneys and Romney crosses in the world than any other breed of sheep. At the Rye Market more than 400 Romney rams are sold annually for export to all the other five continents. In 1970 they fetched £52 apiece, in 1982 £114.75.

And, strange to behold, there are now several dairy herds on The Marsh. In the old days this was not possible because as there is no flow of water along the ditches and dykes, in summer these become stagnant and brackish, which no cow could stomach and survive. Today paradoxical as it may seem, abundant fresh water is piped to The Marsh.

In the early 1970s the Kent River Authority carried out a plan to improve the drainage of 23,800 acres in the low-lying land of the Rother levels. But by the 1980s the Southern Water Authority had evolved a whole new scheme whereby "summer feeds to the marshes" is pumped from the Rother itself into the Royal Military Canal, and "winter water" is pumped from the Union Channel, Playden, into the Rother at a rate of $2\frac{1}{4}$ million gallons per hour. An ingenious way of making the River Rother function as either reservoir or drain.

Now Puck undoubtedly could put a girdle round the Earth in next to no time, so why didn't he tell me that Lydd was going to do something of the sort. But he never whispered, not even when I was listening to the marsh frogs croaking and burping in the sewer. For suddenly the ugly chorus of the frogs was drowned by the roar of aero-engines—Lydd Airport, Ferryfield, was opened. That was in 1954, and for twelve years the airport went from strength to strength. Operating base for Silver City Airways, and owned and operated by the British United Airways Group, it was, to quote their brochure "the first international airport in Britain to be designed by an independent airline for the use of independent operators." It is only 37 miles from the continent and "ideal for economic cargo shipment by air, for passenger flights to Europe . . . and for private flying. During 1965 over 7,000 tons of cargo and 50,000 cars were handled at Lydd, while passenger traffic amounted to 160,000."

And now, only seven years later, I can hear the frogs again! Ferryfield is silent, or nearly so. Why oh why? Everything seemed so right, proximity to France, perfectly laid out, well appointed, first-rate modern airport, fine runways, tiptop equipment and communications, fog free—only two days in a year unserviceable through bad weather conditions—and yet silent. I cannot answer why. For a while the airport remained open and was used by a flying school, and it played an important part in air traffic control across the Channel. But all the brave expectations have faded, for in November 1981 Lydd Airport was closed. I grieve about it; I grieve particularly for Lydd; for just when things seemed so rosy and the Mayor of Lydd wrote in his "Welcome to Lydd" that the airport "had done much to put this former seaport back on the map, this time as a port in the truly modern sense." Yet once again it has "silted up". Lydd has suffered, and survived, disasters in the past, and I feel sure it will come successfully through this set back—and put the croaking frogs to shame.

The curious thing about the whole affair is that Lympne, up on the old cliff, which was a state-owned grass airfield, had become by 1953 "inadequate to handle the fast-growing volume of traffic". Yet three years later the airport was purchased by Skyways International. By April 1968 a brand new paved 1350 metre runway was completed. In 1969 the passenger lounge and office block were built, and Lympne became Ashford Airport. But alas, it too folded. The Airport ceased to operate in 1975 and now an industrial estate replaces it.

And what is The Marsh doing, or going to do, for you and me, for the general public, for the populations of the other five continents? Its influence is secretive, insidious, unseen; its tentacles reach out far and wide to the very ends of the Earth; they touch, tease, tantalise and lure with thoughts and facts and fantasies of things past and things to come. Peoples' minds are captivated by the puzzling record of upheaval and disaster, of events dramatic that changed the course of history, of unique terrain alive with flowers and birds, of the strange changing struggle for survival of ships and sheep and crops and towns—and men, particularly men.

This is why they come to The Marsh. They come to see for themselves. They come in hundreds of thousands. Mind you The Marsh proper is almost as empty as it ever was. Lose your way on the winding lanes at twilight between Lydd and Brookland and never a soul will you meet to tell you your way. Even the guide posts are missing. Tom said, "Ye get all turned round in broad daylight." At dusk it is alarming, and I know, I've been lost. But an old Romney Looker once gave me good advice:

"an' ever ye get lost an' dunno which way to turn acrost 'er, keep yer eye on Rye, keep yer eye on Rye".

I was intrigued by the fact that the old shepherd referred to The Marsh as "her", just as Tom Shoesmith had done, but the advice was sound. The outline of Rye is unmistakable, the buildings, particularly the church tower, are sufficiently high above the levels to be distinguished from many miles away, and in the evening the silhouette against the western glow is discernable till nearly an hour after sunset. You can be bedevilled by ditches and sewers, by single-track lanes which double back like contorted serpents, by G.P.s non-existent or broken down, by a new moon which seems to be rising out of the east, but at every fork, at every crossroads, wherever an alternative is offered to you, and they will be offered to you at every quarter of a mile, make your choice as that which appears most likely to take you to Rye. And at Rye you will arrive.

All roads lead to Rye. Pardon a cliche, but for once in this Fifth Quarter of the Globe, it is the truth. From Hythe to Pett, from Appledore to Dungeness, the hundreds of thousands of visitors wherever or however they may be accommodated, in hostel or hotel, guest house or holiday camp, tent or caravan, they will eventually all come to Rye. Rye is bursting at the seams, and by that I do not mean that this wonderful Antient Town is in danger of modernisation, tower flats, garish hotels, and all the rest of the hideous "amenities" which are supposed to make life "fuller" for the tourist. The Mayor and Corporation have a tight hold, and no ancient beam, or brick for that matter, may be altered, and no house even painted without express permission. They know full well that the attraction of Rye is in what it is, in what it was. So within the walls little or no structural change can take place. Outside the walls in Rye Foreign, that is the area north of the town quite considerable new accommodation has been built. At Rye Harbour there has been some development particularly industry-wise. There is a big enough timber wharfe to attract ships of moderate tonnage and once again they come from as far as the Baltic.

Nor must we forget temporary accommodation. Within a

radius of some three miles of the Land Gate, from Camber through Rye Harbour to Winchelsea Beach, the Rye authorities have sites for no less than eighteen hundred caravans. And every one of these is occupied.

And in Rye itself there is an air of business and bustle that was unknown twenty years ago. Boat building has taken a new lease of life. The modern craze to go sailing has boosted the business skyhigh. "Craze" is not fair, I apologise, the urge to go to sea is as old as the Portsmen and seems inborn in every Englishman. No wonder the boatbuilders are doing well. They are now building lifeboats for the R.N.L.I. Two hundred yachts come up or lie up the Rother. What if a Marina be constructed in the Saltings? No need for a crystal ball—the need is cash.

In Rye there are other industries, specialised engineering, pottery, there are the markets, the lamb sales, the ram sales, but the biggest business. of all is the tourist trade. The Town Clerk has told me that in the last twenty years the number of visitors to Rye has trebled. Why in one holiday camp alone (ought I to call it a palace), at Camber, capacity accommodation for *one week* is 4,500, greater than the entire population of Rye. There is in Rye a little museum, which was reopened in 1954. At a small charge (note Victoria and Albert) in those early years it attracted about 3000 visitors per annum. Eighteen years later 30,000 visitors paid to go in. That is treble trebled.

Bravo Rye! I have the greatest admiration for all who live within the Borough, and in particular the Mayor and Corporation. There have been mayors in Rye since A.D. 1289, and at long last Lady Mayors. The first was Councillor Mrs E. Philpott, and recently, already three years in office, Cllr Mrs J. Kirkham. I was granted the privilege of an interview with this 'Mr Mayor', and to my delight I discovered a lady who is determined that the good name, the honour and the prestige of the Antient Town shall not be found wanting.

Thus while Rye retains in effect its Mayor and Corporation, I must add that now its affairs are largely administered by the Rother District Council.

* * * * *

One of the great problems for me in writing the story of Romney Marsh has been not so much the recording of events over ten thousand years, complex as this has sometimes been, but rather keeping up with the rapid changes which have taken place over the last thirty years. This may sound absurd but it is simply astonishing what has been happening since the first edition of this book in 1953.

For five hundred years the remarkable pastures created by the reclamation and innings of the marshes were inviolate, sacred pastures for sheep, yet in thirty years the whole farming practice has changed. More than 60% is now arable. Instead of 250,000 sheep there are barely 40,000 breeding ewes.

In the same period two airports were developed, each in its own way became important, each had great expectations, and yet both Ashford Airport and Ferryfield are no more.

On a happier note consider Romneyrail, the delightful Romney, Hythe & Dymchurch Ry. The line has suffered severe financial problems—what railway in the world has not?—particularly relating to the need for capital re-investment. But in spite of many difficulties the railway has developed enormously since the early 1970s, with much track and building work being undertaken together with the reconstruction of its passenger coaches. It has even become a 'school bus' and conveys some 250 children daily from Hythe to New Romney. The line will soon have a new diesel locomotive constructed specially for the purpose. In 1982 it has loaned its magnificent *Black Prince* to the Ravenglass & Eskdale Ry., on the shores of Cumbria, and in exchange the R. & E. Ry.'s diesel hydraulic *Shelagh of Eskdale*, built in 1969, will be running on the R.H. & D.Ry.

Eight years after Hiroshima who would have dreamt, in the wildest nightmare, that the imposing monstrosities of nuclear power stations would arise on the flowery deserts of Denge Beach? And who could with dismay have foretold that Station A would suffer temporary closure, that Station B would be unfinished, and that the drawing-board with the plans for Station C apparently lost?

Professor R. D. Burrowes, who perceived how the unique

terrain of Dungeness could be a naturalist's paradise, almost
bankrupted himself in his prolonged single-handed fight to
save it for posterity. Yet today not only is the R.S.P.B. firmly
established but there is the remarkable creation of the Rye
Harbour Local Nature Reserve, already by 1982 expanded to 219
hectares, with no fewer than eight Councils, Societies, Authorities,
etc. interested in its maintenance and preservation.

Writing ten years ago about the establishment of the Rye
Reserve and the encouragement it gave me I said: These things
augur well. Dare I prophesy that there might yet come a time
when the whole Marsh will be a reserve for wild life?

It can be foolish to prophesy, but Puck is a very unpredictable
sprite, and maybe he had a hand in this, for look you 16,600
acres of Walland and Guldeford Marshes were declared in 1977 a
Site of Special Scientific Interest (what in modern jargon is
called an SSSI), an enormous area from Appledore following the
Royal Military Canal through to Iden Lock, right down to
Camber and through to the boundaries of Denge Beach—all in
measure protected.

Do I harp overmuch on natural history? When this book was
first published it was kindly and quite well received. But I
remember one sharp criticism: Why did I spend a page on
Spotted Redshanks and only two lines on Henry James? How just!
But then you see the story of Romney Marsh is like a fabric, a
tapestry, woven on the loom of time. The weft shuttles to and
fro, constantly changing, as the acts of men produce marvellous
patterns of pageantry and history. But the warp is constant, its
many strands which are the acts of nature remain unchanged
throughout the whole texture of the tapestry. Redshanks, a
strand of nature, are, in their way, more enduring than any
author.

When we began our exploration of Romney Marsh we entered
the region by train. Since then we have employed every kind of
device from back-stays to the Time Machine to assist us in our
adventures through time and space. Now I recommend before
we leave that we charter a plane and take our farewell from
the air.

The flight must be in the early morning and the day crystal clear, with the beams of the rising sun striking across the levels and casting long, sharp shadows. We rise over Hythe, its long high street deserted and its houses straggling up Quarry Hill to its fine church, and see the glint of the canal among the trees. We turn southwards along the beach, a miniature Dungeness, until suddenly the shingle ends and the green lands of Romney Marsh leap to the very edge of the sea. What a slender barrier the Dymchurch Wall looks from up here, a mere thread between the dark high tide and the vivid greens of The Marsh.

Up, up; and as the whole vast extent of the levels flattens out into one enormous intricate mosaic of pastures and arable, crops and ploughlands threaded and intersected with countless dykes and waterlets, the full significance of what has happened is impressed upon us. The sea-bed that has been up and down, up and down, and that eventually man himself reclaimed—this vast area that was sea and mud-flats, creeks and islands, is now firm ground rich and fertile.

We are now above the Foreland of Dungeness. From the air the forcefulness of this monster thrusting outwards into deep water cannot be mistaken, and how remarkable the shingle fulls look in the level light of the rising sun. They look like furrows of a giant plough, they are drawn so even and so regular, sweeping round at "the nose" and shooting long fingers into the green ripes of Lydd.

How queer and how slight look the piers at the mouth of the Rother! Beyond them, Nook beach, Pett Level and the new, sweeping concrete wall, and the old groins like broken teeth in a new comb. We turn, the whole Marsh seems to gyrate below us.

> "Look you our foreshore stretches far
> Through seagate dyke and groin,
> Made land all, that our fathers made,
> Where the flats and fairway join.
> They forced the sea a league back,
> They died and their work stood fast,

We were born to peace in the lee of the dykes,
But the time of our peace is past."

Kipling's prophetic words have been more than fulfilled, for not only have two world wars broken across the levels, but the sea again challenges. There is no peace yet in the lee of the dykes.

We follow the doubling Rother. Rye and Winchelsea slip away below us. It seems incredible that the history of England took shape there. But we know that the Barons of the Cinque Ports were not found wanting in their country's service. It was their destiny to hold the Narrow Seas, and how valiantly 'twas done!

And now our charter plane is at such an altitude that there is no longer any detail left, only shape. It is the shape of things past. It is The Marsh, lying a-dreaming under the summer sun, its broad acres, its green pastures, irregular as a patchwork quilt, feather-stitched with reedy dyke and glinting sewer.

My story's done, and if you find it as ravelly as witch-yarn on the spindles, I beg you blame Puck for that.

BIBLIOGRAPHY

History of Romney Marsh. Wm. Holloway.

The Invasion of England by Julius Cæsar. Thos. Lewin.

Froissart's Chronicles.

Chronicles. Holinshed, 1577.

Great Britain. Camden, 1586.

Itinerary. Leyland, 1539.

Caius Julius Cæsar's Expeditions and the subsequent formation of Dungeness. F. H. Appach.

Formation of Dungeness Geographical Journal, Vol. 80. W. V. Lewis.

Evolution of Romney Marsh Archæologia Cantiana, Vol. 45. C. J. Gilbert, F.G.S.

Constitutional History of the Cinque Ports. K. M. E. Murray.

History of Winchelsea. W. D. Cooper.

The Level and the Liberty of Romney Marsh. M. Teichman-Derville, O.B.E.

England's Outpost. A. G. Bradley.

An Old Gate of England. A. G. Bradley.

Chronicle of Rye. L. Grant.

A New History of Rye. L. A. Vidler.

The Land of the Cinque Ports. S. P. B. Mais.

The Romney Marsh Problem. G. H. Garrod.

The Shape of Ships. William McDowell.

The Sailing Ship. R. & R. S. Anderson.

Bird Life on Pett Level (British Birds, Vol. 41). R. Cooke.

Romney Marsh Investigation. Agricultural Land Commission, 1949.

Soils of Romney Marsh. R. D. Green, Rothamstead Experimental Station, 1968.

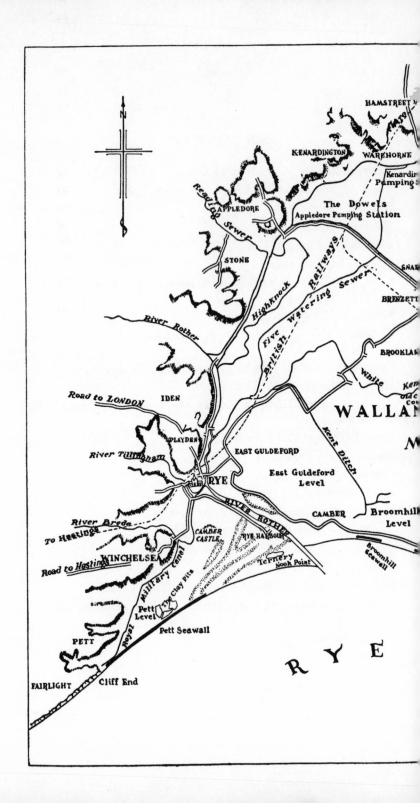

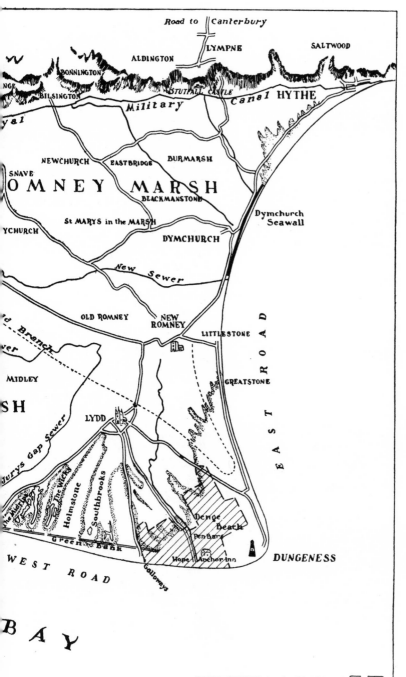

ROYAL SOCIETY for the PROTECTION
of BIRDS. area shown thus

INDEX